Linking Developmental Assessment and Curricula

Prescriptions for Early Intervention

Stephen J. Bagnato
Pennsylvania State University
Hershey, Pennsylvania

John T. Neisworth
Pennsylvania State University
University Park, Pennsylvania

AN ASPEN PUBLICATION®
Aspen Systems Corporation
Rockville, Maryland
London
1981

Library of Congress Cataloging in Publication Data

Bagnato, Stephen J.
Linking developmental assessment and curricula.

Bibliography: p. 329.
Includes index.
1. Education, Preschool—Curricula.
2. Child Development—Evaluation.
I. Neisworth, John T.
II. Title.
LB1140.4.B33 371.9 81-3468
ISBN: 0-89443-367-9 AACR2

Library of Congress Catalog Card Number: 81-3468
ISBN: 0-89443-367-9

Printed in the United States of America

1 2 3 4 5

Table of Contents

Preface

There is a gap between assessment of exceptional preschoolers and programming for them. Too often, assessment reports furnished to teachers are irrelevant or only remotely useful for designing individual educational programs. We have worked for years with numerous agencies, teachers, and parents who are concerned with quality early education for handicapped preschoolers. Repeatedly, the same problem occurs when it comes time to apply assessment findings to the formulation of instructional and developmental objectives. Skilled developmental school psychologists and other professionals usually collect varied information about each child. Expert early educators, equipped with excellent curriculums and other instructional materials, wait eagerly for the assessment findings to help them in selecting and creating appropriate objectives and methods for working with each child. The critical job of writing meaningful individualized educational plans demands that assessment and programming be purposefully and pragmatically joined. Typically, however, the contributions of assessment experts are of little direct help. Often, unfortunately, assessment results are confusing, global, and concerned with traits or dimensions that must be interpreted to be of instructional relevance.

Because of the mismatch between assessment and instructional activities, we have attempted to develop a straightforward approach for uniting these two important elements. This book emphasizes the critical importance of linkage between developmental diagnosis and intervention. Within the eight chapters are the logic, procedures, and descriptions of materials for bringing assessment and programming together to optimize the diagnostic-prescriptive approach for young handicapped children. We believe this book can serve as a practical resource for preschool teachers, school psychologists, early childhood special educators, infant stimulation specialists, and administrators who are intimately involved in the assessment-intervention process.

S.J. Bagnato
J.T. Neisworth
August 1981

Acknowledgments

The many children, parents, and teachers who worked with us over the last six years are the most fundamental contributors to this book. The numerous problems and suggestions presented to us by preschool teachers and school psychologists concerning the match or mismatch between assessment and intervention gave us the motive and content for the material in this book.

Several colleagues were of special help in preparing this manuscript. Their specific contributions are:

Andrea Berger, The Pennsylvania State University
Compiler, Appendix B: Selected Preschool Curriculums Useful in Constructing Prescriptive Linkages

Maria Bianchianello, University of Maryland
Compiler, Appendix A: Selected Preschool Developmental Scales Useful in Constructing Prescriptive Linkages

John Breen, The Pennsylvania State University
Contributor to Chapter 2: Developmental Assessment of Young Exceptional Children: Principles and Procedures; and to Chapter 7: A Developmental Model for Prescriptive Linkage

Frances Moosbrugger Hunt, The Pennsylvania State University
Compiler, Appendix B: Selected Preschool Curriculums Useful in Constructing Prescriptive Linkages

Elizabeth A. Llewellyn, The Pennsylvania State University
Author, Chapter 5: Close-ups of Prominent Preschool Curriculums; and coauthor, Chapter 8: From Assessment to Individualized Programming: A Case Study

Sally Mascitelli, The Pennsylvania State University
Coauthor, Chapter 8: From Assessment to Individualized Programming: A Case Study

Jonathan P. Smith, The Pennsylvania State University
Contributor to Chapter 5: Close-ups of Prominent Preschool Curriculums

Many thanks also to Howard Gallop for his help in proofreading the manuscript and his suggestions for improving its readability. We are particularly grateful to Janis Leitzell for her rapid and accurate typing, turning our pen and pencil scrawls into a professional appearing document. Finally, we are pleased to thank Erika Wolf for producing an accurate and useful index, so important to the proper and full use of a reference book.

Part I

Assessment of the Exceptional Preschooler

Chapter 1

The Gap between Child Assessment and Programming

Developmental assessment of handicapped preschoolers can be the key to quality programming. Early educators know the value of good diagnostic information in formulating individual educational plans. Unfortunately, however, assessment reports made available to teachers are frequently useless for program planning. Assessment often provides only remote, if any, implications for early educational programming. Yet, forging effective "linkages" between assessment and treatment is vital for the developmental progress of handicapped infants and preschool children. "Screening without intervention and eventual program planning is futile and maybe even detrimental. . . . Considerable additional research must be done regarding optimum matches and most efficacious approaches to screening, evaluation, and intervention for young children at developmental risk" (Meier, 1973, p. 529).

Traditionally, there has existed a voiced interest in the need for early identification and comprehensive assessment of developmental problems but little direct concern with constructing individualized educational plans upon the results of such assessments. Thus, the crucial *bond* between assessment and intervention usually has been bypassed. Preschool teachers and early childhood specialists have received little direct, practical guidance from psychologists and other diagnostic specialists regarding the design of individualized treatment plans for the developmentally disabled child.

Federal Public Law 94-142 (94th Congress, 1975) represents a major step toward ensuring that comprehensive assessment methods serve as guides to individualized educational planning for all handicapped children. The following provisions of P.L. 94-142 define the impact of mandated procedures upon the role of school psychologists, educational specialists, and other individuals who must program for the handicapped child:

- "A free, appropriate, public education . . . to all handicapped children between the ages of 3 and 21 by no later than September of 1980" (p. 8).

- The use of comprehensive, nondiscriminatory methods of assessing major areas of child developmental status with no single measure as the sole criterion of diagnosis and placement.
- A written "individualized educational program" (p. 4) for each handicapped child developed by an educational unit representative, teacher, and parents which details: (1) present levels of educational performance, (2) annual goals and specific instructional objectives and interventions, (3) specific services to be provided, and (4) specific evaluation procedures and objective criteria to monitor progress.
- An ongoing program of screening and identifying children with developmental and educational problems.

The central theme implicit in P.L. 94-142 is educational accountability for the educational progress of handicapped children. In essence, "assessment yields data on current educational performance in a sequence of instructional objectives which lead to individually planned goals for each handicapped child" (Tano, 1976, p. 4).

Although such individualized assessment and programming procedures mandated by P.L. 94-142 are not new to many diagnostic specialists, the unique thrust of this law is that individualized methods and procedures will be increasingly required for the young and severely handicapped child within the public schools. The impact of this aspect of the law on the typical roles, functions, and relationships of school psychologists, teachers, and parents is enormous.

Central to the role and function of the school psychologist is the assessment of and prescription for psychoeducational problems. However, the process of assessment is devoid of practical, functional significance unless it "serves as a *blueprint* for designing individualized instructional programs" (Ysseldyke & Bagnato, 1976, p. 283). The growing interdisciplinary involvement of school psychologists, special educators, and other specialists with exceptional preschool populations alerts us to the need and potential for devising pragmatic and integrated methods that match assessment and intervention. The procedure of matching or linking assessment to individualized instructional planning for the handicapped preschooler is central to this book. Before detailing this procedure further, it is important first to analyze some problems that delimit school psychological practice with the handicapped preschooler.

THE SCHOOL PSYCHOLOGIST AND PRESCHOOL POPULATIONS

Because of their training focus and their traditional role within the schools, most school psychologists have had little or no practical experience with children younger than five years of age (Valett, 1967). Knowledge of how to interact with and assess the capabilities of very young handicapped children who do not or cannot respond consistently to structured situations is lacking. Similarly, direct familiarity with the types of developmental behaviors and preacademic functional skills expected of children between birth and five years of age is often sketchy. Therefore, the comprehensive assessment of developmental skills and the design of individualized instructional plans have been left completely to the preschool teacher and the preschool teacher's aides without the advantage of educational and psychological programming based on a comprehensive assessment of skills. Such educational planning has traditionally been based upon information derived from the administration of informal measures, parent reports, and subjective classroom observations without specific purpose. With the inception of P.L. 94-142, this situation is changing dramatically. School psychologists and other specialists must prepare themselves to be able to adapt, generalize, and update professional skills to meet the new service demands of the preschool population.

DEVELOPMENTAL ASSESSMENT AND INDIVIDUALIZED PROGRAMMING

A comprehensive, functional analysis of developmental skills is vital to the establishment of individualized educational programs for each handicapped preschooler. The unique skills of the school psychologist are important in implementing such assessments. However, because of the school psychologist's traditional diagnostic focus on older school-age children to remedy their educational problems, little concern has centered on prevention to identify *developmental* deficits and their potential impact on learning. Most school psychologists have limited practical knowledge and direct experience with assessment devices, curricula, and intervention strategies that can be applied and adapted to normal as well as handicapped preschool populations. Such popular measures as the WISC-R, Stanford-Binet, ITPA, WPPSI, and other similar tests tap isolated, global and separate intellectual and language abilities and are not precise and comprehensive enough to measure developing processes in the young child. The most frequently utilized tests designed for school-age populations are inappropriate and impractical when applied to infant and preschool populations.

Without familiarity with preschool children or appropriate assessment devices, the school psychologist's potential effectiveness in planning educational programs based upon diagnostic results is greatly reduced. Since, frequently, little continuity exists between screening, assessment, and programming, the school psychologist tends to have limited, practical input regarding the planning of individualized instructional programs. Therefore, the crucial "linkage" between diagnostic assessment and curriculum planning is rarely achieved (Chase, 1975; Simeonsson & Wiegerink, 1975).

Nevertheless, school psychologists are now mandated to function in the roles of infant-preschool assessment and individualized curriculum planning. The emergence of this mandate regarding the education of handicapped infants and preschoolers necessitates the development and implementation of systematic purposes and procedures for ''linking'' screening, assessment, and individualized instructional programming.

MAKING ASSESSMENT RELEVANT TO INSTRUCTION: THE ISSUES

The essence of school psychological practice is to determine the match between a handicapped child's capabilities and the effective features of a treatment program. There are several important practical issues related to why assessment has not been as helpful as it could be and why school psychologists have had difficulty in providing teachers with instructionally relevant reports.

Issue 1: Traditional Assessment Purposes and Practices

Traditional practices in assessment—which emphasize the exclusive use of global, norm-referenced, intellectual measures for the purpose of describing a child's range of general abilities—are clearly inappropriate when applied to normal preschool populations, let alone handicapped preschoolers. Beyond their inappropriateness and lack of precision in an evaluative sense, such methods are ineffective in terms of creating a link between developmental diagnosis and intervention (Haeussermann, 1958; Chase, 1975; Meier, 1976; Valett, 1972).

The ambiguity, lack of precision, and absence of continuity in testing and teaching the handicapped preschooler appear to result from a failure to understand the purposes of assessment with such children. Haphazard and ill-suited goals and methods lead to gross misjudgments and considerable wasted effort.

> The main reason for evaluation in special education is to make better decisions about the character and direction of each child's instructional program. . . . The assessment of a child's performance and the collection of data for subsequent use in the design of an instructional program should not be done in a haphazard way. There are many real and potential problems involved in administering tests to children without a clear rationale. . . . (Smith & Neisworth, 1975, pp. 94, 122)

Assessments are conducted for a variety of purposes but primarily to make individual decisions about the essential features of a child's treatment program. The type of decision made dictates the kind of skills assessed and the type of measure selected. Most often the following purposes guide assessment:

- screening and identification
- comprehensive assessment and program placement
- individualized instructional planning
- child progress and program evaluation

Whereas traditional assessment practices operate as if these were separate operations, functional developmental assessment seeks to merge these purposes. Based on the developmental task model, infant-preschool assessment is a continuous, general-to-specific process of defining functional capabilities and establishing treatment goals. Like the wide angle sighting scope on a highpowered telescope, screening information should provide a wide view of a child's functioning and guide fine-focus diagnostic assessment. Detailed assessment should then provide a baseline for curriculum planning and establish the criteria for monitoring child progress and evaluating program effectiveness. Philosophy, purpose, and practice merge to link developmental diagnosis and curriculum planning. When instructional planning is the explicit purpose of assessment, even traditional developmental assessment devices can be administered and analyzed to design practical programs. As Valett (1972) contends, "Most [traditional] psychological test results can be analyzed from a developmental task point of view" (p. 129). In its entirety, the approach aids in delineating the child's current functional levels, in specifying deficit areas, and in constructing interventions and strategies based on a developmental task analysis of functional skills and the environmental conditions necessary for learning and adjustment to occur.

Issue 2: Categorical Versus Functional Developmental Orientation

Traditional assessment has been aimed at diagnosis of a child's "condition;" that is, the main purpose has been identification of a child's primary disability area or diagnostic category. The result is usually an assessment report that tells a teacher what a child *is,* rather than what the child *does*. "Billy is retarded," "Bertha is learning disabled," "Martha is sociopathic," or "Harvey is emotionally disturbed." Notice that these are *diagnostic* statements that label a child with some categorical so-called underlying condition. This approach may be termed *genotypic assessment* because it attempts to identify a general, underlying problem. In contrast, a more useful approach, *phenotypic assessment,* attempts to describe and summarize what capabilities a child *does* or *does not* display (genotypic vs. phenotypic assessment is discussed in greater detail in chapter 2). Unfortunately, categorical or genotypic diagnosis does not provide much guidance for instruction. The major limitations of the genotypic diagnostic approach are (1) various exceptionalities are not distinct or pure; a diagnostic label does not automatically accurately describe a child's functional problems; and (2) identification of a disability area does not automatically suggest preferred treatment.

Categorical methods provide only the most general diagnostic-intervention data. Effective intervention depends upon precise phenotypic descriptions of functional skills and abilities (see Table 1-1). A functional, developmental approach seeks to define the handicapped child's levels and ranges of behavioral strengths and weaknesses. The objective is to analyze the child's developmental/learning status (Meier, 1976) in such a manner as to establish an initial treatment plan that is handicap-appropriate and everchanging based on functional gains.

Table 1-1 Categorical (Genotypic) vs. Functional (Phenotypic) Orientation in Assessment

Categorical Approach:

- Attempts to systematize views re: different exceptionalities
- Highlights the area of "primary disability," i.e., mental retardation, emotional disturbance, etc.
- Ensures political allocation of service funds for exceptional groups
- Perpetuates the faculty assumption that exceptionalities are exclusive and distinct entities

Functional Approach:

- Focuses on functional descriptions of each individual's range of capabilities and limitations within and across behavioral areas regardless of "exceptionality"
- Stresses that exceptionalities are not distinct entities but share dysfunctions across functional domains
- Emphasizes the complex set of interactions between developmental and learning disabilities (DLD) (Meier, 1976)
- Expands the scope of individuals eligible to receive special services

Issue 3: Translating Assessment Results for Goal-Planning

The psychological report is one of the prime vehicles through which school psychologists and other diagnostic specialists demonstrate the value and effectiveness of their services. Moreover, this report is a vital step in the process of clearly communicating information regarding a child's capabilities to parents and teachers and of translating data for instructional planning. With the rise of specialized services to young exceptional children, the critical importance of quality reports increases. However, criticism by parents and teachers (supported by the results of descriptive research) suggests that traditional diagnostic reports are ineffective as guides to individualized curriculum planning (Sattler, 1974; Bagnato, in press). Traditional reports are often test-centered, ambiguous, authoritarian, confusing, and contribute little to the current programming needs of the child. In practice, there are three difficulties with traditional reports:

1. Failure to identify the purpose of the assessment
2. Vague, imprecise presentation of functional information
3. Failure to link assessed child needs to specific intervention goals and targets

Assessment Purpose

Failure to identify correctly the reason for conducting an assessment directly affects the meaningfulness of the information provided, given the needs of the child and the expectations of those who work with the child. Often, the primary assumed purpose of assessment is to predict future cognitive performance and adaptive functioning. However, contrary to the usual perspective, prediction contributes information of only limited use to teachers or parents. The apparent need for predictive data is often reflected in such questions as "How far behind is my child in developing speech?" or "Why doesn't my four-year-old talk yet?" Or, particularly, "What can we do to help our child learn to talk?" Without answering these questions regarding degree of dysfunction, cause, and strategies, the psychologist who provides only "predictive" data leaves the parents of a handicapped child with a sense of confusion, hopelessness, and helplessness. Furthermore, predictive data provide no precise information to guide intervention and are often based on a limited sample of behavior that frequently leads to erroneous conclusions regarding later functioning. The assessment of infants and preschoolers is particularly relevant, since traditional developmental scales have limited predictive validity because they sample primarily sensorimotor behaviors at the earlier age levels while later intelligence tests tap verbal and analytical skills.

However, traditional developmental scales are reliable measures of *current functioning* and provide a practical baseline for intervention. Problems arise when "prediction" is misconstrued as the primary purpose for assessment. The real-life diagnostic reports presented in the following examples illustrate both the stylistic problems inherent in typical psychological reports and the gross errors that can result from lack of caution in predicting later performance from infant functioning (see Exhibit 1-1). The report of Psychologist 1 easily evokes the criticism of parents and teachers in its authoritarian style, absolute tone, limited focus, and test-centered quality. Furthermore, it fails to detail specific functional skills, offers no leeway for the effects of stimulation, and provides no recourse to the parents. Its sole predictive purpose leads to serious errors in judgment about the child's later functioning and unjustifiably limits the parents' expectations—as evidenced by David's superior WISC IQ of 132 at 7 years of age. These real examples are admittedly extreme, but they point up how easy it is to err seriously when assessment is centered on prediction rather than on current functioning and goal-planning.

Effective Presentation of Information

Correctly identifying the purpose of assessment enables the correct measures to be selected and the appropriate skills and processes to be sampled. Nevertheless, a broad collection of performance data is meaningless unless it is presented in an organized, highlighted, economical, and easily accessible form. These features are particularly important when programming for young and severely handicapped children.

Traditional diagnostic reports can be modified so that they "translate" assessment results more effectively for planning treatment. The organization, content, and style in the application of reports must be modified to maximize their usefulness to the teacher.

Bersoff (1973) has discussed the poor qualities of traditional psychoeducational reports by focusing on their test-centeredness, lack of scope, and limited relevance to a child's functioning in educational contexts. "The point is that a psychological evaluation is not a report of test results but a report of relevant behavior that serves to answer the referring questions and leads to decisions about the person evaluated . . . the report is more helpful in all ways when it describes a person and not his test productions" (p. 5).

With these deficiencies in mind, we suggest the following points as guideposts in organizing, describing, and applying assessment information within diagnostic reports.

Exhibit 1-1 Early Childhood Assessment: A Case of Lack of Caution in Predicting Intelligence

Report 1: Child at 8 Months

Adaptive Development—16 weeks

No less mature behavior is seen; more mature behavior at 20 weeks indicated in grasping with the near hand only and visual pursuit of the lost rattle.

Language Development—20 weeks

Less mature behavior is seen as Scott does not laugh out loud very much; more mature behavior is indicated in spontaneous vocalization of his toys.

Personal Social Behavior—16 weeks

Less mature behavior is seen in not sitting propped 10-15 minutes; more mature behavior is indicated in patting his bottle when feeding.

Griffiths Mental Development Scale– C.A. 32.0 weeks (8 months)
D.A. 16.67 weeks
Developmental rating—mentally deficient

Summary:

It becomes more and more apparent as I see Scott periodically and as he becomes older that he is quite a damaged baby and may not develop much beyond the crib stage. Even though I am correcting for 8 weeks prematurity, this infant is now measuring about 8 weeks below this. The picture seems rather total in that it is apparent in motor growth, language growth, and play behavior. There is certainly very fleeting attention in this baby and an irritable pattern that certainly suggests that things are not right with him. I feel the foster mother finds him rather frustrating, but, reality-wise, this certainly would be a very difficult infant to live with. He does not respond much to whatever stimulation is given to him. I contrast him with the older boy infant in the home who is also somewhat slow but has responded very nicely to the parental stimulation and love. I feel that Scott may need to be planned for as an institution baby. At this point, I see no real possibility of his ever being considered normal. I am not requesting reevaluation on Scott unless he remains in your care for an extended period of time before permanent plans are made for him. The diagnosis seems so clear-cut to me at this point that I feel that repeated examinations would not add much.

Psychologist 1

Exhibit 1-1 continued

Report 2: Child at 7 Years

Wechsler Intelligence Scale for Children	Verbal scale—126, Performance scale—129, Full scale—132
Vineland Social Maturity Scale	S.A—9-2, S.Q.—130
Bender Gestalt Test	
Drawing	

Scott is an alert, bright youngster who made an excellent subject for testing. He was interested, cooperative, and willing to do his best. There is no significant difference between the verbal and performance areas, in both of which he seems to be superior in ability. Verbally he had good command of himself and is aware of what is going on around him. This boy shows promise of having leadership abilities as well as contributing to group learning situations. He is alert, can reason well, and can plan and synthesize. The subjects on the WISC are especially interesting in estimating these qualities.

WISC Subtests

Verbal		*Performance*	
Information	15	Picture completion	18
Comprehension	14	Picture arrangement	11
Arithmetic	12	Block design	17
Similarities	14	Object assembly	15
Vocabulary	16	Coding	10

Verbal—126 IQ Performance—129 IQ Full scale—132 IQ

Vineland Social Maturity Scale

This 7-year-old boy is socially competent in that his basal social age was 7 years but he reached an age equivalent of 9-2 on the total test. His social quotient is 130. He is a very personable child who expresses himself exceptionally well for his age.

Psychologist 2

Organization. Test-centered reports tend to restrict descriptions of child functioning and to perpetuate the use of confusing terminology and abstractions. Reports appear to be more communicative when they emphasize the qualitative features of a child's performance rather than the quantitative, comparative aspects. For purposes of individualized goal-planning, organizing a report by *functional developmental domains* (e.g., language, motor, social, cognitive) serves to facilitate a comprehensive description of current levels. A section of the report devoted to integrating "commonalities" in multisource data helps to focus the reader's attention to relevant strengths and weaknesses. The use of "advance organizers," summaries, lists, and paragraph headings also facilitates clear organization.

Content. A comprehensive description of a child's current levels of functioning requires the use of multiple methods and sources of data collection about behavior. Bersoff (1973) describes a process of "psychosituational assessment" in this context. The use of such multiple methods provides descriptions of performance across fields of behavior by integrating subjective, observational, interview, and performance data with an eye toward program planning (Bagnato & Neisworth, 1979).

A report that balances descriptions of deficits with strengths enables teachers to capitalize on these skills in programming and instruction. Moreover, analyses that focus on individual "process" variables (Keogh, 1972) such as cognitive style, persistence, attention, organizational approach, speed of response, and need for feedback highlight individual differences and have greater application to individualized goal planning.

Style in application. An essential similarity must exist between the behaviors assessed (reported) and the behaviors taught, that is, sampled and predicted behaviors. By focusing on behavioral skills that are common to both the assessment and instructional process, school psychologists and teachers begin to merge their efforts to help the child more effectively. Often short outlines and sequences of information concerning developmental ceilings, strengths and weaknesses, instructional needs, readiness skills, and test modifications present assessment-based data in a more economical, eye-catching manner. Such behavior information is infinitely more useful than comparative statistics and can be readily transformed into initial goals and strategies for instructional planning. Specifically, the use of "developmental ages" as functional reference points instead of IQ-like developmental quotients helps to define both understandable current levels of operation and child needs.

Examples of traditional and "translated" formats of writing diagnostic reports for young handicapped children are presented in Exhibits 1-2 and 1-3. The use of "translated" reports has been shown to be more effective in writing individualized educational plans.

Exhibit 1-2 Example of a Traditional Psychological Report on a Handicapped Preschooler

Developmental Test Report

Michelle
Hershey Medical Center

DOT: 77-2-25
DOB: 74-5- 9
CA: 2-9-16 (34 mo.)

Observation, Evaluation, and Analysis:

Michelle, age 34 months, was evaluated in conjunction with a developmental followup study on premature children conducted by the pediatrics unit of Hershey Medical Center. Placement within a preschool program as a result of this examination is indicated.

Michelle was seen in a teaching apartment of the pediatrics unit with the mother, a sister, and an educational specialist present. Michelle was initially a little shy and apprehensive in the situation, but after some rapport building she readily accompanied the examiner and worked with him on a number of developmental activities. Michelle was easily interested in a number of the different activities and toys presented; however, in general, she exhibits a very short attention span and erratic listening and is also very distractible and impulsive in her responses in structured tasks.

In general, Michelle's performance on various developmental tasks suggests the existence of delays of between 12 and 18 months in all functional areas; however, within her own pattern of performance Michelle shows individually well-developed skills in the area of language development, particularly in labelling objects and pictures on cards. In contrast, Michelle's weakest area appears to be the domain of gross motor skills. Delays in these areas are to be expected because of the congenital hip problem she experienced.

The Gesell Developmental Schedules were administered in order to obtain a comprehensive estimate of Michelle's developmental status. The following age ranges describe her current functional levels:

Motor	= 15-18 months
Adaptive	= 18-24 months
Language	= 21-30 months
Personal-social	= 18-24 months

Exhibit 1-2 continued

These developmental age ranges indicate the acquisition of functional skills expected of a developmental quotient (DQ) of 61. By this estimate, Michelle's developmental/intellectual functioning is within the moderately retarded range. Overall, Michelle's level of developmental functioning appears to be most comparable to that expected of approximately the average two-year-old child.

Recommendations:

Based upon Michelle's performance, the following recommendations are offered as guidelines for her future educational placement and programming:

1. Immediate placement within a mainstreamed preschool setting.
2. Stress on language, motor, and problem-solving experiences.
3. Development of attention, listening, and direction-following skills.
4. Procurement of the services of a physical therapist to refine and increase Michelle's motor skills.
5. Reevaluation suggested within six months.

____

School Psychologist
Preschool Program

Exhibit 1-3 Example of a "Translated" Developmental Diagnostic Report

AN ASSESSMENT/CURRICULUM LINKAGE FOR PRESCHOOL CHILDREN

NAME	Michelle	DOT	77-2-25
ASSESSMENT PURPOSE	Developmental Assessment	DOB	74-5-09
		CA	2-9-16 (34 mo.)

COMPREHENSIVE DEVELOPMENTAL ASSESSMENT PROFILE

I. QUANTITATIVE FUNCTIONAL ANALYSIS

The following measures were employed to determine Michelle's *current functional levels in major developmental areas and to identify targets to guide individualized instructional goal-planning. The profile below provides a comprehensive estimate of* Michelle's *pattern of skill development compared to that expected for his/her chronological age.*

TEST	CURRENT AGE FUNCTION
Gesell Developmental Schedules (GDS)	Motor = 15-18 mo.
	Adaptive = 21 (18-24) mo.
	Language = 24 (21-30) mo.
	Pers.-Soc. = 21 (18-24) mo.
Preschool Attainment Record (PAR)	Devel. = 31 mo.
(parent report)	

TEST	GESELL					PAR
BEHAVIOR	Motor	Adaptive	Language	Pers.-Soc.		Devel.
69						
66						
63						
60						
57						
54						
51						
48						
45						
42						
39						
36						
33						
30						
27						
24						
21						
18						
15						
12						
9						
6						

Exhibit 1-3 continued

II. *Qualitative Functional Analysis*

A. Background Information and Behavioral Observations:

Under a developmental follow-up study directed by Dr. Jeffrey Maisels at the Hershey Medical Center, Michelle, age 34 months, was administered a comprehensive developmental evaluation. The Gesell Developmental Schedules were given for the following purposes:

1. to delineate Michelle's current range of developmental capabilities and functional skills
2. to suggest less well developed skills requiring educational programming
3. to aid in providing a basis for home-based parent/child instruction

Michelle was seen in a teaching apartment in the pediatrics section of the medical center with the mother, a sister, and an educational specialist present. Michelle was initially a little shy in the situation, but after some rapport building readily accompanied the examiner and worked with him on a number of developmental tasks. Michelle was easily interested in a number of different activities and toys presented. However, in general, Michelle exhibits a very short attention span. During the course of testing, she seemed quite distractible and fairly impulsive on a number of activities. Her distractibility required the quick administration of different items. It was necessary often to present one object at a time and to limit any distracting circumstances and to make sure that the object and materials used were high-interest objects.

At this point, Michelle is quite observant but also impulsive in working on a number of activities. It appears that she needs some structure and reinforcement in the form of praise, hand clapping, or smiling in order for her to perform well and to maintain her attention. In this respect, some attention training and behavioral control may be needed. Such a tactic as saying "You can have the next toy after we finish working on this one first" appeared to work often with Michelle during the course of testing.

In general, Michelle's performance on various developmental tasks suggest the existence of developmental delays of between 12 and 18 months in all functional areas; however, within her own pattern of performance Michelle shows individually well-developed skills in the area of language development, particularly in labelling objects and pictures on picture cards. In addition, good imitation skills and developing imitation skills indicate the expansion of her abilities in these areas.

In contrast, Michelle's weakest area appears to be the area of gross motor skills. Delays in these areas are to be expected because of her hip problem. In

Exhibit 1-3 continued

the same respect, her fine motor skills also appear to lack fine motor coordination that is often necessary to complete more focused kinds of tasks and to manipulate objects. Some eye-hand coordination problems were noted also. However, Michelle appeared to be adjusting well to her glasses, and her eye-hand coordination problems did not seem to be very evident when objects were presented on either side and her attention was directed to each of the tasks by way of prompting her face and directing her eyes and giving her specific instructions on what she was supposed to do.

B. Description of Observable Developmental Skills/Functional Area

The following analysis provides a comprehensive estimate of Michelle's range of functional skills based upon her performance on a series of developmental tasks. Although delays are evident, her emergent progress in many areas speaks well for significant skill acquisition with appropriate structure and programming.

1. *Communication Skills*

Michelle's range of demonstrated language skills appears to be comparable to those expected of approximately the typical 2½-year-old child. Although delays are evident, this area represents Michelle's strongest individual capabilities. Michelle's functional vocabulary is expanding and is reported to be about 50 words. She has discontinued the use of jargon and is beginning to elaborate on her sentence structure also. During testing, Michelle named 50% of the pictured objects and concrete objects presented to her and identified approximately 70% of them correctly, including such pictures and objects as dog, shoe, cup, potty chair, ball, key, truck, pocketbook, bell, and spoon. In addition, Michelle's ability to imitate words and gestures spontaneously speaks well for continued progress in this area. Michelle is able to combine two to three words into a more complex sentence form ("What's that Mommy?"; "That's baby's potty chair.") and to ask questions. However, the usage of various parts of speech except personal pronouns was noted during testing. Similarly, Michelle does not appear to know her full name or to use it, nor to understand and express the function and use of many objects beyond labelling them.

It is suggested that some training in the home using large cards with three to four pictures in each corner and requiring Michelle to pick out specific pictures may go a long way toward expanding her capabilities in the language area. In addition, it would be helpful to set out a series of objects and also ask Michelle to tell what they are used for. These kinds of activities would be helpful in the home to expand some of her skills.

Exhibit 1-3 continued

2. *Self-Care Skills*

The level of development of Michelle's interpersonal and self-help skills appears to be comparable to that expected of the average 1½- to 2-year-old child. Michelle is reported to be very cautious of strangers; however, her behavior during testing gave no indication of this, as she allowed being held by the examiner and immediately expressed interest in interacting on a number of tasks. Her emerging cooperative play was very evident here. Nevertheless, she appears to need some control in knowing the limits of her behavior and obeying rules in structured situations. Her impulsive and distractible behavior are normal for her age but need to be limited by directing her attention purposefully. It was reported that Michelle eats and drinks independently but still spills quite a bit. In dressing she experiences difficulty in putting on pullover garments as well as pants. Her hip problems conceivably may contribute to difficulty in this area.

3. *Gross/Fine Motor Skills*

Michelle's hip problem undoubtedly affects the development of skills in the gross motor area. Her current range of skills appears to be comparable to those expected of a 15-18-month-old child. Such capabilities as walking with one hand held, momentarily standing with support on both legs, creeping up stairs, and throwing a ball represent typical skills for Michelle. Cruising along furniture and creeping on the floor and up stairs are her principal means of moving about.

In the fine motor area her skills are individually more highly developed, although delays are evidently involved with some apparent difficulties in eye-hand coordination in timed object manipulation tasks (peg placement and pellet dropping). Her performance suggests the acquisition of fine motor capabilities much like those expected within the 18- to 24-month range. Michelle built a tower of two cubes but experienced difficulty with three to four cubes. Similarly, in drawing tasks she spontaneously scribbles and makes a stroke imitatively but fails to make a circular or letter-like stroke (V, H, +). Finally, Michelle is able to consistently place circle and square shapes in the formboard but fails to place the triangle consistently or even to adapt to errors and self-correct her mistakes. Although some fine motor coordination problems appear to be evident, when Michelle worked on more focused manipulation tasks it was apparent that her distractible and impulsive manner of responding on such activities contributed very much to low performances on such activities as stacking cubes, dropping pellets into a bottle, and placing

Exhibit 1-3 continued

pegs in a peg board, as well as discriminating shapes and placing them in a formboard. Such activities require attention that Michelle is only developing within an emergent stage at this point.

4. *Problem-Solving Skills*

Although it is inappropriate at this time in her development to pinpoint intellectual abilities, Michelle's performances on imitative and expressive and receptive language tasks in addition to fine motor activities provide evidence of emergent problem-solving capabilities much like those expected of approximately a 2- to 2½-year-old child. Her individual strengths in the language area speak well for continued acquisition and refinement of more complex cognitive skills. Nevertheless, Michelle shows deficits in such activities as attention to focus tasks, building block forms, discriminating shapes, imitating folded paper forms, and recalling and repeating numbers and phrases from memory. The following tasks suggest Michelle's more well developed skills:

- naming and identifying pictures and objects
- using an elaborated sentence form
- imitating words and gestures
- rudimentary description of action in pictured situations

EDUCATIONAL RECOMMENDATIONS AND CURRICULUM LINKAGE

Based upon Michelle's *performance on a series of developmental tasks, the following set of recommendations, curriculum objectives, and strategies are offered as suggested guides for designing an individualized educational plan:*

Based upon Michelle's performance on a variety of developmental tasks, the following recommendations are offered as suggested guidelines for her future educational programming as well as current home-based instructional efforts.

Exhibit 1-3 continued

1. Increase attention to structured activities by physically directing chin and eyes to the task. Such instructions as "Look at all the parts of the picture" and "Watch what I do carefully" paired with directing facial, head, and eye orientation may help. Increase attention to and understanding of rules by such tactics as "This is what we are going to do first" and "You can play with that toy after we do this first" will help in using preferred activities as a way of getting less preferred tasks done. Also, situations such as "time out" may help Michelle to begin to learn the limits of her behavior. Time out can be done by placing her in a chair by herself in another room with instructions that she can come out when she decides not to act up anymore.

2. Emphasize home-based educational work on these developmental tasks:

- Combines parts of speech to make three- to four-word sentences
- Responds with action word to "What's _____ doing?"
- Draws circle in imitation of adult
- Draws verticle line from a model
- Draws horizontal line from a model
- Draws recognizable face
- Assembles simple puzzles
- Washes and dries face and hands
- Attempts to brush teeth
- Responds to "Where is the _____?" and "Show me the _____."
- Points to picture in an array in response to "Show me the _____" and "Where is the _____?"
- Names object in response to "What's this?" or "Who's that?"
- Recognizes object misplaced in an array of other objects
- Responds to "Which is bigger?"

3. It is recommended that further developmental assessment be conducted within the next year in order to analyze further Michelle's range of developmental and cognitive skills with emphasis particularly on the areas of fine motor coordination skills and the acquisition of more complex language capabilities.

Home-based Educational Specialist	School Psychologist Preschool Assessment and Programming

Exhibit 1-3 continued

ASSESSMENT-BASED CURRICULUM-ENTRY TARGETS

Child Michelle ________ Curriculum ________

Test Gesell Developmental Schedules C.A. 34 months

	PERFORMANCE CEILINGS (TEST)	LINK INDEX	CURRICULUM-TARGET OBJECTIVES
	D.A. = 24(21-30) Mo.	COMMUNICATION	
±	Follows 2-4 simple directions		
±	Uses 20+ vocab. in speech		
-	Names pictures & Objs 8-12		
±	Uses I, me, you & plurals		
±	Identifies objs & pictures		
-	Imitates 5-6 word phrase		
-	Gives full name-requested		
±	Answers personal/factual ques.		
-	Combines 3-4 words in sent.		
±	Tells action & experiences		
±	Asks for food, toilet, drink		
-	Attends & listens to a story		
	D.A. = 21(18-24) mo.	SELF-CARE	
±	Uses spoon, spilling little		
±	Asks to use toilet		
±	Tries to contrl bowels/blad.		
±	Pulls on simple garment		
-	Puts on shoes		
-	Removes coat		
±	Washes/dries hands & face		
-	Plays near others, no disturb.		
-	Unbuttons		
-	Helps put toys away		
±	Words/tell wants, food, toilet		
-	Careful with toys or hazards		
	D.A. = 15-18 mo.	MOTOR	
±	Stands momentarily alone		
-	Walks a few steps		
±	Pulls self to standing		
±	Climbs into small chair & sits		
±	Rolls, throws, walks into ball		
-	Turns book pages singly		
-	Builds 3-4 block tower		
-	places ○ □ in puzzle board		
-	Draws horiz & vert lines-imit.		
-	Draws circular stroke-imitat.		
-	Holds crayon with fingers		
±	Puts cubes in-out of cup		

Exhibit 1-3 continued

D.A. = 21(18-24) mo.		PROBLEM-SOLVING	
-	Matches ○□△ shapes in puzzle		
-	Ident., match, sort colors		
±	Understands concept of "one"		
±	" prepositions & positions		
±	Imit fine motor beh-drawing		
±	Names & ident. objects & pict.		
-	Imitates a sequence of blocks		
-	Repeats 2 digits imit. adult		
-	Folds paper imitat. adult		
±	Identifies "big" & "small"		
-	Follows 2 simple directions		
-	Gives use of objects		

	COMMUNIC	SELF-CARE	MOTOR	PROB-SOLV	TOTAL	
TEST						
CURRIC.						
%						

Source: Bagnato, S. J., & Neisworth, J. T. Between assessment and intervention: Forging an assessment/curriculum linkage for the handicapped preschooler. *Child Care Quarterly,* 1979, 8(3), p. 192.

Construction of Assessment/Curriculum Linkages

The diagnostic developmental report is one of the major methods through which the school psychologist translates diagnostic results into meaningful goals for developmental intervention. Through the clear synthesis, integration, and practical communication of diagnostic information from multiple sources, the report should comprehensively describe current levels of child functioning upon which individualized goals and interventions can be constructed.

Bagnato (1980) employed inservice workshops and simulated exercises with groups of early childhood teachers (N = 48) to analyze the characteristics of diagnostic reports that make them useful to teachers for individualized curriculum planning. Thus, this study was designed to explore general differences between two styles of writing diagnostic reports: traditional and translated. Moreover, the study sought to analyze the differential accuracy with which teachers could "match" diagnostic results to curriculum goals as an outcome of using both reporting styles. An expert panel of six school psychologists and early special educators evaluated the accuracy of teacher-constructed linkages in practice Individualized Education Programs (IEPs). This study will be discussed in detail since it directly compares the usefulness of the usual assessment report with the translated, functional type of report advocated by this book.

A COMPARISON OF TRADITIONAL AND TRANSLATED ASSESSMENT REPORTS FOR USEFULNESS IN INSTRUCTION

Forty-eight teachers in early childhood programs for handicapped children enrolled in workshops that taught them to analyze developmental reports to identify diagnostic data that could be "linked" with curriculum objectives to form individualized instructional goal-plans. All teachers in the study had 1 to 5 years experience working with handicapped infants and preschoolers as well as familiarity in using developmental curricula for child programming. In addition, the teachers represented a wide-range spectrum of training, ranging from child-care aides to masters-level training in special education.

First, teachers were assigned to an experimental or control group. The experimental and control groups received specific training on how to link assessment results to curriculum goals. The experimental group received a "translated" report to help in designing instructional objectives while the control group received the usual traditional report. The assessment information contained in these two different reports provided the basis for constructing linkages.

A diagnostic report dealing with the developmental performance of a handicapped preschooler was selected from clinic pediatric files by an expert panel. The psychoeducational assessment data from the diagnostic report were first used in original form to represent the traditional diagnostic report typically provided by school psychologists. This traditional report involved both a quantitative and qualitative breakdown of assessment results. It was organized by traditional subheadings of background information, behavioral observations, results, analysis, and discussion. Global recommendations were suggested (see Exhibit 1-2).

In contrast, diagnostic data from the traditional report were reanalyzed and reorganized to form the translated psychoeducational report. The translated format consisted of three major divisions: (1) a diagnostic profile of variations in age-level functioning across several behavioral areas; (2) a narrative organized by functional and developmental domains that involved behavioral descriptions of the child's capabilities, deficits, learning style, and instructional needs; and (3) a description of developmental/learning targets to guide program planning as derived from the assessment results (see Exhibit 1-3).

Using the traditional and translated reports as a basis, teachers in the experimental and control groups selected instructional objectives from the developmental curriculum they employed in their programs that best matched the developmental problems discussed in each diagnostic report (see Table 1-2). Results showed that the experimental group teachers who used the translated report were more stable, accurate, and productive in constructing individualized linkages than the control group teachers who used the traditional diagnostic report. While the inservice training was moderately effective, the greatest impact on focusing teacher judgments about matching diagnostic and programming data can be attributed to the efficacy of translated over traditional diagnostic reporting procedures (88 vs. 54 percent) (see Tables 1-2 and 1-3).

Table 1-2 Total Assessment-Curriculum Links Correctly Matched by Report/Training Condition

Training/Report	*Total Linkages*
E1 (Translated report)	677
E2 (Translated report)	650
C (Traditional report)	260

Table 1-3 Percentage Teacher Linkage Agreement with Expert Standard by Report/Training Condition and Curriculum Area

Training/Report	*Communication*	*Self-care*	*Motor*	*Prob.-solv.*	*Total*
E1 (Translated)	.85	.88	.95	.85	.88
E2 (Translated)	.88	.83	.89	.79	.85
E (Traditional)	.48	.57	.62	.54	.54

SUPPORT FOR THE ASSESSMENT-CURRICULUM LINKAGE CONCEPT

When an assessment report is specific with respect to a child's actual behaviors—deficits and strengths—it can be used to pinpoint instructional targets within a program curriculum.

The assessment-curriculum linkage concept has had its widest application with school-age individuals in the form of criterion-referenced measurement. Nevertheless, the full application of linkage in school settings has been tenuous because no common approach or philosophy underlies school-age testing and teaching and because the behaviors focused upon are often very different—for instance, specific reading skills versus general intellectual abilities.

Fortunately, early assessment devices and early educational curricula share a common framework: a "developmental task-process" orientation. This common denominator makes possible the use of the linkage concept with the most practical impact. Diverse educational, clinical, and research support exists for linkage applied to early intervention settings.

Developmental Curricula and the Diagnostic-Prescriptive Approach with the Handicapped Preschooler

The notion of functional developmental assessment as a guide to individualized programming is intimately linked to the use of developmentally sequenced curricula. Jordan, Hayden, Karnes, and Wood (1977) stress this integrated relationship in examining preschool curricula. They state that there should be "clear logical links between what the curriculum is attempting to do (rationale), how it is organized to accomplish the specific aspects of its effort (content and objectives), and how accomplishment can be determined (evaluation)" (p. 153). This perspective implies the importance of a structured diagnostic-prescriptive approach within the framework of a clear rationale.

Scriven (1967), speaking of methodology in evaluation, underscores the need for three types of matches in the development of effective curricula:

1. A match between the goals of the curriculum and the content of the assessment.
2. A match between the goals of the curriculum and the content of instruction.
3. A match between the course content and the assessment content.

However, traditional practices rarely achieve these necessary "matches," as evidenced in Kamii and Elliott's call (1971) for developmental measures that will more effectively match the objectives of new curriculums for handicapped children.

The Diagnostic-Prescriptive Approach

The diagnostic-prescriptive model emphasizes assessment in order to delineate patterns of strengths and weaknesses and matching interventions designed to enhance deficit skills. Observable skills and measurable objectives are the keys to the reliability, validity, and practicality of such an approach (Ysseldyke & Bagnato, 1976). Preschool programs that combine comprehensive skill analysis with a normal developmental approach are called "developmental prescriptive" (Anastasiow & Mansergh, 1975). Hewett, Taylor, and Artuso (1968) support the notion of curriculum planning based on comprehensive skill assessment and developmental sequencing. Such an approach bridges the "translatability gap" between assessment and intervention.

Peter (1967) and Gearhart and Litton (1975) adhere to the prescriptive teaching model in programming for handicapped children. Instructional modifications are individualized and result specifically from an individual diagnostic profile of functional skills directed toward enhancing learning and developmental progress in children. The intent is to match the specific elements of the education program to diagnostic information. With the handicapped infant, Banus (1971) views comprehensive developmental diagnosis as the foundation of physical and educational therapy prescriptions.

Gillespie and Sitko (1976) perceive the diagnostic-prescriptive model as a method of systematizing the assessment and programming process. The operations of *in situ* teacher assessment, experimental teaching, program modification, and reevaluation make the teacher the major contributor to diagnosis and assessment.

Smith and Neisworth (1975), adhering to the developmental diagnostic-prescriptive model, assert that the major purpose of assessment is to make individual modifications in a child's educational program. "Teachers need to decide what curricular goals are appropriate for each youngster who possesses a particular constellation of behaviors. Within a very broad range, there are hierarchies of skills in which certain behaviors are dependent on the prior acquisition of other more elementary skills" (p. 206).

The developmental diagnostic-prescriptive model is best summarized in the approach of Stellern, Vasa, and Little (1976): "Functional assessment provides a basis for the development of a profile of student learning characteristics. To accomplish an effective *match* between student [capabilities and deficits] and materials to be used in instruction, the selection of materials should be based on the student's learning characteristics [functional assessment]" (p. 189).

Functional developmental assessment serves as the diagnostic basis for individualized educational programming, but developmental sequencing provides the common structural framework that links the two.

APPROACHES AND RESEARCH THAT SUPPORT THE LINKAGE PROCEDURE

Functional Assessment Approaches

The comprehensive functional approach to assessment and programming recognizes that evaluation of the handicapped child is a multidimensional process requiring the use of both norm-referenced and criterion-referenced measures. Both measures are employed in order to delineate the child's functional levels and to plan individual instructional goals. Several clinical approaches to assessment and programming lend support to this functional mode of operation and, thus, to the linkage concept.

Drew, Freston, and Logan (1972) claimed that "the gap between normative and criterion-referenced assessment may be bridged utilizing the strengths of both approaches" (p. 4). Within a functional approach, one must focus upon both interindividual and intraindividual differences in order to detail each child's profile of "primary distinguishing characteristics" (PDC) that indicate the child's specific instructional requirements. The greater the interface between a child's PDCs and instructional goals, the greater the potential for educational growth. Ongoing skill acquisition, in terms of enhancing deficit PDCs, then "serves as the criterion measure of success" (p. 7). Hammill (1971) advocated a similar "total evaluation" concept to guide individualized diagnostic-prescriptive teaching. Both formal and informal teacher-initiated assessment should be employed to increase the sample of a child's behavior, since school psychologists rarely have a knowledge of differential interventions. "Instruction and evaluation are not separate worlds but . . . are inseparably meshed" (p. 343).

Within the same concept, Lambert, Wilson, and Gleason (1974) described a purposeful process of using multiple measures to profile the educationally retarded child's functioning across several cognitive and adaptive areas. This multidimensional assessment process enables the psychologist to obtain specific diagnostic information in order to design educational objectives.

Bell (1975), while focusing on the visually impaired preschooler, emphasized a continuous, comprehensive assessment process that details present developmental levels, prescribes educational and service options based on a profile of strengths and weaknesses, and ensures continuous monitoring of the child's progress. This approach is implemented by adapting assessment to the child's problems and by using both normative and criterion-based measures as a basis for diagnostic-prescriptive teaching. Spungin and Swallow (1975) advocated an identical mode of operation in assessment, but stressed that the school psychologist needs to know "how to develop an appropriate strategy of intervention" (p. 67).

Modifying the Haeussermann (1958) approach with multihandicapped preschoolers, Jedrysek, Klapper, Pope, and Wortis (1972)developed an educational evaluation format that permits one to adapt assessment to survey the child's intact functioning across several sensory and cognitive areas. The results of the assessment serve as a curriculum guide, that is, a psychoeducational profile, that identifies deficits and instructional goals.

Whereas the Haeussermann approach used adaptive assessment of the handicapped child as a guide to intervention without a specific curriculum, Kamii and Elliott (1971) took the assessment process a step further by calling for the development and application of measurement techniques that effectively match the program objectives of new curricula for young children. Meier (1976) attempted to operationalize the "match" between developmental assessment tasks and infant curriculum objectives by suggesting a practical format that merged similar assessment and curriculum tasks. This format perceives the developmental inventory, that is, traditional norm-referenced developmental scales, as a "profile and base for curriculum planning" (p. 190). A child's pattern of skills and deficits on specifically numbered test activities are extracted and used as the basis for constructing task-analyzed sequences of entry, task, and terminal behaviors. In this way, "the behavioral series contained in infant assessment instruments will comprise not only an initial profile of the child but also a skeletal framework for the infant curriculum" (p. 194). Meier provides a strong rationale for the linkage procedure detailed in this book:

> It is unnecessary to be apologetic or surreptitious about employing the current and rather well conceptualized series of behaviors contained in various infant assessment instruments, at least as the skeletal framework for an infant curriculum . . . provided that the items sample behaviors which are universally recognized as essential indices of normal infant growth and development and constitute critical experiences in optimal human development. (p. 191)

Supporting Research

Few controlled studies have dealt with the practical problem of matching assessment tasks from traditional instruments with activities from curricula in order to facilitate diagnostic-prescriptive teaching. However, the results of peripherally related studies lend research support to the linkage concept (Meeker, 1969; MacTurk & Neisworth, 1978; Caldwell & Drachman, 1964; Fowler, 1972; Gordon, 1975; Morrison & Potheir, 1972; Valett, 1967).

Meeker (1969) devised a method of assigning Stanford-Binet items to cells in Guilford's Structure of the Intellect. Using interjudge reliability and factor analysis procedures to validate the match, Meeker demonstrated that congruent behaviors were being sampled within both test activities and Guilford's theoretical structure when groups of children performed on both sets of tasks. Furthermore, case studies on gifted children gave evidence that patterns of abilities and deficits on the congruent Binet-Guilford tasks could be reliably matched with activities from commercially available curricular materials to facilitate individualized programming in perceptual, language, and problem-solving areas.

In a study that compared the differential utility of normative and criterion-referenced measurement procedures in a mainstreamed preschool setting, MacTurk and Neisworth (1977) evaluated the developmental progress of 20 handicapped and nonhandicapped preschoolers across a 6-month period. Intercorrelations between Gesell diagnostic results from a psychologist and teacher-evaluated curriculum progress ranged from $r = .61$ to .93 for both groups with a mean correlation of $r = .91$ for the handicapped group. The results reflected a developmental similarity between Gesell test behaviors and HICOMP curriculum objectives and supported the usefulness of traditional developmental scales as reliable criterion-based measures of individual child progress and intervention effectiveness. Moreover, other similar studies (Bagnato, 1980; Bagnato & Neisworth, 1979) demonstrate that preschool teachers can easily learn to extract norm-based developmental data and targets from psychological reports and to match accurately such targets to appropriate curriculum objectives ($r = .88$).

Similarly, Caldwell and Drachman (1964) compared three methods of assessing the current developmental functioning of 52 infants, aged 1 to 2 years. The Griffiths, Cattell, and Gesell scales were chosen because of their mutual inclusion of similar developmental tasks. Results indicated that the correlations across age levels among the three scales were described by a range of $r = .77$ - .98, significant at the .01 level. The study supported the objectivity of the scales as measures of current functioning and the developmental similarity of tasks comprising the infant scales.

Fowler (1972) reported a Canadian study in which individualized assessment-based programming was instituted for 39 infants, ages 2 to 30 months. Multiple developmental domains were surveyed using the Bayley scales, the Stanford-Binet, and the Infant Behavior Inventory, and sequenced developmental objectives were established for each child. Significant increases in skill acquisition were revealed over a 1-year period. Success was attributed to the individualized programming based upon "diagnostic developmental monitoring" (p. 153) in which teachers received periodic profiles of each infant's rate of learning within multiple areas.

Gordon (1975) studied the impact of an intensive inpatient developmental program on 40 multihandicapped children, aged 18 to 36 months, and their parents. Results demonstrated that assigning developmental age levels to matching performances on test activities and instructional tasks yielded significantly more relevant information about child progress.

In a similarly designed study, Morrison and Potheir (1972) evaluated the developmental progress of 30 mentally retarded preschoolers with a mean age of

49 months. Sensorimotor activities were individually prescribed based upon performances on traditional developmental scales. The results demonstrated the significant advantage of employing a detailed analysis of sensorimotor deficits as a basis for selecting specific remedial activities.

In summary, the conclusion to be drawn from an array of clinical assessment approaches and research studies is that traditional developmental scales can be reliably employed as measures of current functioning and as criterion-based guides to individualized programming for handicapped preschoolers.

As Stellern et al. (1976) contend,

> functional assessment is a criterion-referenced approach to the systematic analysis of the learning behavior of students. Functional assessment focuses on how the individual learns, and compares individual performance to a fixed continuum of skills rather than to the mean performance of a group. Functional assessment augments traditional assessment procedures and provides additional information from which more effective individualized educational programs can be designed. (p. 175)

DEVELOPMENTAL DIAGNOSIS, INTERVENTION, AND LINKAGE: GUIDING CONCEPTS

Effective early intervention programs owe their success to systematic methods of integrating the processes of screening, comprehensive assessment, developmental intervention, and program evaluation. Subsequent chapters present a pragmatic system for integrating assessment and intervention; we call this procedure *assessment-curriculum linkage*. To serve as an ''advance organizer'' for understanding these phases of the system, this final section briefly discusses concepts that facilitate the forging of developmental linkages for young handicapped children. Each topic will be discussed in greater detail in later sections of the book.

Comprehensive Developmental Assessment

The process of functional developmental assessment of young handicapped children involves the collection of diagnostic information from many sources, covering many areas, and using a variety of measures, that is, it is a process of multisource, multidomain, multimeasure assessment.

Multisource means combining information about child functioning from a variety of perspectives: parent-teacher ratings, interviews, actual child performance, and curriculum-based records.

Multidomain concerns the wide-range coverage of functional skills across several behavioral areas: language, gross-fine motor, cognitive-perceptual, readiness, and personal-social.

Multimeasure involves the employment of diverse types of scales to tap child functioning. Norm-based measures serve to "compare" the exceptional child's skills with those of other children who are most like the child along several dimensions. Criterion-based scales serve to monitor the "individual" child's mastery of sequential developmental-behavioral objectives that are stressed in instruction. Adaptive-process scales are instruments that contain special tasks and procedures to circumvent partially the impairments of certain handicaps in assessment.

Developmental Intervention

Contemporary preschool programs for exceptional youngsters can differ in a number of ways: in underlying theory, characteristics of the curriculum employed, intervention methods, training of staff, type of program evaluation, or degree of parent involvement. Yet, although they may differ in these respects, *almost all effective programs use a developmental approach as the basis for assessment and instructional objectives*. Regardless of handicap, exceptional children are viewed *first* as requiring a program that promotes progress across all areas of development. Secondly, exceptional children need a program that addresses the specific deficits and demands of their handicapping condition.

With respect to assessment and educational objectives, an effective preschool program is concerned with the following questions:

- What is the child's current developmental status *in each* area of development? Assessment activities can provide information concerning the child's capabilities in language, motoric, social, and cognitive functioning. These four areas are part of almost all developmental assessment measures and almost all developmentally based curriculums.

- What special objectives are appropriate for the child because of the handicap? Depending on the child's sensory or response differences, certain special goals and objectives are important to permit progress. An obvious illustration is the objective of teaching blind children special mobility skills, or teaching children with no use of arms and hands how to use their feet for many purposes.

- What instructional objectives should be selected to start with, and which ones should follow? Fortunately, the teacher does not always have to "invent" objectives for every child. Numerous developmental curricula are available that include hundreds of instructional objectives. Accordingly, the teacher need only select a good curriculum (see chapter 4) and use it systematically. Appropriate developmental assessment will provide a profile of the child's current capabilities. This information can be used to determine entry points in a developmental curriculum. After that, the scope and sequence of the curriculum will guide the selection of subsequent objectives.

- How can the child's program be evaluated so that methods and materials can be adjusted? A good developmental curriculum provides objectives that are taught until mastery is achieved. As the child reaches whatever criterion of mastery is used for each objective, a check-off system can be used as a record of progress. This record of progress within the curriculum should be quite similar to progress on developmental assessment measures. This should not be surprising since both the assessment instruments and the curriculum contain similar developmental-skill items. Test-retest results between time 1 and time 2 and progress in the curriculum from time 1 to time 2 should correlate highly.

Early educators who use developmental assessment and curricula experience relatively little difficulty in determining initial objectives, in prescribing the sequence of objectives, and in monitoring progress. In brief, a developmental, functional approach unites assessment with curriculum and makes the design of individual educational plans a straightforward, systematic procedure.

The Developmental Task Approach: A Bridge

The developmental task approach presents the notion that human development is composed of a series of sequential processes and tasks that arise invariantly within certain age ranges and stages for all individuals. The tasks emerge during "sensitive" periods in the lives of all individuals when the psychological, social, and neuro-motor systems are most receptive to stimulation and growth. Successful mastery of tasks makes it possible to attain more complex life skills later. Most developmental scales and infant-preschool curricula contain task-sequences that reflect to general or specific degrees this philosophy. The assessment-curriculum linkage systems attempt to capitalize on the "developmental task" approach to bond assessment and intervention.

Developmental Assessment-Curriculum Linkages

The linkage procedure operates on the assumption that there must be an essential similarity between the behaviors *tested* and the skills *taught*. Using the developmental task sequence as the unifying bridge, the assessment process generates a series of developmental "targets" representing the child's range of deficits and emerging capabilities. Similar targets within a developmental curriculum are then selected to match the levels of the assessment targets. These "developmental linkages" or skill targets comprise the child's individual intervention plan.

As stated earlier, Individualized Education Programs or IEPs are actually the tangible products of the linkage system. In essence, the child's current levels of functioning in several developmental areas are defined. Goals for intervention are established on the basis of the comprehensive assessment results. Individualized instructional objectives are written in congruence with the assessment results. Thus, a match is established between a child's needs and instructional objectives.

Chapter 2

Developmental Assessment of Young Exceptional Children: Principles and Procedures

The Education of All Handicapped Children Act (1975) and the Developmental Disabilities Act (1978) make significant changes in the organization and provision of developmental and educational services to handicapped learners. The new laws provide guidelines that influence how specialists perceive, assess, and plan treatments for exceptional learners, particularly handicapped infants and preschoolers.

The Individualized Educational Program (IEP) is the direct and tangible outcome of these new trends. The well-designed IEP clearly outlines instructional objectives and related methods and materials for working with a specific child. Further, an acceptable IEP *must* be based on a full assessment of the child's current developmental status. The IEP, then, is a plan for going *from* current capabilities *to* higher levels of functioning. *Assessment should provide the baseline of where a child is and give help in specifying targets for achievement.*

To be instructionally relevant, assessment must serve dual roles of determining current *and* projected developmental status. In order to fulfill both of these purposes, assessment must meet certain criteria to ensure its usefulness in designing IEPs.

Unfortunately, few school psychologists and other diagnostic specialists have had specific developmental training applicable to the birth to 5-year-old child, let alone the developmentally disabled preschool child. The elements of federal legislation and current educational trends underscore the need to enhance the training of psychologists and early educators in developmentally based assessment and programming. In order to ensure more appropriate and useful assessment, contemporary professional preparation now stresses several guidelines regarding assessment, program planning, and evaluation for developmental intervention. This chapter discusses these qualities or criteria for assessment of young handicapped children. When met, these guidelines ensure that developmental assessment will be highly direct and relevant for instructional planning and evaluation.

SUGGESTED QUALITIES FOR DEVELOPMENTAL ASSESSMENT

For purposes of program planning, developmental assessment should be

- phenotypic, rather than genotypic
- comprehensive, rather than narrow
- multisource and multimethod, rather than built on a single or few sources and methods
- adaptive to the handicap, rather than follow (nonhandicap) standardized administration procedures
- purposeful and applied, rather than aimless and abstract

Each of these criteria is discussed in this section.

Phenotypic

"Phenotypic" refers to observable, manifest characteristics. When assessment methods use a phenotypic approach, they provide a clear analysis of what the child can *do* and *not do*. On the other hand, a "genotypic" approach is one that attempts to assess a child's "condition" or "underlying problem," that is, what a child *is*. A developmental or psychological report is phenotypic if it describes a child's actual behavior and apparent capabilities. "Jimmy has trouble in adding beyond two places, showing errors in carrying numbers"—is an example of an observation of what Jimmy currently can do or not do. A report couched in genotypic language refers to alleged, unseen processes that supposedly account for the child's problems. "Jimmy suffers from dyscalculia and poor numeric memory" describes presumed underlying (genotypic) conditions but does not specify actual performance. When such genotypic reports are furnished by school psychologists or other professionals, it would be wise to ask them to "decode" their reports and to translate them into phenotypic language. When it is clear what a child can do or not do, instructional planning is much more direct and on target.

Comprehensive

Testing and assessment are related but not identical activities. Each of us has had our abilities *tested* in our school experience, but few of us have had our capabilities *assessed*. The critical differences between these two operations are magnified when treating children with developmental and learning disorders. The prime distinction directly involves the quality, scope, and usefulness of the information obtained during the process of evaluation. As Salvia and Ysseldyke (1978) state,

> *Testing,* then, means exposing a person to a particular set of questions in order to obtain a score. That score is the end product of testing. . . . *Assessment* in educational settings is a multifaceted process that involves far more than the administration of a test. When we assess students, we consider the way they perform a variety of tasks in a variety of settings and contexts, the meaning of their performances in terms of the total functioning of the individual, and likely explanations for those performances. . . . It provides information that can enable teachers and other school personnel to make decisions regarding the children they serve. (pp. 3-4)

Assessment must be a *comprehensive process* of collecting information about child functioning across all developmental areas. Information must be gathered that permits analysis of the child's status in language, personal-social, motor, and cognitive development. Seldom are developmental problems "pure" and specific. An infant with motor problems may not be able to move around the environment as much as another child. As a result of restricted mobility, other areas of development may suffer, for example, cognitive development. Often, also, language and social growth are stunted when mobility problems are severe. It should be clear, therefore, that problems in one area of functioning may be related to problems in others. Assessment, accordingly, must cover all areas of development in order to provide the whole picture of the child's functional development. Comprehensive assessment is often *diagnostic,* that is, it seeks to describe a child's strengths, weaknesses, and psychological and educational needs. The end result is very practical—the creation of *individual plans of therapy and instruction* that meet special needs and lead to more positive child functioning. The school psychologist and the teacher are generally the pivotal individuals in this diagnostic/assessment process.

Multimeasure and Multisource

Reliable developmental assessment of handicapped infants and preschoolers demands both a multimeasure and multisource approach.

Multimeasure refers to the use of a variety of assessment devices and approaches in order to obtain a more thorough view of a child's developmental profile. Combining various kinds of measures provides a solid basis for more accurate program planning. Norm-referenced, criterion-referenced, task-analytic, standardized, informal, and adaptive measures (these will be discussed later) can all provide important information.

Multisource assessment means seeking a wider perspective of the child by obtaining information from various persons in contact with the child. Observations and data from a team—developmental school psychologists, early special educators, physical and occupational therapists, speech/language specialists, parents, and child psychiatrists—are crucial in planning for the needs of young exceptional children. When assessment information comes from only a single source—for example, the school psychologist—it may be limited, at odds with teacher judgments, or fail to take into account behavior that is situation specific. We all know of children who are expressive in one setting but not another, who are toilet trained at home but not elsewhere, or who are aggressive in selective settings. Observations from only one source could be misleading and unreliable.

Multimeasure, multisource assessment provides the strong, stable collection of findings across types of measures, across persons, and across settings that permits accurate and comprehensive program planning.

Adaptive to the Handicap

Most developmental measures have been standardized on normal children. That is, both the content and administration of most testing and information-gathering devices do not take into account the sensory and response problems of handicapped youngsters. Limitations in sight and hearing can, of course, create developmental problems for a child. With regard to assessment, such limitations can seriously alter a child's performance during testing or observation. When a child cannot see test materials or hear instructions, test results will obviously be depressed. The solution is to *adapt* items and procedures in order to minimize the distortion of results.

This adaptive approach is not without problems. A standardized instrument should be administered just the way it was with the children on whom it was standardized. When items and procedures are varied, it becomes difficult to compare a child's standing with the original reference group. Nevertheless, this variance from standard procedure is necessary if some instruments are to be used at all. While the results may be questionable from a strict psychometric perspective, they gain credibility when seen in conjunction with other results and clinical judgment.

Problems of response limitations likewise demand adaptive procedures. A cerebral palsied child with no control of hands or arms obviously cannot perform in tasks calling for manipulation of objects. For such a child, either the item must be changed or some alternative response mode (e.g., a head wand) must be employed. The point is that we must adapt our assessment to meet the differences of each child, otherwise assessment may be a futile psychometric exercise.

Purposeful and Applied

Accurate and meaningful developmental assessment is a continuous, general-to-specific procedure that proceeds according to some clear purposes. A purpose in assessment guides the selection of measures and facilitates individual programming. There are several reasons for testing and observing children: screening, identification, comprehensive assessment, curriculum linkage, individualized programming, program evaluation. Depending on the purpose, assessment measures and procedures will differ. An instrument designed for screening cannot be used for comprehensive assessment or program evaluation. If the purpose of assessment is to guide instructional programming, especially linkage to a program's curriculum, then certain standards, which otherwise would not be necessary, must be adhered to. It is this purpose—assessment for instruction—that is the central concern of this book. When the purpose is instruction but assessment is conducted and reported for other purposes, the results are often useless and confusing to the teacher. It is incumbent on the teacher to demand instructionally relevant assessment when that is the purpose of the assessment effort.

TRENDS AND CONSIDERATIONS IN DEVELOPMENTAL ASSESSMENT

Recent trends in the field of early special education stress the crucial importance of early detection of developmental problems in infants and preschool-age children (Meier, 1976). The emphasis is on early identification as well as the continuous monitoring of skill acquisition in order to prevent problems and to intervene before secondary disabilities emerge (Capute & Biehl, 1973). As Chase (1975) notes, "When problems are identified . . . and treatment plans formulated and executed . . . the psychologist is engaging in the 'highest order' evaluation, *preventive assessment*" (p. 342).

It is apparent that the notion of systematic intervention is linked to the operation of identification and assessment in theory but often not in practice. The nature of this link between assessment and intervention is especially critical when serving the handicapped preschooler. However, numerous issues, problems, and considerations concerning the processes and diagnosis of normal and abnormal development must be addressed so that this assessment/programming linkage can be achieved.

The psychological assessment of the preschool child begins with an appraisal of the nature and rate of the child's development and seeks to detect possible factors that may be deterring growth. "Assessment is part of an overall process that is a starting point and not an end in itself. Assessment is a dynamic and ongoing process" (Erickson, 1976, p. 1). Knowledge of normative principles of growth and development can aid in the planning and implementation of systematic interventions for handicapped youngsters.

Knobloch and Pasamanick (1974), advocating the clinical approach of Gesell, support the concept of using the principles and sequences of normal behavior in development as a framework on which to base assessment and intervention. As they state, "development is subject to diagnosis, because the construction of the action system of the infant and child is an orderly process" (p. 4). In this perspective, normal behavior development displays specific patterns across motor, adaptive, language, and personal-social areas. Since behavior patterns serve as indicators of the maturity and integrity of the child's developing nervous system, developmental assessment can detect imbalance in a child's behavior repertoire in comparison with normal, characteristic patterns of development. The developmental-behavioral approach to assessment is the fundamental perspective and method employed in evaluating both normal and abnormal development (Knobloch & Pasamanick, 1962; Palmer, 1970; Illingworth, 1970; Haeussermann, 1958; Capute & Biehl, 1973). The approach is a fundamental one because it is based upon established principles of development and growth derived from research and clinical practice. The following list of principles and trends underscores the developmental behavioral approach to assessment and is particularly relevant when focusing on the handicapped preschooler:

- Developmental sequences are generally the same for all children, although each child progresses at his or her own rate within variable patterns.
- Individual variations in development are evident at an early age and show substantial consistency with increases in age.
- Development proceeds in a hierarchical and nearly "building-block fashion" in which competency at rudimentary skills is viewed as a prerequisite for the acquisition of more complex capabilities.
- Critical, "sensitive" periods appear to exist when susceptibility or readiness for new learning is greatest and when focused assessment and structured intervention have the most impact.
- Development proceeds in a cephalocaudal (head to foot), proximodistal (body midline to extremities) direction and reflects a progression from diffuse or general to more specific functioning.
- Individual progress in development is highly variable and marked by accelerations, regressions and plateaus. Such variability helps account for low correlations between early and later intellectual functioning.
- Development is multidimensional and occurs simultaneously across several behavioral domains.

- Development is a function of the interaction between individual maturation and environmental stimulation; problems in development must be attributed to this interaction, rather than to the child or the environment alone.
- Developmental-skill acquisition shows a progression from predominantly sensorimotor behaviors early in infancy to verbally mediated behavior in later childhood.
- Infant development and assessment should be perceived as a dynamic, continuous, multidimensional, and individual process. The more specific the measures employed to assess this process, the more that individual variability becomes evident.

Working within the framework of the developmental-behavioral approach, the psychologist, through assessment, can determine *where* the child stands within the developmental sequence, *what* the child's capabilities and deficits are, and *how* and *under what conditions* the child learns best. "If early assessment leads to early intervention, so that those closely involved in the care and training of the child glean directions for fostering development, the appraisal is worthwhile" (Chase, 1975, p. 341).

Issues and Problems in Developmental Assessment

There is a dilemma in preschool assessment—the critical need for early identification and assessment of developmental problems versus, first, the questionable adequacy of the many measures employed and, second, the limited and variable developmental patterns of the children assessed.

Numerous studies summarized by Yang and Bell (1975) and Thomas (1970) present data that question the reliability and validity of developmental measures. However, other clinicians and researchers (Illingworth, 1970; Knobloch & Pasamanick, 1974) dispute these results, both by presenting conflicting data and by pointing out the existence of widespread misunderstandings about the purpose and function of developmental diagnosis. Several factors account for these contradictory perspectives. Early child development is characterized by a limited behavioral repertoire that is predominantly sensorimotor in nature. Also, early developmental skills are quantitatively and qualitatively different from later skills. Infant "intelligence," for example, does not seem to be defined and measured in the same fashion as adult intelligence (Lewis, 1973). This view underscores the necessity for focusing upon multiple factors and domains in developmental diagnosis rather than on intelligence per se.

Another side of the issue concerns the care in maintaining standardized procedures in preschool assessment. The tenuous reliability and validity of preschool assessment scales would seem to demand standardized administration, yet the child's limited behavioral repertoire, distractibility, transient responsiveness, and functional disabilities suggest the need for adapting procedures and testing to the limits (Chase, 1975). This dilemma gains in magnitude when dealing with handicapped preschoolers. In fact, approaches such as Haeussermann's (1958) favor the use of adaptive rather than standardized procedures with cerebral palsied and other multihandicapped preschoolers.

Simeonsson and Wiegerink (1975) focus the issue directly on the handicapped preschooler by asserting that scales designed for the normal child are often inappropriate for the handicapped child. The problem is compounded by the fact that while children are developmentally more similar than different, diverse individual differences exist among handicapped children (Wolf & Anderson, 1969; Simeonsson & Wiegerink, 1975). "Real interest lies not in knowing how a handicapped infant or youngster would function if he were normal . . . but rather in knowing how his handicaps have influenced the sequence and pattern of his development" (Simeonsson & Wiegerink, 1975). Despite the soundness of this perspective, critics warn against the dangers of early labelling and premature diagnosis (Chase, 1975). In the end, the problems and issues are reduced to the basic questions of the purpose of developmental assessment and the best approach to be employed.

Purpose in Developmental Assessment

In traditional assessment procedures, no logical or practical link is recognized between evaluation and actual instruction (Chinn, 1975). But beyond the role of screening and identification, developmental assessment should guide individualized curriculum planning. Chase (1975) stresses this point by noting that, "as with any appraisal of an individual's functioning, the most important first consideration is the purpose. . . . Unless the findings are translated into action, particularly in the early stages of life, assessment becomes merely an exercise" (p. 341).

Critics have overemphasized the predictive validity question and have misconstrued developmental assessment as being intellectual in nature (Capute & Biehl, 1973; Knobloch & Pasamanick, 1974). In doing so, they have lost sight of the basic function of developmental assessment—to provide insights into *current levels of functioning* (Bayley, 1969; Illingworth, 1970). Viewed in this manner, the process of developmental assessment provides a "baseline" from which to plan instruction fitted to individual patterns of skills and deficits (Meier, 1976; Banus, 1971). With the emphasis on curriculum planning in assessment, the issue of labelling loses its relevance.

In serving multihandicapped, preschool populations, various specialists propose a flexible, purposeful, and practical approach that emphasizes the assessment of current functional levels across multiple areas, the planning of individualized goals, and the continuous monitoring of skill acquisition. Capute and Biehl (1973) highlight this approach regarding the handicapped preschooler.

> Knowledge of the child's current developmental level can be shown to be necessary when plans are formulated for his education or habilitation. . . . For purposes of habilitation [intervention], a functional profile must be determined wherein all of each child's important weaknesses and strengths, functional attainments and lags, are identified. A plan of therapy whereby the child is helped to use his individual portfolio of abilities in the achievement of the next higher level of personal independence must then be developed. (pp. 3, 4)

A Pragmatic, Integrative Approach in Developmental Assessment

Proposed solutions to the dilemma of assessing the capabilities of handicapped preschoolers have centered on three basic alternatives: (a) developing test materials standardized on the handicapped group in question, (b) adapting existing instruments to meet the response capabilities of the handicapped group, (c) giving age-appropriate instruments to estimate the child's functioning under realistic demands without regard to handicap. All three approaches present serious limitations regarding reliability, validity, limited behavior samples, and an emphasis on exclusion with the handicapped child.

The more realistic and practical approach in the developmental assessment of the handicapped preschooler appears to be that promoted by Haeussermann (1958) and Dubose, Langley, and Stagg (1979), which integrates elements of the previously cited modes of operation. Essentially, developmental assessment is viewed as encompassing both norm-referenced and criterion-referenced qualities. The developmental sequencing of tasks and skills enables one to compare the handicapped child's performance to that of the comparably aged normal child, while the child's intraindividual pattern of capabilities and deficits provides a basis for planning instructional goal-sequences. The approach combines the use of both standardized and nonstandardized tasks in a "systematic sampling strategy" to test the limits of the child's ability to function while adapting tasks to the particular handicap and response mode. This approach has gained greater educational focus for teachers through the modifications of Jedrysek et al. (1972).

Simeonsson and Wiegerink (1975) and Bagnato and Neisworth (1980) advocate a similar "practical" versus "purist" orientation in combining multiple measures to assess the handicapped preschooler. In this perspective, indexes of test progress and indexes of intervention progress are interrelated through a sequence of clearly defined developmental skills and objectives. The resulting "efficiency index" (p. 475) underscores the advantage of using developmental scatter and age-level scores rather than global developmental quotients as measures of functional skills. "It is essential that strategies be adopted to measure developmental changes which are functionally related to programmatic intervention" (p. 450). "The question is how to select, modify, and use instruments and approaches which will enhance documentation in comparative analyses of child and program progress" (p. 475). In similar approaches, Chase (1975) and Lewis (1973) advocate matching the evaluation of the child's skills and the monitoring of intervention progress by using specific developmental tasks and activities rather than global scores such as developmental quotients.

A REVIEW OF BASIC DEVELOPMENTAL ASSESSMENT APPROACHES

Developmental diagnosis is a process of detailing and analyzing a child's capabilities and deficits as they affect functioning across many interrelated areas of behavior. Most experts in the early intervention area stress that the fundamental purpose of developmental assessment should be the planning of individualized treatment programs. Yet, disagreement often centers upon the most effective procedure to reach this goal with young handicapped children. Various excellent reviews of general developmental diagnostic approaches have appeared in recent years (Simeonsson, 1977; Dubose et al., 1979; Chase, 1975). In general, a multimeasure, multisource approach to assessment is advocated, consisting of vital child information gained through norm-referenced, criterion-referenced, adaptive, behavioral and subjective judgment sources. In this manner, a comprehensive assessment of the handicapped child's developmental skills that pinpoints goals and strategies for intervention can be achieved.

The following paragraphs examine each of these major developmental assessment approaches.

Norm-Referenced Assessment: Comparative Evaluation

Basically, norm-referenced (NR) scales are designed and used to compare a particular child's skills and abilities with other children who are most like the child along several dimensions, that is, age, sex, socioeconomic status, and so on. Norm-referenced assessment (NRA) most often results in age or functional-level scores that provide a comparative index for describing the child's status. The process is basically *quantitative* in nature presenting an indication of average functioning across multiple skills and abilities.

NR developmental assessment typically yields a developmental age score or range that represents the child's most stable level of skill development. For example, a child with a chronological age of 42 months may be able to perform effectively only those tasks that the average 30-month-old child can complete. Thus, the 42-month-old child's functional skills are limited and more typical of the 2½-year-old child. However, unless an analysis is made of the kinds of tasks which the child failed to complete and the child's usual approach to problem solving, only *general* information about learning needs and educational goals is provided. In addition, NR developmental assessment provides a "developmental quotient" (DQ), which is a standard score describing the general status of a child's capabilities much as the developmental-age score does. The DQ basically reflects the relationship between a child's level of functioning and chronological age. For example, whereas the normal or average 42-month-old child may have a DQ of 90-110, child A, also 42 months old, may have a DQ of 75, indicating significant dysfunctions in developmental functioning compared to the average 3½-year-old child.

NR scales are vitally important in the process of determining global levels or ranges of skill acquisition. When separate age ranges are provided for different developmental domains—that is, cognitive, language, motor, personal-social—a valuable profile of strengths and weaknesses is provided that can serve as a baseline for curriculum planning.

Despite the value of NR scales, when used alone they convey only general information about functional capabilities and do not precisely pinpoint skill deficits in such a manner as to be useful in teaching. These measures have their most justifiable use in providing a diagnostic "entry point" and in evaluating overall child progress and program effectiveness. When, however, NR developmental scales are matched with other measures in a multidimensional battery, their educational relevance is enhanced. Evidence suggests that where a strong similarity exists between the behaviors tested and the behaviors taught, NR scales have much greater instructional application when matched with developmentally sequenced curricula. The normal developmental task sequence aids this integration process since most infant-preschool tests and curricula have this as their foundation (MacTurk & Neisworth, 1978; Bagnato & Neisworth, in press; Meier, 1976).

Finally, caution should be exercised in employing NRA, since the tasks and standardization are very often incompatible with the handicaps of many developmentally disabled children. Only adaptive assessment procedures that allow alternate methods of responding can hope to determine accurately individual differences that are often obscured in NRA.

Examples of norm-referenced developmental scales discussed in the next chapter include the Bayley Scales of Infant Development (Bayley, 1969) and The Gesell Developmental Schedules (Knobloch & Pasamanick, 1974).

Criterion-Referenced Assessment: Skill-Mastery Evaluation

While norm-referenced developmental assessment compares a child *quantitatively* to a normative group of children, criterion-referenced assessment (CRA) evaluates individual *quality* of performance. Thus, stress is placed upon individual mastery of well-defined sequences of developmental skills rather than on the relative status of children. Criteria or levels of mastery for such skill objectives are established, and the children's performances are rated against these criteria. In effect, however, the children are being compared to themselves over time as their progressive mastery of more complex, sequential skills is monitored. For example, CRA allows the teacher to determine in a *task analysis* the specific breakdown of skills the child has or has not developed along the developmental sequence. In this manner, the individual quality of performance is determined, that is, in terms of acquired (+), absent (−), and emerging (±) capabilities. This analysis provides specific entry points at which instruction can be appropriately started. Once this is accomplished, the teacher then teaches the needed skills toward mastery. Follow-up assessment using the same criterion-referenced sequence of developmental tasks evaluates both child progress and program effectiveness. CRA is the one procedure that effectively imbeds assessment within programming; it has thus been called the "test-teach-test" model. CRA enables one to pinpoint not only deficit skills but, often, the processes, and strategies typically used by a particular child to solve problems and master skills.

One of the major differences between norm- and criterion-referenced developmental assessment is the specificity of tasks and sequences included within the scales. NR developmental measures, like screening tests, focus on various "landmark" tasks or skills that are necessary prerequisites to later development and learning, but in a more comprehensive manner than screening tests. Yet, these landmark tasks are often only the first step in a longer chain of developmental behaviors. For example, although we may know a child has not acquired the skill of "walking independently," the NR scale may give us no information about the child's acquisition of prerequisite "walking skills" earlier in the developmental sequence. Thus, NR scales have limited utility for handicapped children.

On the other hand, CR measures provide much longer and more detailed sequences of developmental skills that more accurately define the handicapped child's specific capabilities and deficits. However, as you may expect, CR measures are generally more cumbersome and time-consuming to administer. They are usually employed only periodically within an educational program.

The most familiar types of criterion-referenced developmental measures of varying quality are those that are curriculum-imbedded devices. These include the Learning Accomplishment Profile (Sanford, 1978), the Memphis Comprehensive Developmental Scale (Quick, Little, & Campbell, 1974a, 1974b), and Developmental Programming for Infants and Young Children (Rogers, D'Eugenio, Brown, Donovan, & Lynch, 1977).

Adaptive-Process Assessment: Functional Evaluation

Assessing children's developmental capabilities can be effectively accomplished only when comprehensive information is gathered through a variety of sources. This involves combining norm-referenced, criterion-referenced, and subjective judgment data across multiple areas of functioning. However, the limitations of each of these methods are most evident when the method is employed exclusively. The limitations of any one approach are further magnified when diagnostic specialists must assess young children who suffer multiple handicaps and therefore cannot adequately demonstrate their capabilities on traditional instruments. Various physical, neuro-motor, sensory, and emotional impairments present a special dilemma in this regard. Modifications in the assessment process must be made in a flexible, but systematic, manner to enable children to respond through a variety of alternative modes. Table 2-1 presents an outline of several adaptive options.

As mentioned previously, several approaches have emerged over the years to alleviate the handicapped assessment dilemma. Common solutions have involved designing special normed tests for a specific handicapped group (Hiskey, 1966; Newland, 1973), altering the response modes required on certain scales (French, 1964; Sattler & Tozier, 1970), and administering traditional scales in the usual manner to look at deficit child functioning under "realistic" conditions (Louttit, 1957). It is obvious, however, that all three options present unique disadvantages that limit their effectiveness in serving young exceptional children.

On the issue of assessing the young, multiply handicapped child, most specialists in early intervention advocate a multimeasure approach that combines vital elements of norm-referenced and criterion-referenced assessment. This approach is called *adaptive-process* assessment. The views of Allotti (1977), Haeussermann (1958), Dubose et al. (1979), Simeonsson (1977), and Chase (1975) are most representative of this approach. These observers advocate a flexible, yet systematic method of evaluating upper and lower limits of the child's ability to complete tasks. In particular, they stress the need to modify activities in a structured manner to compensate for a particular impairment and to allow for alternative response modes. Adaptive-process assessment combines testing and teaching as part of a single adaptive diagnostic *process*. On the one hand, diagnostic specialists can determine a normative developmental range/level of functioning for the young child while also detailing individual strengths and limitations in a criterion-based manner. Adaptive modifications are employed to further individualize the assessment process. For instance, the size and construction of blocks and puzzle boards can be altered, the complexity of four choice-discrimination tasks can be modified,

Table 2-1 Adaptive Strategies in Assessing the Young Exceptional Child

- Stress looking at tests not only as predictive measures, but as the initial stage in individualized goal-planning, and as samples of *current functioning.*
- No test is inherently unfair, only the user—lack of validity refers not to the test, itself, but rather to the purpose to which the results are applied. "Invalid for what?" (Cronbach, 1971).

1. *Combine and group tasks within one or various instruments that tap certain behaviors or functional characteristics that you want to focus on in assessment (Smorgasbord).*

- Memory span, form discrimination, receptive language skills categorization and sequencing, auditory-visual discrimination.

2. *Systematically alter the response mode required to function on and complete various tasks.*

- Pointing vs. expressive language, headpointing vs. fingerpointing, eye localization vs. gesturing, steady child's hand on motor items.

3. *Alter the method of evoking the response.*

- Tasks requiring completion, filling in, and elaboration through language changed to yes-no, multiple-choice formats; use of pantomime directions and responses.

4. *Omit task that you believe biases the results due to the child's handicapping conditions, and modify scoring criteria on selected items to accommodate child's persistence and behavior.*

- Omit beading-stringing and block-building activities for the C.P. child—eliminate timed criteria on motor tasks, check for goal-direction, persistence, and quality of completion.

Table 2-1 continued

5. *Decision to utilize nonverbal vs. verbal tasks for the language-impaired, C.P. and multiply handicapped child.*

6. *Rearranging order of presentation of items within a test.*

- Administer nonverbal items before verbal ones to facilitate establishment of rapport.

7. *Alter size and composition of objects and tasks within a test to accommodate child's limitations.*

- Alter activities by using larger pictures, blocks, handles on formboards, or by rearranging order of pictures and their spacing; use of concrete and three-dimensional objects rather than pictured-symbolic items.

8. *Combine multiple measures that sample similar skills to increase reliability of results and scope of behavior samples.*

9. *Use norm-referenced tasks in a criterion-referenced manner.*

- *Test-teach-test model.* Give item in standardized way and note performance, then instruct child in the activity by highlighting relevant cues to the solution, reducing number of pictures on a card by covering up, asking focal questions, and using demonstration on the item; then administer the same or similar test task to evaluate the effect and transfer of your instructional strategy.

10. *Task-analysis and work-sample approach to assessment.*

the use of concrete objects versus the same objects in pictures can be included to appraise intact functioning at a lower level of comprehension. In addition, pointing, eye localization, yes-no, multiple choice, and spontaneous toy-play response modes can be used to determine the level of understanding of concepts. In practice, this adaptive-process approach is a functional evaluation method that merges assessment and curriculum elements in order to

- determine functional developmental levels in multiple areas,
- identify alternate methods of responding,
- discover the child's typical strategies for solving problems,
- select "entry points" to guide curriculum planning,
- modify tasks to compensate for functional impairments, and
- arrange child-management strategies to promote individual developmental progress.

It must be remembered that assessment of young multiply handicapped children is further confounded by the fact that their disabilities often prevent or limit access to stimulating learning experiences during "critical" developmental periods. Their receptivity to stimulation is blunted, and therefore critical cognitive, language, and personal-social skills necessary for later complex learning are not intact. For example, the physically impaired and blind infant has significant sensorimotor dysfunctions that tend to blunt the development of a conception of object permanence.

Because so many handicapped youngsters have had restricted sensory and motor experiences, adaptive developmental assessment must also be viewed as a continuous stimulation/learning activity. The process seeks not only to determine current levels of operation but also to teach the young child the critical features of novel problems and situations. This facilitates the development of selective attention, orientation to the task, interpersonal skills, and basic problem solving. In this manner, testing and teaching are interdependent phases of the same diagnostic process.

The primary outcome of adaptive-process assessment is to effect a "match" between a child's capabilities and the instructional environment. Developmental skills must be assessed within different situational contexts, that is, home versus preschool and teacher/specialist versus parent. In this way, the influences of different people and different environments in eliciting behavior can be appraised. Also, the virtues of certain adults and helpful situational factors, such as low distraction and secure surroundings, can be incorporated within the intervention program. Evidence of generalization and learning is provided if a child demonstrates a skill consistently across situations and across teachers. Thus children should experience a variety of professionals who work with them. This will increase skill generalization and result in more stable performance.

Finally, behavior should be assessed within a known context so that the interaction between situational demands and child capabilities can be monitored. For example, a planned play situation within the preschool using a variety of materials can provide valuable diagnostic data. Observing how a severely involved child attempts to obtain and handle a toy or object, searches for a spoon dropped during feeding, or inserts a spoon in a cup provides evidence of object constancy, use of tools and utensils, and comprehension of functional relationships as well as interpersonal relationships.

Measures such as the Developmental Activities Screening Inventory (Dubose & Langley, 1977), the Callier-Azusa Scale for the assessment of deaf-blind children (Stillman, 1974), and the Battelle Developmental Inventory (Guidubaldi, Newborg, Stock, & Wnek, in press) are representative of measures in this expanding area. As yet, however, few commercially available developmental scales are designed using the adaptive-process assessment approach. Most often, the evaluator must put together and adapt a variety of measures that provide functional estimates of capabilities. This tends to increase the reliability of the results, their comprehensiveness, and, ultimately, the instructional confidence we can place in them.

SUMMARY

> Precision prescriptive teaching demands better performance of the evaluator, which frequently results in the criterion-referenced use of instruments that were originally developed on a norm-referenced basis. (Chinn, Drew, & Logan, 1975, p. 73).

This quotation effectively encapsulates the essence of comprehensive developmental diagnosis as it applies to the handicapped infant and preschool child. The nature and course of early development, the effect of multiple disabilities in altering its pattern, and the purpose and effect of early intervention are prominent considerations in designing total services for young handicapped children. The processes of developmental assessment and curriculum planning are interdependent phases in this total service system. *Assessment, in order to be effective, must serve as a functional baseline for individualized programming.* Traditional (norm-based) assessment practices that compare children are ineffective by themselves. Criterion-referenced procedures are more instructionally relevant but often force a view of the child in isolation in relation to some educational standard. Adaptive-process assessment approaches that combine norm-based, criterion-based, curriculum, functional, and judgmental measures enable specialists to more comprehensively assess the capabilities of young developmentally disabled children. In brief, measures must be selected that provide a picture of current child functioning, that compensate for impairments, and that lead directly to educational prescriptions.

Chapter 3

Close-Ups of Prominent Developmental Measures

The developmental capabilities of young handicapped children *can* be validly assessed. Further, the effects of planned individual intervention *can* be detected as progressive gains on such assessments. The outcomes of preliminary research indicate that these assertions are correct *if* measures are selected that (a) are developmentally based, (b) survey functional skills across multiple developmental domains, (c) derive from multiple-source perspectives, and (d) contain tasks that match the goals taught within the curriculum. In this manner, assessment and intervention are intimately "linked." Thus, the processes of screening → identification → comprehensive assessment → individualized goal-planning → child and program evaluation are interdependent and collectively contribute to individualized educational programming (see Figure 3-1).

This chapter provides a series of brief profiles of various developmental scales with which early childhood specialists should be familiar. The coverage is purposefully selective and includes only frequently used measures that lend themselves readily to the process of linking assessment to programming. The measures were selected according to several criteria and are reviewed under the topics of norm-referenced measures, criterion-based curriculum measures, and adaptive-process measures. Appendix A and the test matrixes at the end of the book provide summaries and comparative descriptive information on a variety of developmental and psychoeducational measures covering the birth-to-eight-year age range.

CRITERIA FOR ANALYZING AND SELECTING DEVELOPMENTAL SCALES

To ensure quality programming for young exceptional children, assessment measures must be selected that can be directly linked to a program's available curriculum resources. Early special educators, developmental school psycholo-

Figure 3-1 Interlinking Purposes in Comprehensive Developmental Assessment

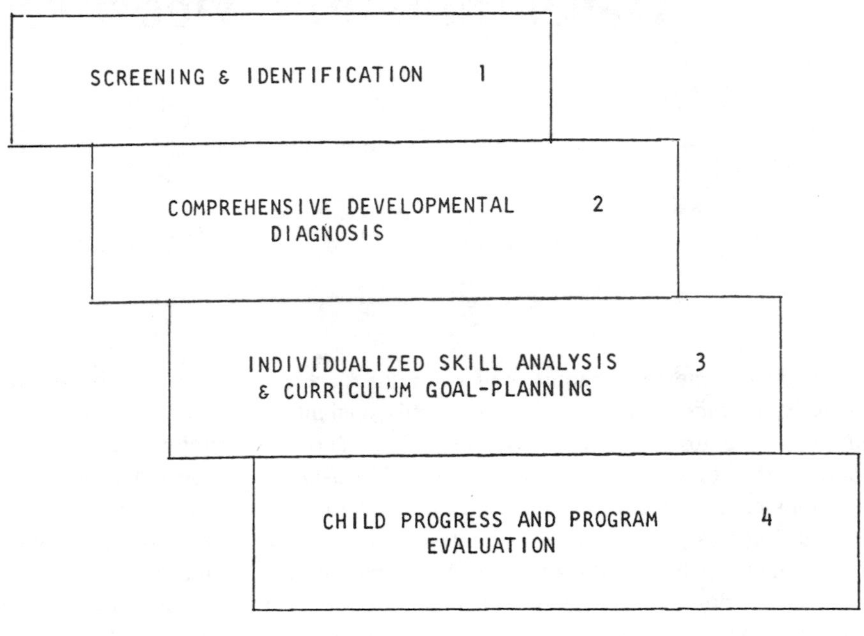

gists, and other specialists need to consider the following criteria when formulating developmental diagnoses and intervention strategies that fit the needs of exceptional children in their programs.

Developmental Base

Are the activities within the assessment instrument sequenced according to a developmental-task approach, and are they hierarchically arranged? The most useful assessment measures are those that combine norm- and criterion-based qualities. Specifically, tasks that sample various functional abilities are arranged along a developmental task-analysis continuum according to age level or operational stage. The smaller the increments between each major task in the sequence and the next one, the more useful the measure is for fine-focus diagnosis and for individualized curriculum goal-planning, particularly for multihandicapped children. Developmental sequencing tends to provide a common and reliable underlying framework for assessment and intervention. In addition, it establishes functional, behavioral criteria for testing, teaching, and program evaluation.

Comprehensive Coverage

Does the assessment instrument survey broad-range functional domains and provide a developmental profile that details skills, deficits, and emerging capabilities within each domain? Linkage between an assessment device and a curriculum is facilitated most by scales that cover multiple developmental areas commonly contained within the educational program, that is, receptive-expressive language, fine-gross motor, personal-social, self-help, perceptual-cognitive, and readiness. Skill analysis in separate developmental areas is crucial to effective individualized intervention, particularly for the young and severely handicapped. Such separate area coverage is, however, somewhat artificial, since capabilities in one domain are intertwined with abilities in other areas, as in the emergent relationship between language and thinking.

Multiple Sources

Does the selected assessment instrument or battery of measures incorporate the perceptions about the young handicapped child of different people across different situations? With multihandicapped children, continuous, multisource assessment is not only desirable but crucial. Multisource appraisal helps account for behaviors that are emerging and situation-specific. It helps to standardize the judgments of teachers, parents, psychologists, and other specialists regarding the child's current status and developmental progress. Also, increasing the sample of assessed skills, in turn, increases the reliability of estimates about child functioning and, therefore, enhances the confidence to be placed in those results. Thus, accountability is facilitated. Recent research in this area (Diebold, Curtis, & Dubose, 1978; MacTurk & Neisworth, 1978; Bagnato and Neisworth, 1980, in press) suggests that an approach that combines subjective judgment, child performance, and curriculum estimates is the most reliable, practical, and adaptive assessment strategy for young handicapped children. See Tables 3-1 and 3-2 for suggested multimeasure, multisource developmental assessment batteries.

Curriculum Links

Are the assessment instruments compatible with the type of curriculum employed in the preschool? Actually, the concept of curriculum linkage is a practical method of making traditional developmental scales more useful in the initial stages of individualized curriculum goal-planning. Developmental linkages depend upon each of the previously cited criteria: developmental basis, comprehensive coverage, and multiple sources. When selecting scales, remember that it is important to

Table 3-1 Comprehensive Developmental Assessment Battery: 18-24-Month-Old Child

Measure	*Age Range*	*Domain*	*Source*
1. Bayley Scales of Infant Development (BSID)	2-30 mo.	Developmental	Performance
2. Receptive-Expressive Emergent Language Scale (REEL)	0-36 mo.	Language	Performance & judgment
Communication Evaluation chart	3-60 mo.	Language	Performance & judgment
3. BSID Mental Scale	2-30 mo.	Cognitive/Readiness	Performance
4. BSID Motor Scale	2-30 mo.	Neuro-motor	Performance
5. BSID Infant Behavior Record (IBR)	2-30 mo.	Personal-social	Behavior ratings
Developmental Profile	0-12 yrs.	Adaptive	Judgment
6. Early Intervention Developmental Profile	0-36 mo.	Curriculum	Curriculum ratings

seek an essential similarity between the "testing tasks" and the "teaching tasks," or between sampled and predicted behaviors (Newland, 1973). Similar developmental items in the scale and congruent developmental tasks within a curriculum facilitate effective assessment/curriculum linkages.

Adaptive Procedures

Do the assessment instruments contain adaptive administration strategies or tasks that have the potential to be modified for use with young multihandicapped children? Currently, few of the frequently employed developmental scales have organized adaptive administrative strategies. Nevertheless, some have the potential for substituting modified objects and activities to alter the mode of response required of the child. The work of Haeussermann (1958) provides guidelines in this respect. A few newly developed preschool scales and specialized intellectual assessment devices contain both adaptive administration procedures and special-handicapped norms (see for instance the Battelle Developmental Inventory—Appendix A).

Table 3-2 Comprehensive Developmental Assessment Battery: 36-48-Month-Old Child

Measure	Age Range	Domain	Source
1. Gesell Developmental Schedules (GDS)	1-72 mo.	Developmental	Performance & Judgment
2. McCarthy Scales of Children's Abilities (MSCA)	2½-8½ yrs.	Cognitive/readiness	Performance
Pictorial Test of Intelligence (PTI) [Alternate]	3-9 yrs.	Cognitive	Performance (Nonverbal)
3. Assessment of Children's Language Comprehension (ACLC)	36-72 mo.	Language	Performance
4. Developmental Test of Visual-Motor Integration (VMI)	2-15 yrs.	Perceptual-motor	Performance
MSCA Perceptual-Motor Scales	2½-8½ yrs.	Perceptual-motor	Performance
5. Preschool Attainment Record (PAR)	1-84 mo.	Personal-social	Judgment
6. Brigance Diagnostic Inventory of Early Development (BDIED)	0-72 mo.	Educational	Criterion-referenced Ratings

A REVIEW OF DEVELOPMENTAL SCALES

Comprehensive Norm-Based Measures

Most traditional infant-preschool scales are constructed on a developmental model based on psychometric methods, that is, on statistically derived norm groups. Early efforts in assessing cognition and overall development in infants and young children sought to evaluate a series of global abilities that were thought to represent an individual's *general* status. However, most experts now agree that no unitary factor of infant cognition exists. Thus, many newer scales sample multiple abilities across multiple functional areas in order to effectively assess the status of young children.

The Bayley Scales of Infant Development

The most technically adequate of the comprehensive developmental scales, the Bayley Scales of Infant Development (BSID) (Bayley, 1969) survey the 2-30-month-age range. The comprehensive analysis of infant development skills encompasses three major subscales that involve over 244 separate tasks and behavioral characteristics:

1. The mental scale (163 items)—performance yields a Mental Developmental Index (MDI).
2. The motor scale (81 items)—performance yields a Psychomotor Development Index (PDI).
3. The infant behavior record—a descriptive rating scale of several infant behavior traits.

Within the context of the three measures, the following types of functional capabilities are surveyed: sensory-perceptual skills, object permanence, discrimination, generalization, classification, memory, problem-solving, receptive-expressive language, body control, fine-gross motor skills, balance, and eye-hand coordination. In addition, the quality of certain behavioral characteristics is assessed, that is, attention, responsiveness, temperament, attachment, goal-directness, endurance, and so on.

In its entirety, the BSID is an excellent measure of current developmental functioning and provides a reliable basis for generating profiles of skills and deficits.

The "developmental quotients," that is, the Mental Developmental Index (MDI) and Psychomotor Developmental Index (PDI), provide a statistical basis for comparing an infant's performance with that of same-age infants in the standardization sample of 1,262 infants. Furthermore, developmental ages can be derived that provide a much more functional basis for profiling the capabilities and limitations of handicapped children. Few attempts have focused on modifying BSID tasks for exceptional infants; however, Hoffman (1975) suggests certain clinical procedures for substituting tasks, reconstructing objects, and altering the administration of activities for handicapped children with visual, hearing, and neuro-motor dysfunctions.

Regarding the practical quality of the BSID for curriculum planning, most clinicians agree that the developmental sequencing of skills provides a useful starting point for goal-planning. Meier (1976) asserts that scales such as the BSID offer a unique "profile and base for curriculum planning" (p. 190). Nevertheless, important cautions must be observed in this process.

The developmental items contained in most norm-based scales like the BSID are usually insufficient in number to allow the diagnostician to pinpoint targets precisely for intervention in any particular developmental domain. In addition, the increments between sequenced items are too broad for precision programming with handicapped children. Yet, performance on selected items within the sequences can provide an idea of the upper and lower limits to target intervention. Table 3-3 presents a reorganization of Bayley items for a particular functional area to demonstrate these increments. When the BSID is used in conjunction with a task-analyzed developmental curriculum, the usefulness of its tasks is enhanced.

Considerations. The BSID represents the best organized and technically developed of all the comprehensive scales currently available. The standardization, content, and skill coverage make it acceptable not only as a diagnostic measure but also as an initial guide to curriculum goal-planning. The scale is painstakingly normed yet contains valuable clinical features regarding how to test very young children and how to adapt activities to their interest and level of responsiveness. Use of the "developmental age" ratings rather than the PDI or MDI indexes is more appropriate and meaningful when serving handicapped children. Finally, if the authors were to expand the age range of the BSID to 5 years, the scale would be indispensable for preferred use in programs serving a birth-to-5-year population.

The Gesell Developmental Schedules

The Gesell Developmental Schedules (GDS) (Knobloch & Pasamanick, 1974; Ames, Gillespie, Haines, & Ilg, 1979) stand as the patriarch of traditional developmental measures from which all other scales have been directly or indirectly modeled. Because of Gesell's original longitudinal research in charting child development, the GDS was designed as a clinical research tool rather than a statistically and technically adequate test according to current psychometric standards. For this reason, the scales have come under heavy pressure to be restandardized. Despite this criticism, the GDS provides a truly functional and clinical assessment of the infant's and preschooler's broad range of developmental skills not contained in many other similar measures. In fact, the GDS is particularly useful for identifying neurological dysfunctions and predicting moderate levels of retardation (Knobloch & Pasamanick, 1974).

Covering the 4-week- to 72-month-age range, the GDS samples more primitive reflexes and progressive developmental skills than most other measures (350-400 behaviors). The GDS comprehensively surveys five major functional tracts: language, fine-motor, gross-motor, adaptive (problem-solving), and personal-social (see Table 3-4). The additional use of the essential developmental history format and the neurological survey make the GDS a very functional, clinical measure of developmental status.

Table 3-3 Reorganized Sequence of Cube Tasks from the Bayley Scales of Infant Development (1969)

Item	*Age and Range*	*Item Description*
32T≠	2.5 (1-5)	Regards cube
49	4.1 (2-6)	Reaches for cube
51	4.4 (2-6)	Eye-hand coordination in reaching
54	4.6 (3-7)	Picks up cube
56	4.7 (3-7)	Retains two cubes
60	5.0 (3-8)	Reaches persistently
64	5.4 (4-8)	Reaches for second cube
70	5.7 (4-8)	Picks up cube deftly and directly
77	6.3 (4-10)	Retains two of three cubes offered
82	7.6 (5-14)	Attempts to secure three cubes
86	8.1 (6-12)	Uncovers toy
96	10.5 (8-17)	Unwraps cube
111	13.8 (10-19)	Builds tower of two cubes
119	16.7 (13-21)	Builds tower of three cubes
143	23.0 (17-30+)	Builds tower of six cubes
154	26.1 (19-30+)	Train of cubes
161	30+ (22-30+)	Builds tower of eight cubes
162	30+ (21-30+)	Concept of one

Source: Adapted from Bayley, N. *Manual for the Bayley scales of infant development.* New York: Psychological Corporation, 1969.

Table 3-4 An Example of the Gesell Developmental Schedules' Multidomain Coverage of Skills Across the 24-36 Months Levels

Gesell Developmental Schedules

Age	Motor	Adaptive	Language	Personal-Social
2	Walks: runs well, no falling Stairs: walks up and down alone Large ball: (no dem.) kicks Cubes: tower of 6-7 Book: turns pages singly	Cubes: tower of 6-7 Drawing: imitates V stroke Formboard: places blocks on separately (G) Formboard: adapts after 4 trials Color Forms: does not identify any	Speech: jargon discarded Speech: 3 word sentence Speech: uses *I, me, you* Picture Vocabulary: 2+ correct	Toilet: may verbalize needs fairly consistently Play: domestic mimicry Play: hands cup full of cubes Play: parallel play predominates Feeding: inhibits turning spoon Dressing: pulls on simple garment Commun: verbalizes immed. experiences Commun: refers to self by name Comm: comprehends & asks for "another" Temperament: gentle, easy
2½	Stands: tries, on 1 foot Cubes: tower of 10 Drawing: holds crayon by fingers	Cubes: tower of 10 Cubes: aligns 2 or more, train Drawing: imitates V & H strokes Drawing: scribbles to circular stroke Inc. Man: adds 1 part Formboard: inserts 3 blocks on presentation Formboard: adapts repeatedly, error Color Forms: places 1	Interview: gives first name Interview: tells sex (G) Prepositions: obeys 1-2 Picture Vocab: 7 correct Action Agent: 3 correct	Play: pushes toy with good steering Play: helps put things away Commun: refers to self by pronoun "me" rather than by name Commun: repetition in speech and other activity Self help: can put on own coat (not necessarily fasten) Temperament: opposite extremes
3	Walks on tiptoe, 2 or more steps Stands on 1 foot, momentary balance Skips: tries Rides tricycle using pedals Stairs: alternates feet going up Jumps down: lands on feet (G) Broad jump: distance 12" Pellets: 10 into bottle in 26" (G); 24" (B)	Cubes: adds chimney to train Cubes: imitates bridge Copy Forms: copies circle Copy Forms: imitates cross Inc. Man: adds 3 parts Formboard: adapts, no errors or immediate correction of error Color Forms: places 3 Counts with correct pointing: 3 objs. Pellets: 10 into bottle in 26" (G); 24" (B)	Speech: uses plurals Interview: tells age (G) Interview: tells sex (B) Prepositions: obeys 3 Digits: repeats 3 (1 of 3 trials). Picture Vocab: 11 correct Comprehension Question A: answers 1 Action Agent: 6-7 correct Picture Vocab.: 11 correct	Feeding: feeds self, little spilling Feeding: pours well from pitcher Dressing: puts on shoes Dressing: unbuttons front and side buttons Commun.: asks questions rhetorically Commun: understands taking turns Commun: knows a few rhymes Temperament: cooperative

Source: Ames, L.B., Gillespie, C., Haines, J., & Ilg, F. *Gesell developmental schedules* (Revised). Lumberville, Pa.: Gesell Institute for Human Development Book Service and Programs for Education, 1980. Reprinted with permission.

The original normative sample for the Gesell schedules consisted of 107 to 150 infants and preschoolers between the ages of 4 weeks and 6 years, with approximately 26 to 35 children represented at each "key" developmental age. The sample was limited by the fact that no handicapped children were included in the group, which consisted of children of northern European ancestry in New England. Nevertheless, developmental skill expectancies were established for each "maturity level." Recent limited changes in the normative basis and organizational format of the GDS reveal that the norm group based on the 1960 census consisted of 320 boys and 320 girls (40 at each age level) covering the age levels from 2½ to 6 years. The sample was stratified but included mostly Caucasians living in Connecticut (Ames et al., 1979). This normative change was much needed, but unfortunately is still technically inadequate. Also, a recent revision of the Gesell schedules covering the birth-to-36-months age range and implementing alterations in item placement was conducted on 927 children in the Albany, New York area (Knobloch, Stevens, & Malone, 1980).

The strongest features of the GDS are its wide age survey, comprehensive domain coverage, and specific behavior samplings. Since the GDS covers the 4-week-to-72-month range, it provides the continuity and scope in assessment required in many birth-to-5-year preschool programs. In addition, the lower age coverage allows the sampling of skills appropriate for many moderately and some severely involved children. Through clearly sequenced developmental progressions (see Figure 3-2), the GDS covers five major functional domains that are congruent with the skills and areas focused on in many early intervention curricula. Thus, the Gesell schedules tend naturally to accommodate assessment/curriculum linkages.

The Gesell "developmental expectancies" or profiles center around functional behaviors that are typical of most children and various "key" ages across the range. Performance is assessed by deriving separate developmental ages, instead of a global score, for each major developmental domain, for example, language—21 months, adaptive—18 months, motor—15 months. Thus, a differential diagnostic profile of individual developmental differences is generated. Furthermore, performance is represented by age ranges and a flexible scoring system that, although somewhat confusing, allows the rating of emerging capabilities and qualitative performance features. For example, scoring is basically accomplished by observing and rating the demonstration of specific developmental skills as absent (−), fully acquired (+), advanced for age (++), or emerging (±). Parental reports of skills performed at home are also accounted for. Moreover, developmental performance is described by providing an age range that "best fits" the child's quality of performance. Thus, a rating of 21 (18-24) months means that the child's most stable level of current skill development is typical of the 21-month level, but the child's performance shows scattered and emerging features spanning the 18-24-month range. This flexible system facilitates the

Figure 3-2 Sample GDS Cube Progression

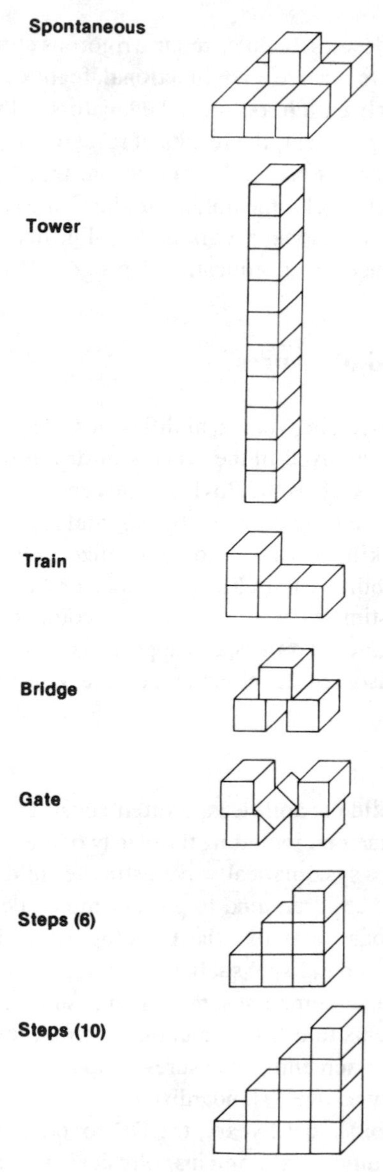

Source: Ames, L.B., Gillespie, C., Haines, J., & Ilg, F. *Gesell developmental schedules* (Revised). Lumberville, Pa.: Gesell Institute for Human Development Book Service and Programs for Education, 1980. Reprinted with permission.

clinical assessment of individual variations in development and is very useful with the young handicapped child.

Considerations. Although the Gesell schedules require rigorous clinical training to be properly used, their comprehensive and functional features make them particularly relevant for aiding early childhood special educators in the process of individualized curriculum planning. In fact, the results of research in programs for both handicapped and nonhandicapped preschoolers indicate that "the Gesell is highly correlated with classroom [developmental curriculum] measures and has utility as a diagnostic device for educational programming. Further, it is a useful measure of a child's progress once in an educational program" (MacTurk & Neisworth, 1978).

Complementary Norm-Based Measures

The multisource approach to assessing the capabilities of young handicapped children demands that parents be involved in the process of developmental diagnosis and goal-planning. Measures such as the Bayley scales and Gesell schedules focus upon actual child performance supplemented by parental reports of demonstrated skills. However, certain skills that have not generalized across situations and people and the functional disabilities of multihandicapped children require that reliable and descriptive parent estimates of functioning be compared with child performance measures. In this regard, certain scales appear to be especially useful as part of a comprehensive multisource developmental battery of measures.

The Developmental Profile

Generally, parent reports of child capabilities are often considered unreliable. Their accuracy depends on many factors, including the clarity of the skills and how the question is asked. Many parents systematically overestimate child capabilities. Yet, parents of severely impaired children tend to portray more accurately their children's status. For these reasons, tests like the Developmental Profile (DP) (Alpern & Boll, 1972) are considered indispensable in comprehensive diagnosis.

The DP is a norm-referenced developmental screening measure that relies on a structured interview with the parents to estimate a child's current levels of functioning. The DP is unique among screening measures in that it is multidimensional, reliable, valid, and extremely well standardized.

Surveying the age range from birth to 12 years, the DP contains 217 developmental tasks ordered within five functional domains: physical, self-help, social, academic, and communication. The tasks are presented as questions that tap the developing child's level of competence in each area. The DP is probably the best standardized interview screening measure currently available, since it is standardized on 3,008 children.

Scoring is done by either circling a zero for a failure or the ''month number'' opposite an item to indicate a pass. Basal and double-ceiling levels are established, as on other measures, to represent the upper and lower limits of functioning. The total number of passes is utilized to determine developmental age scores for each functional domain. Questions are asked in terms of ''does'' and ''can'' the child perform a particular activity to obtain notions of actual functioning and capability (see Table 3-5). Scores representing functioning are interpreted in terms of the degree of ''developmental lag'' between chronological age and current levels of functioning and discrepancies between developmental levels across the multiple domains. The significance of lags is determined from the norm tables.

Considerations. The Developmental Profile presents certain unique characteristics and is invaluable as part of a larger diagnostic battery. It facilitates the use of parent judgments in formulating interventions and aids in standardizing the diverse perceptions of significant adults who know and serve the child. As an interview measure, it is adaptive in accurately portraying the perceived needs of handicapped children and providing a potential basis for counseling and parent training. Finally, it provides a valid and reliable basis for multisource assessment and establishes initial targets for curriculum prescriptions by highlighting perceived capabilities and deficits.

The Preschool Attainment Record

The Vineland Social Maturity Scale (Doll, 1965) was formulated as an alternative method of assessing an individual's degree of personal independence and social maturity through an interview-informant technique. As a type of life-span developmental measure, the Vineland scale can be used to estimate successfully the capabilities of children with multiple sensory impairments. Similarly, the need arose to use the same procedure as a method of assessing the capabilities of handicapped preschoolers in a more focused manner. Thus, the Preschool Attainment Record (PAR) (Doll, 1966) was developed as an expanded, downward extension of the Vineland scale, based on child development research. Although the PAR is a research edition and has no established technical and normative base, the scale is frequently used to assess ''untestable'' multihandicapped preschoolers and holds some promise as part of a larger diagnostic battery. Caution should be observed in following the item placements and derived functional ages too closely; however, the behavioral objectives are instructionally meaningful in assessing children who are difficult to test.

The PAR surveys the birth-to-7-year-age range by focusing upon developmental functioning across three major domains and eight subareas:

1. physical—ambulation, manipulation
2. social—rapport, communication, responsibility
3. intellectual—information, ideation, creativity

Table 3-5 Communication Developmental Age Scale

First ½ Year (Newborn: 0-6 months)

C 1. Does the child use vocal noises for play? The child must *play* with sounds (not just cry or gurgle or laugh when something happens).

C 2. Does the child babble or use some sounds attempting to imitate words or speech? It is as though the child is pretending to talk.

C 3. Does the child usually look toward the source of a sound when it starts, such as a person beginning to talk?

Second ½ Year (Infant I: 7-12 months)

C 4. Does the child sometimes imitate spoken "words" such as "da-da" or "ma-ma?" The child may not know what these words mean.

C 5. Does the child use motions or gestures as a way of talking, e.g., shaking head "no," or holding out arms to be picked up?

C 6. Does the child answer an adult's words with gestures such as waving "bye-bye" when an adult says good-bye, shaking the head up and down for "yes" or side to side for "no" when an adult asks something?

1 to 1½ Years (Infant II: 13-18 months)

C 7. Does the child use some vocal sounds (real words or word-like sounds) to tell what s/he wants? Saying "wa-wa" for water would be an example. Crying or whining for something does not rate a pass.

C 8. Does the child say the names of at least five things (not in imitation and not including names of people)? The words must be said well enough to be understood by a stranger.

C 9. Does the child carry out commands of show, come, go or get? For example, could the child show where its toes are, go to Ma-ma, or get the spoon when asked?

1½ to 2 Years (Toddler I: 19-24 months)

C 10. Does the child use at least 15 different words in the right way?

C 11. Does the child get across, through words or gestures, the idea of wanting "more" or "another?" The words or gestures must be reasonably specific and not merely crying or general handwaving.

C 12. Does the child put two or more words together to form sentences? "Me go," "You give," "Tom want," are all examples of passes. But, if the child *always* uses the same two words together (so that they are really one word to the child), that does not rate a pass.

Table 3-5 continued

2 to 2½ Years (Toddler II: 25-30 months)

C 13.	Does the child either repeat parts of nursery rhymes or join in when others say them?
C 14.	Does the child name (not just repeat) at least 20 things seen in pictures?
C 15.	Does the child use at least 50 different words when speaking? The child must *use* these words, not just understand them when spoken by others.

Source: Alpern, G.D. & Bell, T.J. *The developmental profile.* Aspen, Colo.: Psychological Development Publications, 1972. Reprinted with permission.

The PAR is a type of norm-based child-development screening measure that is useful for highlighting gross disabilities in the above areas, although only eight behaviors are sampled within each 6-month span (see Exhibit 3-1). Parents or others who know the child well are interviewed regarding "typical" behavior, using relatively precise behavioral definitions for each task as a judgment guide. This can be supplemented by direct observation. Performance is rated + if it fits the task completely, ± if functioning is marginal or inconsistent, and − for undeveloped skills. Full and half scores are calculated this way. The Vineland and PAR manuals provide important guidelines regarding the way to interview parents. The use of very general questions, such as, "Tell me how Sally gets about the house?" are used to begin the assessment; then, more specific probes, like, "Does she walk up stairs alternating her feet?" are used to cover unexplored skills. This strategy permits a more conversational and less threatening functional interview for parents of handicapped children. Although attainment age scores and "attainment quotients" can be derived following the evaluation, these must be used with great caution. The use of age ranges, and especially of qualitative information about individual task competence, is a more justifiable and meaningful objective.

Considerations. Although technically inadequate, the PAR is a frequently used scale that is worthwhile as a qualitative measure of "perceived" child functioning. By combining the subjective impressions of several adults who know and work with the child, using the item definitions as structured guides, the judgments of many people can be compared. This strategy increases reliability and focuses the need for intervention in specific areas. Thus, as part of a multisource developmental battery, the PAR provides a diagnostic profile and "base-line for educational planning, treatment, or management" (Doll, 1966, p. 8).

Exhibit 3-1 The Preschool Attainment Record (PAR): An Example of Tasks

PAR

AMERICAN GUIDANCE SERVICE, INC.
Publishers' Building, Circle Pines, Minnesota 55014

AGS

Name__________
Date__________
Examiner__________

SCORES	
In Years	In Months
LA ____	LA ____
MA ____	MA ____
†AA ____	††AA ____
*AQ ____	
IQ ____	

SUMMARY AND PROFILE

	Age in Years	0 to .5	.5 to 1.0	1.0 to 1.5	1.5 to 2.0	2.0 to 2.5	2.5 to 3.0	3.0 to 3.5	3.5 to 4.0	4.0 to 4.5	4.5 to 5.0	5.0 to 5.5	5.5 to 6.0	6.0 to 6.5	6.5 to 7.0	Items Passed by Category
	Age in Months	0-6	6-12	12-18	18-24	24-30	30-36	36-42	42-48	48-54	54-60	60-66	66-72	72-78	78-84	
PHYSICAL	Ambulation	1 Sits	9 Stands	17 Walks	25 Runs	33 Balances	41 Climbs	49 Jumps (1)	57 Hops	65 Circles	73 Skips	81 Jumps (2)	89 Follows Leader	97 Dances	105 Rides Vehicles	Ambulation
PHYSICAL	Manipulation	2 Reaches	10 Grasps	18 Marks	26 Unwraps	34 Disas-sembles	42 Assem-bles	50 Throws	58 Catches	66 Draws Square	74 Blows Nose	82 Draws Triangle	90 Fastens Shoes	98 Colors to Line	106 Cuts and Pastes	Manipulation
SOCIAL	Rapport	3 Regards	11 Attends (1)	19 Initiates	27 Discrimi-nates	35 Complies	43 Plays Beside (a)	51 Plays With (b)	59 Plays Coop. (c)	67 Attends (2)	75 Sings	83 Helps	91 Plays Pretend (d)	99 Plays Compet.(e)	107 Plays (f)	Rapport
SOCIAL	Communication	4 Babbles	12 Vocalizes	20 Imitates	28 Invites	36 Speaks	44 Talks	52 Con-verses	60 Relates	68 Describes	76 Recites	84 Prints	92 Copies	100 Reads	108 Adds	Communication
SOCIAL	Responsibility	5 Nurses	13 Chews	21 Rests	29 Minds	37 Con-serves	45 Takes Care	53 Gets Drink	61 Dresses Self	69 Toilets Self	77 Cleans Up	85 Respects Property	93 Con-forms	101 Coop-erates	109 Ob-serves R.	Responsibility
INTELLECTUAL	Information	6 Recog-Few (a)	14 Recog-Many (b)	22 Recog-Use (c)	30 Recog-His (d)	38 Fondles	46 Knows Sex	54 Tells Name	62 Names Objects	70 Knows D-N	78 Names Coins	86 Knows Age	94 Knows A.M.-P.M.	102 Knows R-L	110 Knows Address	Information
INTELLECTUAL	Ideation	7 Resists	15 Identifies	23 Gestures	31 Matches	39 Counts 2	47 Comp. Size (1)	55 Counts 3	63 Comp. Texture (2)	71 Counts 4	79 Comp. Weight (3)	87 Names Colors	95 Beats Rhythm	103 Counts 13	111 Tells Hour	Ideation
INTELLECTUAL	Creativity	8 Demands	16 Tests	24 Transfers	32 Explores	40 Tears	48 Drama-tizes S. (1)	56 Builds	64 Draws	72 Moulds	80 Drama-tizes M. (2)	88 Paints	96 Invents Stories	104 Solos	112 Experi-ments	Creativity
	Items Passed by Age Periods															Raw Score°

*"Raw Score" is the total number of items successfully passed allowing half credit for ± scores.
†"Attainment Age" in years is determined by dividing raw score by 16 (16 items per year).
††"Attainment Age" in months is determined by multiplying Raw Score by .75 (8 items per 6 months interval).
*"Attainment Quotient" is determined by dividing Life Age into Attainment Age and multiplying by 100.

Source: Doll, E.A. *Preschool attainment record.* Circle Pines, Minn.: American Guidance Service, 1966.

The Perceptions of Developmental Skills Profile

Only a few efforts have focused upon systematically comparing the subjective impressions of significant adults (teachers, parents, psychologists, physical therapists) about the functional capabilities and developmental progress of young handicapped children. Yet, subjective judgments regarding child functioning can be important diagnostic indicators of developmental progress and the need for program modification or auxiliary services, such as parent counseling.

The Perceptions of Developmental Skills Profile (PODS) (Bagnato, Neisworth, and Eaves, 1977) is designed as a screening measure for profiling the subjective ratings of significant adults who work with handicapped preschoolers. Using a format similar to that of Iscoe and Payne (1972), the PODS is a functional-capabilities rating scale focusing upon the 2-8-year-age range and covering 4 major developmental domains and 16 subdomains (see Exhibit 3-2 and Appendix C).

In specific terms, each adult profiles his or her perceptions of the child's functional capability level on a scale of 1 to 7 for each subdomain. A rating of 1 indicates the absence of any perceived deficit, while a rating of 7 denotes awareness of a profound functional impairment. A level of 3 signals a mild functional problem. The research edition of the scale includes behavioral definitions of each developmental domain as well as criteria for each rating level from 1 to 7. These factors help to standardize subjective impressions about child status and to focus individual judgments. Recent research using the PODS suggests that it compares favorably with traditional child performance measures in monitoring developmental progress (Bagnato & Neisworth, in press).

The PODS is particularly useful as part of a diagnostic battery for assessing multihandicapped preschoolers. It is adaptive in that it relies upon the perceptions of diverse individuals for monitoring developmental status. Moreover, it serves to draw attention to deficit areas and highlights dysfunctions requiring more focused assessment. Appendix C includes the entire PODS rating scale.

Considerations. The PODS stands as an initial attempt to standardize subjective impressions about young handicapped children for use in comprehensive developmental diagnosis. The scale is only a research edition and is in need of further revisions, particularly in terms of the wording of behavioral definitions. The measure should be used primarily to gain *qualitative* information about child functioning. The addition of age reference points would significantly improve its utility.

Exhibit 3-2 Mother-Psychologist Functional Ratings on the PODS

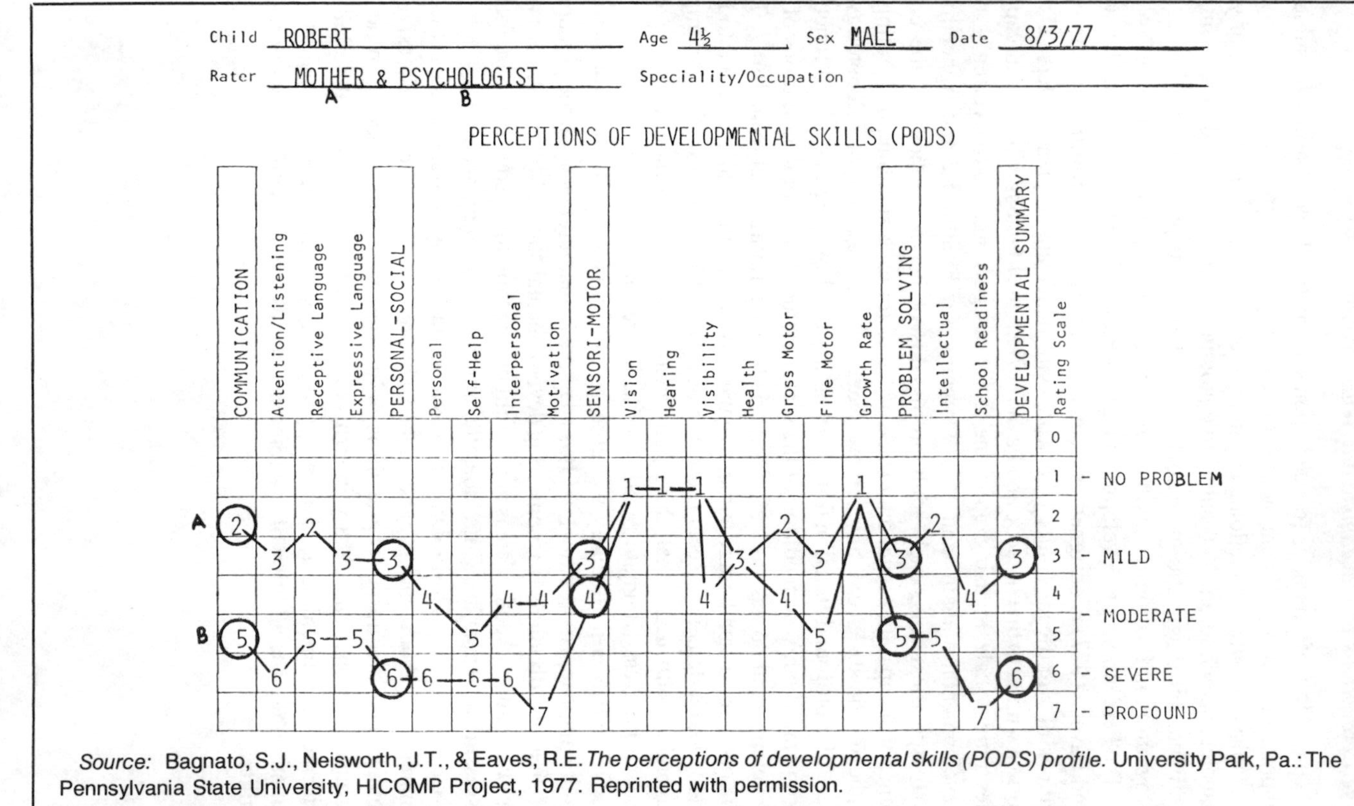

Source: Bagnato, S.J., Neisworth, J.T., & Eaves, R.E. *The perceptions of developmental skills (PODS) profile.* University Park, Pa.: The Pennsylvania State University, HICOMP Project, 1977. Reprinted with permission.

Criterion-Based Curriculum Measures

"Little did Doll and Gesell know that the scales they developed . . . could be better used to plan courses of individualized training and instruction" (Bijou, 1977, p. 10). Bijou's assertion provides an enlightening backdrop to the construction of criterion-referenced developmental curricula and their behavioral scales. Just as most traditional, norm-based developmental scales are modifications of the tasks, procedures, and materials of Gesell, most preschool curricula are expansions of the same developmental tasks and sequences. This similarity in content and basis creates many common aspects between assessment and teaching objectives.

The behavioral scales that form the structural basis of most developmental curricula are extremely useful methods of imbedding assessment within programming, of structuring goal-directed instruction, and of monitoring child progress and program effectiveness. Nevertheless, these scales are often cumbersome and time-consuming to administer, requiring continuous assessment practices. In addition, behavioral checklists most often have undetermined reliability and validity for precise diagnostic purposes and are unfamiliar to most assessment specialists. Yet, they are indispensable within the total assessment-intervention process.

Learning Accomplishment Profile

The Learning Accomplishment Profile—Diagnostic Edition (revised) (LAP-D) (LeMay, Griffin, & Sanford, 1978) and its associated curriculum materials are a product of the Chapel Hill, North Carolina, Outreach Project and represent one of the most frequently used criterion-referenced curriculum scales covering the 0- to 5½-year range. The LAP-D is an expanded compilation of a variety of developmental tasks culled from such traditional scales as the Bayley scale and placed at similar age levels determined by norm-referenced measures. The LAP-D scale combines the advantages of normed sequencing of developmental skills with precise targets for initiating individualized program planning.

The LAP-D is considered a developmental task-analysis diagnostic instrument that details functioning in five distinct areas:

1. fine motor
2. gross motor
3. language
4. cognition
5. self-help

Unlike more limited-scope, norm-based scales, the LAP-D divides its major domains into subareas, including manipulation, writing, matching, object movement, counting, comprehension, and grooming (see Exhibit 3-3). The detailed scale covers the age range of birth to six years across these functional areas and helps generate a diagnostic profile of the child's range of fully acquired (+), absent (−), and emerging (±) developmental capabilities. The profile forms the diagnostic basis for individualized goal-planning by establishing developmental "targets" and age reference points, rather than comparative statistical quotients.

The LAP-D has several features that make it unique among the newer criterion-based measures. First, it is one of the most colorful and interesting of the curriculum scales. The large red carrying case contains a rich variety of tasks—involving formboard, peg placement, drawing, beanbag, color matching, puzzles, block building, bead stringing, octopus dressing toy, and lacing—that are inherently appealing to young children and provide a motivational support for obtaining the child's maximum level of performance. Also, the variety of tasks allows some adaptive accommodations to be made. Next, because of the colorful, high-interest tasks and flip-card administration format, the scale can be given by the teacher in approximately 1½ hours, providing relevant educational goals and qualitative descriptions of the child's developmental and instructional needs. Finally, the LAP-D is based upon continuing research efforts to establish a normative and technical basis in terms of reliability and validity, although the technical manual cites current data on only 35 children. Total scale test-retest reliability is reportedly .98, with subscale correlations of .91-.97.

Considerations. As part of a total assessment-intervention process, the LAP-D helps to formulate an adaptive and individualized program for prescriptive teaching. The relatively recent appearance of the infant LAP provides an extremely practical application of this format to infants and severely handicapped children. In brief, the LAP-D (and the total curriculum program to be discussed in chapter 6) accomplishes six major objectives in early special education: It

1. provides a record of functional skills,
2. establishes an initial developmental task analysis to guide teaching in multiple areas,
3. allows for creative additions to the goal sequence,
4. provides a means for measuring progress,
5. highlights individual strengths and weaknesses, and
6. enables the teacher to initiate curriculum-imbedded assessment within the classroom environment.

Exhibit 3-3 Sample Goal Sequence on Comprehension Skills from the Learning Accomplishment Profile

Language/Cognitive: Comprehension

Developmental Age	Item	Behavior	1st +/−	2nd +/−	Comments
6	LC1	Responds to name			
15	LC2	Looks toward object			
15	LC3	Responds to "look"			
15	LC4	Points to objects			
18	LC5	Points to 3 body parts			
24	LC6	Follows 3 commands			
24	LC7	Hands objects to examiner			
24	LC8	Points to 6 body parts			
24	LC9	Follows 8 commands			
30	LC10	Responds to 2 prepositions			
30	LC11	Follows 2-step command			
33	LC12	Shows use of objects			
33	LC13	Points to objects by use			
36	LC14	Points to 5 actions			
36	LC15	Points to 10 objects			
42	LC16	Points to 15 objects			
42	LC17	Points to 9 actions			
48	LC18	Responds to 4 prepositions			
48	LC19	Relates pictures to story			
48	LC20	Points to numerals 1 - 10			
54	LC21	Matches picture and verbal description			
60	LC22	Selects items in category			
66	LC23	Responds to "who, what, where"			
72	LC24	Follows 3-step command			
72	LC25	Shows left/right			
72	LC26	Points to letters A - Z			
72	LC27	Points to words			
		Last Item Administered			
		Less Errors	−	−	
		Comprehension Score			

Source: LeMay, D.W., Griffin, P.M., & Sanford, A.R. *Learning accomplishment profile: Diagnostic edition* (Rev. Ed.). Winston-Salem, N.C.: Kaplan School Supply, 1978. Reprinted with permission.

The Memphis Comprehensive Developmental Scale

The Memphis Comprehensive Developmental Scale (MCDS) (Quick et al., 1974a, 1974b) represents the first phase of a total three-phase program for enhancing developmental progress in preschool exceptional children. The total program discussed in chapter 6 consists of developmental evaluation, individual educational program planning, and educational evaluation. The Project Memphis program materials attempt to link screening, assessment, programming, and child-program evaluation.

The MCDS is one of the earliest criterion-referenced curriculum scales developed under the auspices of the Federal Handicapped Children Early Education Program. Because it is simple, available, practical, and well-organized, the MCDS is one of the most frequently employed scales in handicapped preschool programs that are just being staffed and implemented. However, some individuals have criticized the Memphis plan for containing insufficient goals and imprecise levels and for proposing "cookbook" methods for preferred use by experienced teachers for multihandicapped young children.

The MCDS surveys the age range of 3 to 60 months across five major functional domains:

1. personal-social
2. gross motor
3. fine motor
4. language
5. perceptuo-cognitive

The scale is intended to be administered by teachers with child information gained in each developmental skill area through observation, report, and actual performance. The authors point out that the MCDS is not a precise developmental measure but "a quickly administered screening and programming device" (p. 36). This is especially important since only about 3 skills for each 3-month interval or only approximately 60 skills in any area across the 3-60-month range are sampled by the MCDS. (See Exhibit 3-4.) This "landmark" quality of skill assessment leads many specialists to question the effective programming qualities of this criterion-based device, particularly for the young handicapped child.

Like many similar scales, the MCDS is viewed as establishing a profile for individualized programming, with more reliable usefulness when coupled with detailed standardized measures. The child is evaluated developmentally by marking P for pass and F for fail beside each functional task. No clear provision is made for detailing emerging skills and qualitative aspects of functioning. However, rough developmental ages can be derived to represent operational levels in each area. This should be done cautiously.

Exhibit 3-4 Memphis Comprehensive Developmental Scale

Name ______________________ Date of Birth ______________________ Date of Evaluation ______________ Raw Score ______________ Chronological Age ______________ Developmental Age ______________

	Years	Months	Pass	Fail	PERSONAL–SOCIAL SKILLS
60			P	F	Plays competitive exercise games.
59	5.00	60	P	F	Dresses self with attempts at tying shoes.
58			P	F	Spreads with knife, partial success.
57			P	F	Uses play materials constructively; builds, does not tear down.
56	4.75	57	P	F	Dresses self except tying shoes.
55			P	F	"Picks up" some after playing with no coaxing.
54			P	F	Attends well for short stories.
53	4.50	54	P	F	Uses paper straw appropriately without damaging.
52			P	F	Washes face well.
51			P	F	Separates from mother easily.
50	4.25	51	P	F	Distinguishes front from back of clothes.
49			P	F	Completely cares for self at toilet, including cleaning and dressing.
48			P	F	Plays with others with minimal friction.
47	4.00	48	P	F	Buttons medium-sized buttons.
46			P	F	Goes on very short distance errands outside the home.
45			P	F	Performs for others; i.e. performs a simple rhyme or song.
44	3.75	45	P	F	Washes hands well.
43			P	F	Brushes teeth adequately.
42			P	F	Attempts help at little household tasks; i.e. sweeping, dusting.
41	3.50	42	P	F	Completely undresses for bedtime.
40			P	F	Removes clothing for toileting.
39			P	F	Buttons large buttons.
38	3.25	39	P	F	Performs toilet activities by self (not dressing, cleaning).
37			P	F	Plays cooperatively, interacts with others.
36			P	F	Puts on shoes and socks (tying not required).
35	3.00	36	P	F	Feeds self with little spilling, both fork and spoon.
34			P	F	Shares upon request.
33			P	F	Avoids simple hazards (hot stove, etc.)
32	2.75	33	P	F	Puts on a coat (buttoning not required).
31			P	F	Dries hands well.
30			P	F	Is not overly destructive with household goods, toys, etc.
29	2.50	30	P	F	Gets a drink unassisted from fountain or sink.
28			P	F	Sucks from a plastic straw.
27			P	F	Eats with fork but spills some.
26	2.25	27	P	F	Recognizes self in mirror.
25			P	F	Uses single words or likenesses to show wants.
24			P	F	Minds–does as told generally.
23	2.00	24	P	F	Removes coat or dress (unbuttoning not required).
22			P	F	At least asks to go to toilet–day and night.
21			P	F	Does not place objects on floor in mouth.
20	1.75	21	P	F	Eats with spoon, spilling little.
19			P	F	Voluntarily "slows down" to take naps or rest.
18			P	F	Plays around other children effectively.
17	1.50	18	P	F	Drinks from cup or glass unassisted.
16			P	F	Pulls off socks, but not necessarily shoes.
15			P	F	Follows simple commands or instructions.
14	1.25	15	P	F	Feeds self with a spoon–some spilling allowed.
13			P	F	Holds out arms to assist with clothing.
12			P	F	Temporarily responds to "no," "stop."
11	1.00	12	P	F	Cooperates with dressing–does not resist.
10			P	F	Chews food.
9			P	F	Places food in mouth with hands.
8	.75	9	P	F	Grasps small objects with thumb and index finger.
7			P	F	Desires personal attention and contact beyond just holding.
6			P	F	Drinks from a cup or glass with assistance.
5	.50	6	P	F	Occupies self with a toy for a short period of time.
4			P	F	Grasps foot or brings hand to mouth.
3			P	F	Pulls at clothing with hands.
2	.25	3	P	F	Sucking and swallowing are present.
1			P	F	Reaches for and wants to be held by familiar persons.

This scale reprinted by permission of the Publisher, Fearon Publishers, Inc., 6 Davis Drive, Belmont, Calif. 94002.

Source: Quick, A.D., Little, T.L., & Campbell, A.A. *Project MEMPHIS: Enhancing developmental progress in preschool exceptional children.* Belmont, Calif.: Fearon Publishers, 1974. Reprinted with permission.

Programming is initiated in each domain when the teacher selects undeveloped or deficit skills within the instructional sequence that the teacher views as appropriate starting points for a particular child. These developmental targets are then expanded into educational lessons using the remaining phases of the Memphis materials.

Considerations. Because of its simplified, practical format, the MCDS and MCDS curriculum materials appear to be most worthwhile as a "starter" package of instruments for newly implemented programs and beginning preschool teachers who are unfamiliar with structured diagnostic-prescriptive methods for developmentally delayed young children. The materials provide an excellent structure for developing integrated components within early special education programs. However, caution should be observed in using these as the sole materials in a program. The MCDS has undetermined reliability and validity and does not contain sufficiently small steps between developmental skills to formulate task analyses for multihandicapped preschoolers.

Early Intervention Developmental Profile

Few criterion-referenced developmental scales exist exclusively for the infant with developmental disabilities. The necessity of formulating early intervention programs for the infants (0-3 population) and their parents has increased the demands for both assessment instruments and curriculum plans to serve their needs.

The Early Intervention Developmental Profile (EIDP) was conceived as the initial phase in a total infant stimulation program, Developmental Programming for Infants and Young Children (Rogers et al., 1977), at the University of Michigan. The scale fulfills a pressing need in this expanding area.

The EIDP is a criterion-based infant assessment measure that covers the 0- to 36-month-age range. It consists of six subscales (see Exhibit 3-5a):

1. perceptual/fine motor
2. cognition
3. language
4. social/emotional
5. self-care
6. gross motor

Exhibit 3-5a Sample Tasks from the EIDP Reflecting Current Research on Developmental Processes

PERCEPTUAL/FINE MOTOR DOMAIN

Age Level	Developmental Task	Process
3-5 mo.	. . . Tracks moving object with head	. . . Visual tracking
20-23 mo.	. . . Completes three-piece formboard	. . Visual-Motor integration

COGNITION

Age Level	Developmental Task	Process
3-5 mo.	. . . Repeats random movements	. . . Primary circular reactions
13-18 mo.	. . . Finds completely hidden object	. . . Object constancy

LANGUAGE

Age Level	Developmental Task	Process
6-8 mo.	. . . Imitates speech sound	. . . Imitation
16-19 mo.	. . . Follows two simple commands	. . . Comprehension
32-35 mo.	. . . Forms questions with verbs	. . . Production

SOCIAL-EMOTIONAL

Age Level	Developmental Task	Process
0-2 mo.	. . . Stops fussing to face & voice	. . . Reflexive social
16-19 mo.	. . . Uses mother as secure base	. . . Attachment

Exhibit 3-5a continued

GROSS MOTOR

Age Level		Developmental Task & Process		
3-5 mo.	. . .	Integrates Moro reflex	. . .	Reflex integration
6-8 mo.	. . .	Protects with "parachute" reaction	. . .	Balance

SELF-CARE

Age Level		Developmental Task & Process		
6-8 mo.	. . .	Begins chewing movements	. . .	Oral motor control
16-19 mo.	. . .	Identifies inedible/edible foods	. . .	Food discrimination

The six scales include 274 milestone tasks that yield a profile of developmental functioning that is invaluable for providing comprehensive services to both normal and handicapped infants (see Exhibit 3-5b). The imminent availability of the expanded EIDP for use with preschool children, ages 3 to 6 years, will greatly enhance the wide use of this system in interdisciplinary settings. The EIDP is considered to be an important adjunct to norm-based developmental assessment. Traditional norm-referenced scales are viewed as important in diagnosing various developmental disabilities, such as cerebral palsy and mental retardation, and in describing the scope and extent of developmental deficits. Criterion-based measures such as the EIDP then provide essential information that qualitatively describes functioning in a comprehensive manner and identifies specific strengths and weaknesses. Thus, ranges of absent (F), acquired (P), and emerging (PF) skills facilitate the *match* between the child's needs/capabilities and appropriate stimulation activities to enhance developmental progress.

Exhibit 3-5b Modified Sample of Matching Developmental Assessment-Programming Tasks from the EIDP

±	*Assessment Tasks*	*Cognitive Domain (9-18 mo.)*	*Instructional Processes*
±	Finds completely hidden toy	Goal:	Child finds hidden toys and objects
±	Understands toy behind screen	Process:	Object constancy
±	Anticipates actions and events	Activity:	1. Hide cookie under one of three bowls in a row; child eats cookie if locates it after watching you.
±	Uses stick to retrieve distant object		2. Change location to third bowl. Child searches and finds.
–	Understands cause-effect relationships		3. Continue until child finds cookie consistently.
±	Imitates sounds and motions	Adaptive:	*Note:* For the *visually-impaired child,* prompt him to explore materials in front of him and find buzzers, bells, and clickers placed in different locations around his body when seated.

Source: Adapted from D.S. Schafer & M.S. Moersch, *Developmental programming for infants and young children.* Ann Arbor, Mich.: University of Michigan Press, 1977.

The EIDP is not a norm-referenced measure; however, assignment of tasks to specific age-range levels was accomplished by calculating averages of item placement from other traditional scales or child development research. Limited reliability and validity studies on the EIDP reveal promising correlations in the .77-.98 range. Congruence with such instruments as the Bayley and Vineland scales is high, and should be, considering the common tasks and item placements among these measures.

Scoring on the EIDP is accomplished by a simple format of P = pass, F = fail, PF = emerging skill, and 0 = omitted item. Unique to this scale is the omission and substitution of items to help circumvent the response/modality handicaps of certain children, that is substituting gestures for words or auditorially directed reaching for visually-directed reaching. Also, the accompanying stimulation activities of the program suggest adaptive activities for handicapped children (see Exhibit 3-6). Once scoring and basal-ceiling levels are established, representative developmental age ranges can be delineated to describe functioning.

Considerations. The EIDP is presently the best available criterion-based device for handicapped infants aged 0 to 36 months. Its developmental sequencing, wide-domain coverage, practical format, and matched stimulation activities attest to its distinct advantages. The following unique features should be considered: The EIDP

- provides a comprehensive six-domain profile of functioning involving 274 tasks;
- enables the selection of individualized objectives for programming;
- reflects current developmental research within its tasks regarding primitive reflexes, Piagetian operations, and attachment and bonding; and
- offers alternative assessment/intervention possibilities for infants suffering various disabilities.

Exhibit 3-6 Sample Visual-Process Stimulation Activities and Adaptive Directions from the EIDP

Perceptual/Fine Motor

0-2 Months

Short-term goal

Child will focus on an object placed 10 to 12 inches in front of his eyes (midline). ***Visual Focusing***

Activities

At various times during the day, position yourself where the child can see you. Talk to the child, make interesting noises, and change your facial expression when the child indicates he can see you.

Place a mobile on the child's crib or chair so that he will have something to focus his eyes on.

Shake a colorful noisemaker in front of the child's face to gain his attention and to promote focusing of his eyes.

Encourage the child to look at his food or bottle when being fed. Reward his looking by feeding him immediately.

Cut out shapes (triangle, star, bull's eye, face) from black or red construction paper. Paste the shapes on a white background or draw shapes directly on white paper. Hang the picture where the infant can see it. Young infants are most attracted to interesting configurations which have highly contrasting components, such as a bull's eye with alternating black and white concentric rings.

Note: If the child's eyes do not focus on the object, move his head to face the object.

Hearing Impaired: *NC*

Motorically Involved: *NC*

Visually Impaired: *Give the child the opportunity to listen to a variety of* sounds *such as noisemakers, records, and voices. Cessation of activity or increased activity is indicative that he is hearing the sounds. Later he will begin to locate the sounds of his environment.*

Exhibit 3-6 continued

Short-term goal

Child's eyes will follow objects that are moving horizontally in front of him (horizontal tracking). ***Visual Tracking***

Activities

1. When the child is looking at you, move your face from one side of the child to the other. Encourage the child to follow you with his eyes.
2. In a darkened room, move a penlight horizontally across the child's face. (Do not shine the light directly into his eyes.) Encourage the child to follow the light visually.
3. Put thimbles on your thumb and index finger and click them together as you move your hand across the midline in front of the child's face, encouraging him to follow visually.
4. Hold a toy or finger puppet about 12 inches from the child's face. Slowly move it from side to side. Be sure the child's eyes are focusing on the object. Gradually increase the distance of the object from side to side.
5. Hang a swinging mobile above the child's crib. Hang it so it swings horizontally. Encourage the child to follow its swing.
6. When the child's eyes are focused straight ahead, present an interesting object to the side. Shake it slightly and try to attract the child's attention.

Short-term goal

Child will voluntarily grasp an object in his palm using only his pinkie, ring, and middle fingers (ulnar-palmar prehension). ***Grasp***

Activities

Offer the child one of your fingers to grasp. Encourage him to close his last three fingers around it.

Give the child plastic clothespins or doughnut rings to hold on to. Decrease your assistance until the child can grasp a toy by himself.

Give the child a teething biscuit. Encourage him to grasp it by himself.

Hearing Impaired: *MA*

Motorically Involved: *If fist is closed due to stiffness, drop the wrist to relaxed position before offering the object.*

Exhibit 3-6 continued

Visually Impaired: *Give the child safe objects (teething ring, rattle) and encourage him to bring them to his mouth. Mouthing is another way to learn about objects.*

Support the child on your lap in front of a table, or sit on the floor and set the child between your legs for support. Help the child explore objects which have been placed in front of him. Close his hand over objects. Later encourage him to explore the surface in front of him and grasp on his own.

Ulnar-palmar prehension

Short-term goal

Child will look at his hands. ***Visual Focusing***

Activities

Put lightweight mittens on the child's hands or tie a ribbon around each hand to call the child's attention to them. Encourage him to look at them by raising them into his visual field.

Bring the child's hands into the child's field of vision and move them around (e.g., pat-a-cake, swiping at or reaching for objects).

Tie small bells to the child's hands so they will ring when he moves them.

Hearing Impaired: *MA*

Motorically Involved: *MA*

Visually Impaired: *Use bells to call child's attention to his hands. Spend time rubbing his hands with terry toweling and/or lotion after bathing. The child will not be able to watch his hands but needs to develop awareness that his hands are a part of him.*

Source: Schafer, D.S., & Moersch, M.S. *Developmental programming for infants and young children. (Vol. III)* Stimulation Activities. Ann Arbor, Mich.: University of Michigan Press, 1977. Reprinted with permission.

The Brigance Diagnostic Inventory of Early Development

The diagnostic specialist who works most frequently with handicapped infants and preschoolers (under the mandate of P.L. 94-142) is the school psychologist. However, as noted before, differences in training and the typical emphasis on school-age children limit the school psychologist's training, and the typical emphasis on school-age children reduces the school psychologist's readiness to serve fully such a population. Recent changes involving more developmentally based training models have promoted school psychological services to young children. Although it is most often given by teachers, the Brigance Diagnostic Inventory of Early Development (IED) (Brigance, 1978) is an aid in this direction for specific reasons: it was constructed by a school psychologist, it is based on a developmental model, and it combines criterion- and norm-based assessment qualities with a task-analytic curriculum format.

The IED covers the age range from birth through 6 years and assesses 98 task/skill sequences in the following functional domains and subdomains (see Exhibit 3-7):

1. preambulatory motor skills and behaviors (4 subdomains)
2. gross motor skills and behaviors (13 subdomains)
3. fine motor skills and behaviors (9 subdomains)
4. self-help skills (11 subdomains)
5. prespeech behaviors (3 subdomains)
6. speech and language skills (10 subdomains)
7. general knowledge and comprehension (13 subdomains)
8. readiness skills (5 subdomains)
9. basic reading skills (11 subdomains)
10. writing skills (7 subdomains)
11. math skills (12 subdomains)

Because of its wide-range, multidomain coverage, the IED is a truly comprehensive, criterion-based measure for assessing developmental functioning. It is easily administered, using its durable, flip-card, ring notebook format. Information is collected on child functioning through a variety of sources: observation, parent judgment, and child performance. In addition, the author recommends that common home and classroom materials be used to administer the test while informally altering materials and response styles to obtain "best" performances and to circumvent the impairments of the developmentally disabled. Though no standard procedure is suggested for these modifications, various response styles are required, that is, verbal, pointing, and paper-pencil behaviors. In administration, certain tasks are selected depending upon whether they are appropriate for the

Exhibit 3-7 Selected Visual-Motor Tasks from the Brigance Diagnostic Inventory of Early Development

C. FINE MOTOR SKILLS AND BEHAVIORS

59-65

General Eye/Finger/Hand Manipulative Skills:

0-7 1. Uses inferior pincer grasp.
2. Pokes or examines objects with index finger.
3. Uses neat pincer grasp.
4. Puts objects in container.
5. Squeezes squeaking toy with hand.
6. Eyes follow movements of hands or object in hand.
7. Picks up small objects, such as raisins, with pincer grasp.
1-0 8. Unwraps loosely wrapped small objects.
2-0 9. "Nests" objects graduated in size.
10. Turns knobs (on TV, radio, toys, etc.).
11. Turns door knob to open door.
12. Makes stirring movement.
13. Cuts dough or soft clay with cookie cutter.
2-6 14. Strings one-inch beads.
15. Unscrews and screws three-inch lid.
3-0 16. Folds paper.
17. Strings half-inch beads.
3-6 18. Winds up toy.
19. Unscrews and screws on a one-inch lid.
20. Sorts dissimilar objects.
4-0 21. Puts paper clip on paper.
22. Creases paper with fingers.
5-0 23. Folds paper diagonally and creases it.
24. Opens lock with key.
25. Sews through holes in sewing card.
26. Opens and closes large safety pin.
6-0 27. Builds structure with blocks, Tinker Toys, etc.
28. Uses pencil sharpener.
29. Uses eraser.
30. Dials telephone number given in writing.
31. Drives large nails in soft wood.
32. Draws line with ruler.
33. Threads large needle. 7-0

Developmental Age: 0-7 — 1-0 — 2-0 — 2-6 — 3-0 — 3-6 — 4-0 — 5-0 — 6-0 — 7-0

Notes:

Source: Brigance, A.H. *Brigance diagnostic inventory of early development.* Worcester, Mass.: Curriculum Associates, Inc., 1978.

child's age, functional level, and assessment purpose. Performance levels are "scored" by circling the tasks successfully completed and commenting upon the quality of performance. Developmental age levels accompany each skill sequence indicating when learning usually begins and when mastery typically occurs. Rough age estimates are derived in this manner. Color-coding with different pencils is suggested as a method of recording the results of successive assessments and, thus, the sequential planning and accomplishment of objectives.

Once this recording and coding have been completed, a profile of child functioning is provided that indicates the

- functional level at first assessment,
- specific acquired and deficit skills,
- functional level at successive assessments,
- skill progress or gain between assessments, and
- skill sequences or objectives "targeted" for intervention.

Thus, the IED uses an informal developmental task-analysis assessment method to integrate developmental assessment, instructional goal-planning, and child and program evaluation. Since the author is also reportedly publishing matched developmental curricula and since some programs have computerized IEPs from the Brigance inventory, the IED holds promise as a very worthwhile, widely employed instrument for linking assessment → intervention → evaluation.

Considerations. The IED is one of the best of the newly marketed criterion-referenced measures for infants and preschoolers. Its wide skill coverage and flexible format make it a very useful measure with the young and severely handicapped child. As with most criterion measures, technical and normative data are essential to increase its credibility and full usefulness. Suggested adaptive modification of items for handicapped children would further enhance the scale's wide application as a measure of choice in preschool programs.

Adaptive-Process Measures for Young Exceptional Children

Most assessment instruments for use with infants and preschoolers are designed on either a norm-referenced or criterion-referenced basis. The combined use of these dual approaches is advocated by most early intervention proponents. Nevertheless, the diverse needs of young handicapped children and the mandates of individualized services to meet these needs require implementing more flexible, functional-clinical assessment methods. Few available instruments combine norm, criterion, and adaptive procedures (Guidubaldi, Newborg, Stock, & Wnek, in press); thus, knowledge of complementary batteries of devices is essential. This final section on early assessment methods surveys several worthwhile scales that encompass characteristics such as handicapped norms, adaptive administrative procedures, and alternative response modes to accommodate assessment/curriculum linkages.

Developmental Activities Screening Inventory

Designed out of a need to provide functional assessment of young children with sensory impairments, the Developmental Activities Screening Inventory (DASI) (Dubose & Langley, 1977) is an "interim" screening measure that surveys the 6-to-60-month-age span within 6-month ranges. As an interim measure, it is intended to bridge the frequent time delay between identification of developmental problems and the total diagnostic assessment necessary for programming. Through 55 "landmark" developmental tasks, the DASI taps a variety of uncategorized skills that focus on "fine-motor coordination, cause-effect, and means-end relationships, association, number concepts, size discrimination, and seriation" (pp. 1-2).

The scale is easily administered by preschool teachers who are familiar with child development. It includes materials and uses common classroom toys in the administration of each task.

Scoring is readily accomplished by establishing basal and ceiling levels, using a P for passes and an F for failed items. A comments section allows the recording of emerging capabilities and qualitative impressions about performance. The total number of P items are added to the basal level to provide a general developmental age-level reference point. The age-range estimates are intended to provide only a comparative reference point for more comprehensive standardized assessments.

Following the informal skill survey, teachers can then analyze the undeveloped and marginal skills below the child's chronological age and within the functional age range to identify targets for individualized programming. The assessment manual contains clear and detailed suggestions for organizing the teaching of each skill.

Limited research on the DASI suggests positive correlations with similar scales such as the Denver, Cattell, and Merrill-Palmer scales and the Preschool Attainment Record. Clinical application with 200 multiply handicapped children supports the utility of the DASI.

The DASI presents many unique features that should bolster its wide use as an integral part of any multimeasure developmental assessment battery. The inclusion of adaptive administration procedures and congruent instructional goals and procedures is central to its character. The scale is essentially nonverbal and does not penalize children who suffer auditory and speech/language impairments. The

DASI manual clearly and pointedly specifies strategies for adapting assessment for the visually impaired child. For example, on a matching task involving two blocks and a card with two dots, the adaptive strategy suggests substituting a card with "raised" dots.

Finally, the DASI provides a series of instructional suggestions for each assessed skill/task in the sequence. Specifically, a task analysis of the behaviors required to complete the task is provided in outline form by the authors to guide IEP development.

Considerations. The DASI is an extremely worthwhile process measure that provides a model for integrating norm, criterion, and adaptive assessment procedures. It should be viewed as an essential part of a comprehensive developmental diagnostic battery that merges quantitative and qualitative data for planning individualized early intervention programs. Its major practical limitations are its focus on only "landmark" skills and its absence of domain coverage. Its screening quality limits the full application of its unique and invaluable features in comprehensive assessments. The authors are urged to consider modifying and expanding the scale's tasks and domains to facilitate comprehensive assessment purposes.

The Developmental Potential of Preschool Children

The Haeussermann Educational Evaluation. In chapter 7 we will review briefly the Haeussermann approach (1958) for comprehensively assessing the developmental capabilities of young cerebral palsied children. The Haeussermann approach is significant because it seeks to describe a child's skills and methods of solving problems for the primary purpose of establishing instructional goals and strategies. It is one of the few approaches that details "standardized" *adaptive* administration procedures appropriate for various handicaps.

The Educational Evaluation of Haeussermann (EEH) offers a structured and pragmatic approach to the educational and developmental appraisal of children who are between 2 and 6 years of age, or who are functioning on that level, and who exhibit handicaps in sensorimotor and expressive capabilities. The method is the result of experimental exploration rather than statistical computation and compilation, but it also details a structured interview of performance with suggestions for methodical modification of items depending on the child's functional deficits. Valuable suggestions are offered for arranging the testing environment and managing the behavior of physically and emotionally disabled children.

The systematic evaluation detects whether or not a given child can function in all areas related to learning and development and what level the child has reached in each functional area. The essential tasks in the evaluation have been devised so as to require neither manipulation nor speech of the child. Such modifications permit a gradual reduction in demand and difficulty so that there can be a smooth retreat to lower levels of functioning.

As Haeussermann asserts, the approach offers a

> systematic sampling strategy across the child's functional skills and deficit areas with the primary objective of determining the kinds of training and experience that will best promote his own adaptive functional abilities . . . and . . . the special circumstances which are needed to create conditions for learning in the handicapped preschool child. (p. ix)

The evaluation provides a basis for planning individualized instructional plans and strategies by comprehensively assessing such skills as comprehension and use of language, recognition of pictorial symbols, ability to discriminate between colors, concept amounts, ability to perceive, differentiate and recall from memory basic symbols, and visual-spatial orientation (see Table 3-6).

No normative or technical data are presented in the manual. However, the evaluation employs a very pragmatic, clinical method designed to evaluate the status of the individual child rather than compare him or her to the normally developing child. Twenty-five years of clinical experience in medical and special educational settings provide the groundwork for the soundness of this approach for children with multiple handicaps.

The invaluable manual details a structured format for presenting items to the handicapped preschooler; individual item/task modifications are explained that alter the behavioral/response demand of the items as well as the use of differential materials (objects vs. pictures, edible vs. nonedible items). The intent of the assessment is to define those levels of functioning that represent the child's current levels of performance and those strategies which enable the child to respond and learn effectively. Performance is scored pass-fail, but modifications enable lower demand levels to be sampled so that a representative functional level for each child is reached. The structured appraisal of intact sensory, motor, and language skills helps to arrive at a plan for intervention. Inventories of developmental levels also make it possible to derive age levels for generalized functioning.

The Psychoeducational Evaluation of the Preschool Child. The Psychoeducational Evaluation of the Preschool Child (PEPC) (Jedrysek et al., 1972) was formulated by Else Haeussermann's colleagues as a vehicle for applying her functional assessment strategies to the normal preschool child who may experience subtle developmental/learning difficulties. The PEPC is an unnormed teacher-administered instrument that seeks to probe various levels of child functioning to detect the child's "individual style and scope of responsiveness to guided demands" (p. 7). The 41 activities on the scale are developmentally sequenced for ages 3 to 6 in terms of operational complexity and demand features and in terms of covering multiple domains. However, the scale results in no age or grade norms, but rather is intended as a *qualitative* probe to identify learning styles and instruc-

Table 3-6 A Series of Sample Tasks in the Haeussermann Educational Evaluation

Present to Ages	*No. of Item*	*Description of Item*	*Age Level Expected*
II-0 to VI	1.	Recognition of objects, when named	2-0 to 2-6
II-0 to VI	2.	Recognition of objects, described in terms of use	2-6 to 3-0
II-0 to VI	3.	Recognition of sizes, concrete	2-6 to 3-0
II-0 to VI	4.	Recognition of objects in image, when named	2-0 to 3-0
II-6 to VI	5.	Recognition of objects in image, described in terms of use	2-6 to 3-0
III-6 to VI	6.	Recall of missing picture from memory	4-0 to 5-0
II-6 to III only	7.	Recognition of action in image	2-6 to 3-0
III-0 to VI	8.	Recognition of (action in image and) time of day	3-0 to 3-6
II-0 to III only	9.	Recognition of form and symbol, cut-outs, matching	2-0 to 2-6
II-6 to VI	10.	Recognition of form and symbol, on square cards, a) matching	2-6 to 3-6
III-6 to VI	11.	b) finding from memory	4-0 to 4-3

Source: Haeussermann, E. *Developmental potential of preschool children.* New York: Grune & Stratton, Inc., 1958. Reprinted by permission.

tional needs and goals (see Exhibit 3-8). A sense of adaptive learning probes facilitates the construction of an informal diagnostic profile that describes functional patterns and processes across domains. Test items are culled from the classroom as well as cut out or reproduced from the manual. In a large sense, the PEPC is very similar to Valett's profile of basic learning abilities (1972).

Considerations. The main strength of both the EEH and the PEPC is their focus on probing developmental/learning processes in a qualitative manner to establish instructional levels and educational techniques. Both instruments require significant knowledge of developmental processes to be used effectively. Yet, the methods are truly adaptive in orientation and, uniquely, offer structured suggestions for adapting assessment to functional limitations and standard "probes" for extending evaluation to upper and lower limits.

Every psychologist and developmental diagnostic expert should be thoroughly familiar with the methods of Haeussermann. These methods put norm-referenced measurement into perspective and highlight its serious limitations. The Haeussermann approach effectively operationalizes what "assessment" must be, in reference to individualized educational programming.

Assessment of Deaf-Blind Children

The Callier-Azusa Scale. Performance assessments of multihandicapped children are notoriously unreliable and nonfunctional. Because of the serious complicating effects of sensorimotor impairments on child functioning, diagnostic specialists have increasingly depended upon behavioral observation and ratings as an effective method of intervention-based assessment. In fact, Diebold et al. (1978) have demonstrated that for deaf-blind children observation measures correlate significantly with developmental performance scales. The interrelationship is most prominent when the observation and performance measures are ordered according to the normal developmental sequence.

The Callier-Azusa Scale (CAS) (Stillman, 1974) is one of the most widely employed of these measures. Covering the birth-to-9-year-age range, the CAS is composed of five subscales: socialization, daily living skills, motor development, perceptual abilities, and language development. The scale is completed by teachers and/or parents and relies on naturalistic observation of behavior in structured and unstructured situations. Different levels of functioning are numbered in ascending order within each domain; a child's functional level is simply observed and circled on the scale, and a rough developmental age level is derived (see Table 3-7). A diagnostic profile is generated as a result. The scale thus serves to establish functional levels, select instructional goals, and evaluate child progress and program efficacy.

Exhibit 3-8 Sample Qualitative Probes from the PEPC

Name Ricky W. Sex M D.O.B. ______ Age 4-6 School Nursery

Date of Test ______

PSYCHOEDUCATIONAL EVALUATION OF THE PRESCHOOL CHILD

Item No.		Name of Item or Probe	Observations and Teaching Suggestions
SECTION I. PHYSICAL FUNCTIONING AND SENSORY STATUS			
1	+	Manual dexterity	Good coordination and motor control. Graceful movements- In general, active.
2	+	Visual acuity	
3	+	Visual pursuit	
4	+	Depth perception, binocularity	Enjoys physical activity may be used as reward or relaxation.
5	+	Auditory acuity	
	______	Probe A: Simplify task	
6	+	Using touch and vision together	
	______	Probe A. Make task concrete	
SECTION II. PERCEPTUAL FUNCTIONING			
7	+	Color matching	
	______	Probe A. Reduce choices	
8	+	Matching of solid forms on white background	
	______	Probe A. Make task concrete	
	______	Probes B and C. Reduce choices and make concrete	

Source: Jedrysek, E., Klapper, Z., Pope, L., & Wortis, J. *Psychoeducational evaluation of the preschool child.* New York: Grune & Stratton, Inc., 1972. Reprinted by permission.

Table 3-7 Visual Development Ratings on the Callier-Azusa Scale

Perceptual Development

Item	*Example*	*Comments*
A. Visual development		
0. Does not attend to any stimulus in the visual field.		
1. Attends only to light stimulus.		
2. (a) Attends to large object in the visual field within 30 seconds of its presentation.	When an object is presented close to the child's eyes, he will direct his gaze to the object within 30 seconds.	
(b) May look at caregiver's face when held or in close contact with caregiver.		
(c) Eyes follow object from side to center of body.		
3. (a) Looks toward the source of light.		
(b) Visually follows a moving person.		
4. (a) Shows eye-blink response to a quickly approaching object.		
(b) May be aware of familiar faces.		

Source: Stillman, R. D. *The Callier-Azusa scale: Assessment of deaf-blind children.* Reston, Va.: Council for Exceptional Children, 1974. Reprinted with permission.

The Maxfield-Buchholz Scale of Social Maturity for Preschool Blind Children and the Wisconsin Behavior Rating Scale. Two other scales are noteworthy in providing adaptive, observational assessments: The Maxfield-Buchholz (M-B) Scale of Social Maturity for Preschool Blind Children (Maxfield & Buchholz, 1957) and the Wisconsin Behavior Rating Scale (WBRS) (Song & Jones, 1980). The M-B scale is a measure that adapts the Vineland interview format to assess blind preschool children between the ages of birth and 5 years. The standardization was based on 484 children. In organization, items from the original Vineland Scale were relocated or discarded in favor of tactile and orientation tasks more appropriate to the young blind child.

Similarly, the WBRS represents the most recent product of the continuing effort to construct measures combining norm, criterion, and adaptive features. The measure is composed of 11 subscales that are viewed as tapping adaptive developmental behaviors essential for daily functioning, that is, gross motor, fine motor, expressive language, receptive language, play skills, socialization, domestic activity, eating, toileting, dressing, grooming.

The WBRS is an interview-informant measure that attempts to standardize the judgments of significant people in the handicapped child's life. This is accomplished by using a four-level behavior rating format:

- 0 No response or performance—total assistance
- 1 Emergent behavior—independent functioning less than 50 percent of the time
- 2 Independent performance more than 50 percent of the time
- N.O. No opportunity to perform due to situational limitations.

The WBRS is normed on 184 normal and 325 institutionalized, retarded individuals who function below the 36-month developmental level. The scale generates a total "behavioral age" and age equivalents for each subscale. Promising reliability and validity data are reported involving scales such as the Vineland. One of the most unique features of the WBRS is the inclusion of "alternative" items to assess appropriately blind and deaf/blind individuals (see Exhibit 3-9). Due to its effective combination of norm, criterion, and adaptive features, the WBRS appears to be the most promising of the multisource, interview, behavior rating scales in format. However, recent clinical experience with young developmentally disabled children suggests that the WBRS significantly underestimates levels of functioning for these children. A review of its norm structure should be considered.

Exhibit 3-9 Adaptive Receptive Language Tasks for the Deaf/Blind Preschooler on the WBRS

IV. RECEPTIVE LANGUAGE FOR DEAF/BLIND

____ 1. Looks for or searches after objects immediately after being hidden or dropped.

____ 2. Responds appropriately to such words, gestures/signs as "come," "up" or "bye-bye".

____ 3. Distinguishes own name from others.

____ 4. Stops or withdraws from an activity when told, in any form of communication, "no" or "stop that".

____ 5. Follows simple verbal, gestural sign or tactile instructions; e.g., "sit down" or "stand up".

____ 6. Recognizes names of common objects; e.g., table, ball, shoe, spoon, when requested using any form of communication, "Show me ____" or "Give me ____," etc.

____ 7. Appropriately uses three common objects; e.g., when handed a comb, attempts to comb hair (brush, cup, spoon, etc.).

____ 8. Responds to commands given using any form of communication, involving "on" or "in"; e.g., "Put the spoon *on* the plate."

____ 9. Identifies pictures of common objects when appropriate gestures or signs are used.

Alternative item for the blind

____ 9. *Identifies common objects.*

Exhibit 3-9 continued

_____ 10. Points out any (3-5) body parts on a doll when asked via any sensory modality.

_____ 11. Follows a series of two or three related simple commands; e.g., "Turn on the lights and close the door," via any form of communication.

_____ 12. Understands who/what in any form of communication; e.g., "Who is in the chair?," "What do you eat with?."

_____ 13. Identifies two or more verbs (action words in pictures) using any form of communication; e.g., "show me eating," "show me running."

Alternative item for the blind

_____ *13. Demonstrates simple action words such as "eat," "clap hands" in any form of communication.*

_____ 14. Understands concept, tall/short.

Prorated Total

[ ] **Total** × **1.43=** [ ] **Scale IV D/B**

(Round the decimals to the nearest whole number)

Number of N.O. _____

Source: Song, A., & Jones, S.E. *Wisconsin behavior rating scale.* Madison, Wis.: Center for the Developmentally Disabled, 1980. Reprinted with permission.

SPECIALIZED ADAPTIVE INSTRUMENTS

The assessment of general intellectual functioning is of prime importance in diagnosing and placing multihandicapped children, particularly blind, deaf, emotionally disturbed, and cerebral palsied individuals. Although individualized programming requires more precise assessment than that provided by intelligence testing, it is a vital first step in establishing functional baselines. Over the years, two handicapped assessment alternatives have dominated the field: designing response "fair" tests, and norming tests on specific handicapped populations. The cognitive measures discussed in this section reflect these two alternatives and should be considered part of a comprehensive diagnostic battery for the young handicapped child.

TWO COMPLEMENTARY ADAPTIVE MEASURES

The Pictorial Test of Intelligence

The Pictorial Test of Intelligence (PTI) (French, 1964) is designed as a measure of general intellectual functioning for both normal and physically handicapped children even though it was not standardized on physically impaired children. The device's most adaptive feature is the fact that alternate response modes can be incorporated into its structure, that is, eye localization, head-pointing, multiple choice, and yes-no formats. The use of large picture cards allows the child to select one of four pictured stimuli requested by the examiner and thus reveals the child's comprehension of specific areas of information (see Figure 3-3).

The PTI covers the 3-to-8-year age range and surveys six subdomain functions:

1. picture vocabulary
2. form discrimination
3. information and comprehension
4. similarities
5. size and number
6. immediate recall

Three subtests assess developing cognitive "processes" like form discrimination, and three subtests measure "product" information derived through general learning experiences in the environment, for example, picture vocabulary. Raw scores on the total test and on each of the subtests can be converted to mental ages, deviation IQs ($\overline{X} = 100$, $S = 16$), and percentiles by using the norm tables. Thus, a diagnostic profile of cognitive skills is provided.

Figure 3-3 Form Discrimination Task from the Pictorial Test of Intelligence

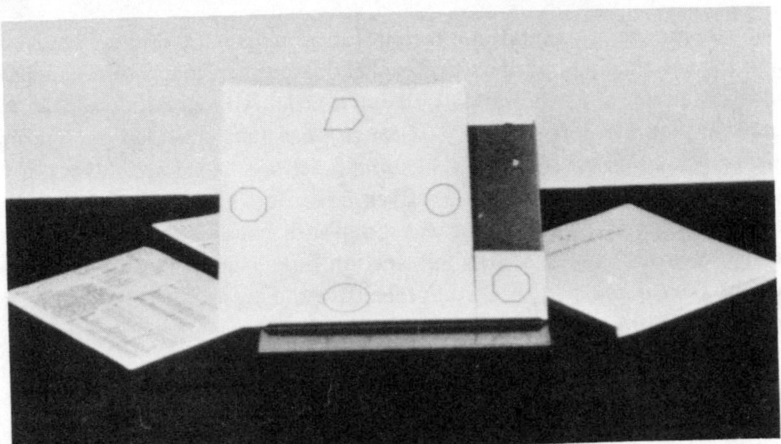

Source: French, J.S. *The pictorial test of intelligence.* Boston, Mass.: Houghton-Mifflin, Inc., 1964. Reprinted with permission.

The PTI is one of the best standardized norm-referenced measures available. The sample consisted of 1,830 children, ages 3 to 8, selected as representative of the U.S. population. The norm group was based on the 1960 census and stratified according to geographic region, community size, occupation level, and sex. Reliability and validity studies on the instrument attest to its adequacy for making instructional decisions.

The PTI should be considered one of the most useful and technically adequate specialized measures. Its excellent alternative response format makes it particularly valuable when assessing young cerebral palsied children, even though its structure is not strictly developmental in nature. The major drawback of the PTI concerns how quickly very young children can become bored and distracted by a format consisting of multiple black and white drawings and what is essentially a repetitive response (pointing) mode. Periodic breaks are essential to temper these limitations. Finally, although the PTI results should be interpreted by a trained school psychologist, the scale can be effectively administered by teachers and used as a general guide to programming. It is an invaluable component of any adaptive diagnostic battery.

The Columbia Mental Maturity Scale

A notable complement to the PTI is the Columbia Mental Maturity Scale (CMMS) (Burgemeister, Blum, & Lorge, 1972). The CMMS presents a format similar to that of the PTI, requiring the child to point out the correct picture in response to the question, "Which one is not like the others?" The child must make "visual perceptual discriminations in order to classify and relate series of pictures, colors, forms, and symbols" (Salvia & Ysseldyke, 1978, p. 266). Essentially, only two types of behaviors are sampled by the CMMS: discrimination and classification. The CMMS is viewed as a nonverbal measure of general reasoning ability. Although the items are colorful, high-interest, well-formed, and very appropriate for the physically handicapped child, the child must have previously acquired the concept of *different* or the instrument will be inappropriate.

The CMMS covers the age range of 3-6 to 9-11 years and involves 92 pictorial items arranged in eight overlapping levels. The level is given that is appropriate to the child's chronological age. Performance raw data yield age deviation scores, and a maturity index reflects basically a mental-age range. After a series of revisions, the CMMS appears to have adequate norms and technical data to be used as an adaptive diagnostic measure.

Considerations

The PTI and the CMMS are complementary adaptive assessment measures. However, the PTI is clearly superior given its comprehensive subscales, handicap-appropriate format, and excellent standardization. Yet, the CMMS is the more "motivating" test because of its colorful, high-interest pictorial stimuli. Both measures are essential adaptive tools for assessing children with diverse handicaps, namely, physical, language and emotional disorders.

The Leiter International Performance Scale

The Leiter International Performance Scale (LIPS) (Leiter, 1969) is a nonverbal age scale originally constructed to assess the global cognitive capabilities of deaf, hearing-impaired, speech/language disordered, bilingual, and non-English speaking individuals. The scale contains approximately 60 items within the 2-to-18-year age range and taps a variety of "process-dominant" skills, including generalization, discrimination, analogies, sequencing, and pattern completion.

The adaptive features of the measure concern its nonverbal, pantomime-direction administration procedure and its essentially match-to-sample answer format. A wooden response frame holds a stimulus card containing a series of color patterns, designs, or pictures. The child then matches blocks containing the same stimuli to appropriate slots in the frame that correspond to the pattern on the stimulus card (see Figure 3-4).

Performance on the LIPS results in a general mental age equivalent and a ratio IQ, both of which are derived through an imprecise and haphazard process. Normative data on the LIPS are nonrepresentative and incomplete, involving only 289 nonhandicapped children. Reliability and validity data are also lacking.

Figure 3-4 Sample Task from the Leiter International Performance Scale Showing Adaptive Format

Source: Leiter, R. G. *General instructions for the Leiter international performance scale.* Chicago, Ill.: Stoetting Company, 1969. Reprinted with permission.

Thus, the LIPS is best employed to analyze *qualitatively* the cognitive processes of handicapped children simply by noting strong and weak skills and by establishing functional ranges. Yet, the constantly changing types of activities and the inherently challenging quality of these tasks make this a highly motivating measure. Its promise rests on its adaptive format and task quality. A reorganization and restandardization of the scale would enhance its usefulness and fulfill its promise.

The Hiskey-Nebraska Test of Learning Aptitude

Covering the age range of 3 to 16 years, the Hiskey-Nebraska Test of Learning Aptitude (HNTLA) (Hiskey, 1966) is designed to assess the "learning aptitude" of both deaf and hearing individuals. Effective use of the test requires training and experience with deaf children. Pantomime administration procedures are employed with the deaf and verbal directions with hearing children.

In addition to the adaptive pantomime procedures, the measure contains separate norm groups for deaf and hearing individuals. The use of a pointing response or motor imitation makes the response mode to some degree more appropriate for the deaf and physically handicapped. The HNTLA employs 12 subtests to assess acquired learning skills:

1. bead patterns
2. memory for color
3. picture identification
4. picture association
5. paper folding
6. visual attention span
7. block patterns
8. completion of drawings
9. memory for digits
10. puzzle blocks
11. picture analogies
12. spatial reasoning

Scoring on the HNTLA results in a learning age and learning quotient for deaf children and a mental age and deviation IQ for hearing children. Technical data for the measure is somewhat limited but is more adequate than for most adaptive measures. The scale was normed on 1,079 deaf and 1,074 hearing children.

Considerations. The HNTLA is the instrument of choice for assessing the learning capabilities of young deaf children. Specific training and experience with the deaf and with psychodiagnostic assessment procedures are vital for effective use of the scale. The HNTLA provides probably the best current example of test standardization involving adaptive procedures. It is obvious that much creative thought and effort were involved in constructing its adaptive items, such as the "plastic digits" for the assessment of memory involving numbers in a series. More thorough work, however, is required to make the HNTLA truly technically adequate.

SUMMARY

Designing procedures for assessing and programming for young handicapped children is a complex process necessitating a multimeasure, multisource clinical approach. Measures must be selected that are *developmental* in nature and that serve to *link* the processes of comprehensive assessment and individualized goal-planning. The collection of both qualitative and quantitative data from norm-based, criterion-based, and adaptive sources facilitates this linkage. Simply, we must "test to the teaching."

An assessment guide presenting comparative data on various assessment methods that are developmental and psychoeducational in nature is presented in Figure 3-5.

Figure 3-5 Developmental Assessment Guide

X Primary focus

O Secondary focus

	AGES	DOMAINS: Language	Fine/gross motor	Personal-social	Cognitive	Educational Readiness	PURPOSE: Screening	Diagnostic/prescription	Evaluation	HANDICAP: Visual	Auditory	Neuro-motor	Language	Socio-emotional	Developmental/learning
Assessment of Child. Lang. Comprehension	3-6 yrs.	X					O	X	O			O	X	O	X
Alpern-Boll Developmental Profile	Birth-12 yrs.	X	X	X	X	O	O	X		O	O	O	O	O	X
Bayley Scales of Infant Development	2-30 mo.	O	X	O	X			X	X	O	O	O	O	O	X
Boehm Test of Basic Concepts	K-2nd grade	O			X	X		X	X						X
Callier-Azusa Deaf-Blind Scale	Birth-9 yrs.	X	X	X	X	O		X	X	X	X	O	O		X
Carolina Developmental Profile	2-5 yrs.	X	X	X	X	X		X	X						X
Cattell Infant Intelligence Scale	2-30 mo.	O			X		X		O						X
Cognitive Skills Assess. Battery	Presch-primary	O			X	X		X	X						X
Communication Evaluation Chart	3-60 mo.	X	O	O	X		X		O				X		X
Developmental Activities Screen. Inventory	6-60 mo.	O	O		X	X	X	X	O		X	O	O	O	X
Denver Devel. Screening Test	1-72 mo.	X	X	X	X	O	X								X
Devel. Programming: Infants & Child.	Birth-36 mo.	X	X	X	X	O		X	X	O	O	O	O	O	X
Down's Syndrome Performance Invent.	Birth-9 yrs.	X	X	X	X	O		X	X	O	O	O	O	O	X
Functional Profile	Birth-6 yrs.	X	X	X	X	O		X	X	O	O	O	O	O	X
Gesell Developmental Schedules	1-72 mo.	X	X	X	X	O		X	X	O	O	O	O	O	X
Haeussermann Educational Evaluation	2-6 yrs.	X	X	O	X	X		X	X	O	O	X	X	X	X

Figure 3-5 continued

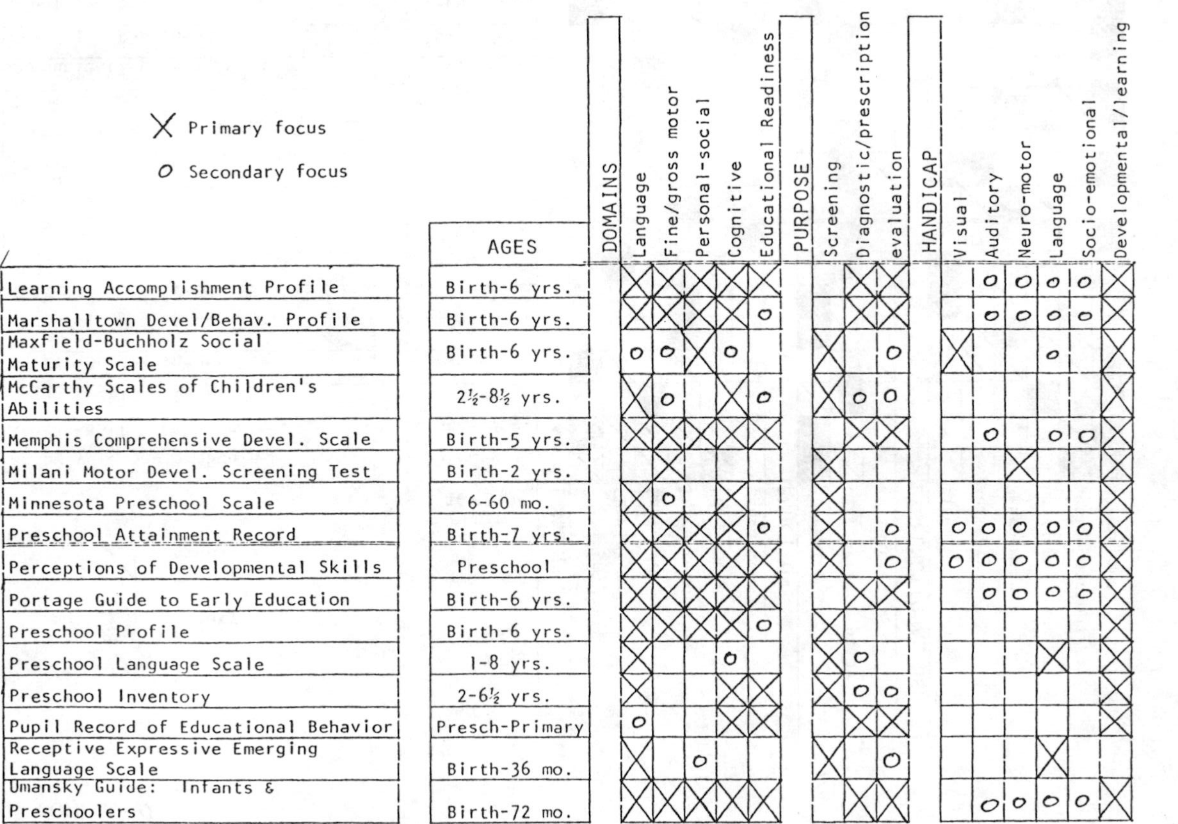

X Primary focus

O Secondary focus

	AGES	DOMAINS: Language	Fine/gross motor	Personal-social	Cognitive	Educational Readiness	PURPOSE: Screening	Diagnostic/prescription	evaluation	HANDICAP: Visual	Auditory	Neuro-motor	Language	Socio-emotional	Developmental/learning
Learning Accomplishment Profile	Birth-6 yrs.	X	X	X	X	X		X	X		O	O	O	O	X
Marshalltown Devel/Behav. Profile	Birth-6 yrs.	X	X	X	X	O		X	X		O	O	O	O	X
Maxfield-Buchholz Social Maturity Scale	Birth-6 yrs.	O	O	X	O		X		O	X			O		X
McCarthy Scales of Children's Abilities	2½-8½ yrs.	X	O		X	O	X	O	O						X
Memphis Comprehensive Devel. Scale	Birth-5 yrs.	X	X	X	X	X		X	X		O		O	O	X
Milani Motor Devel. Screening Test	Birth-2 yrs.		X				X					X			X
Minnesota Preschool Scale	6-60 mo.	X	O		X		X								X
Preschool Attainment Record	Birth-7 yrs.	X	X	X	X	O	X		O	O	O	O	O	O	X
Perceptions of Developmental Skills	Preschool	X	X	X	X	X	X		O	O	O	O	O	O	X
Portage Guide to Early Education	Birth-6 yrs.	X	X	X	X	X		X	X		O	O	O	O	X
Preschool Profile	Birth-6 yrs.	X	X	X	X	O	X								X
Preschool Language Scale	1-8 yrs.	X			O		X	O					X		X
Preschool Inventory	2-6½ yrs.	X			X	X	X	O	O						X
Pupil Record of Educational Behavior	Presch-Primary	O			X	X		X	X						X
Receptive Expressive Emerging Language Scale	Birth-36 mo.	X		O			X		O				X		
Umansky Guide: Infants & Preschoolers	Birth-72 mo.	X	X	X	X	X		X	X		O	O	O	O	X

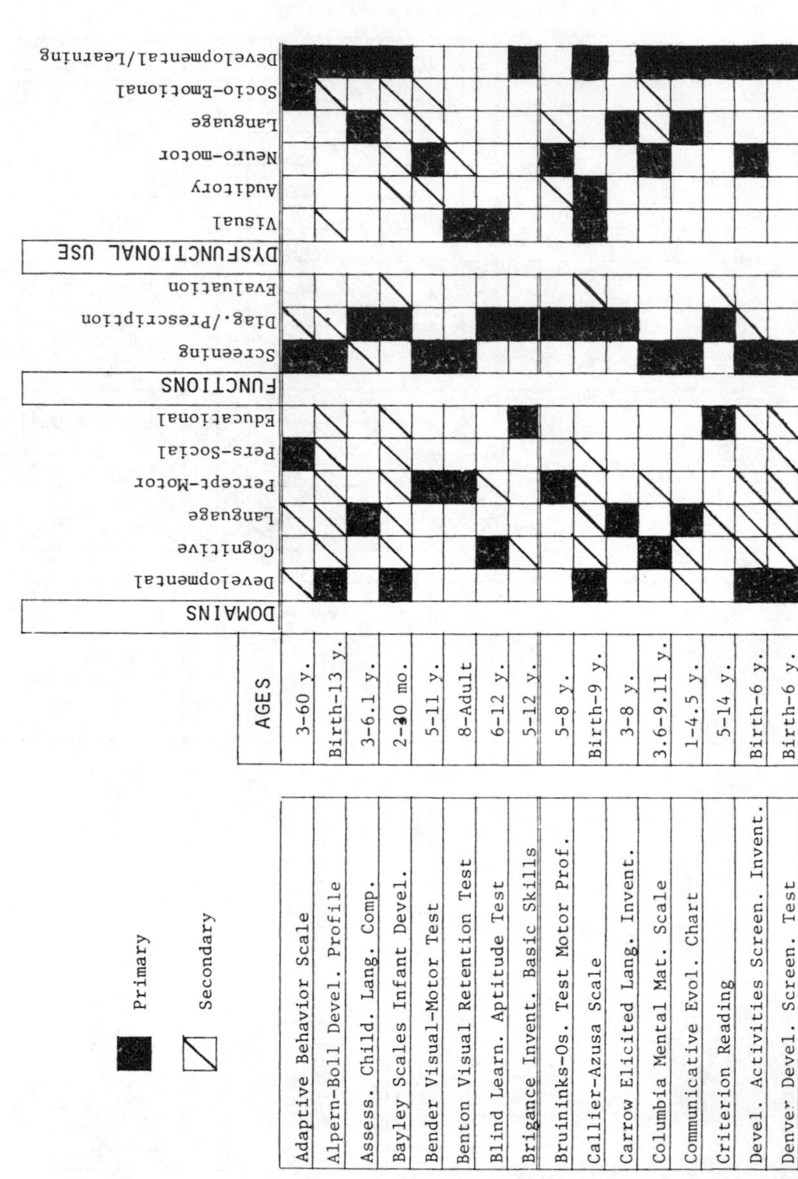

Figure 3-5 continued

Figure 3-5 continued

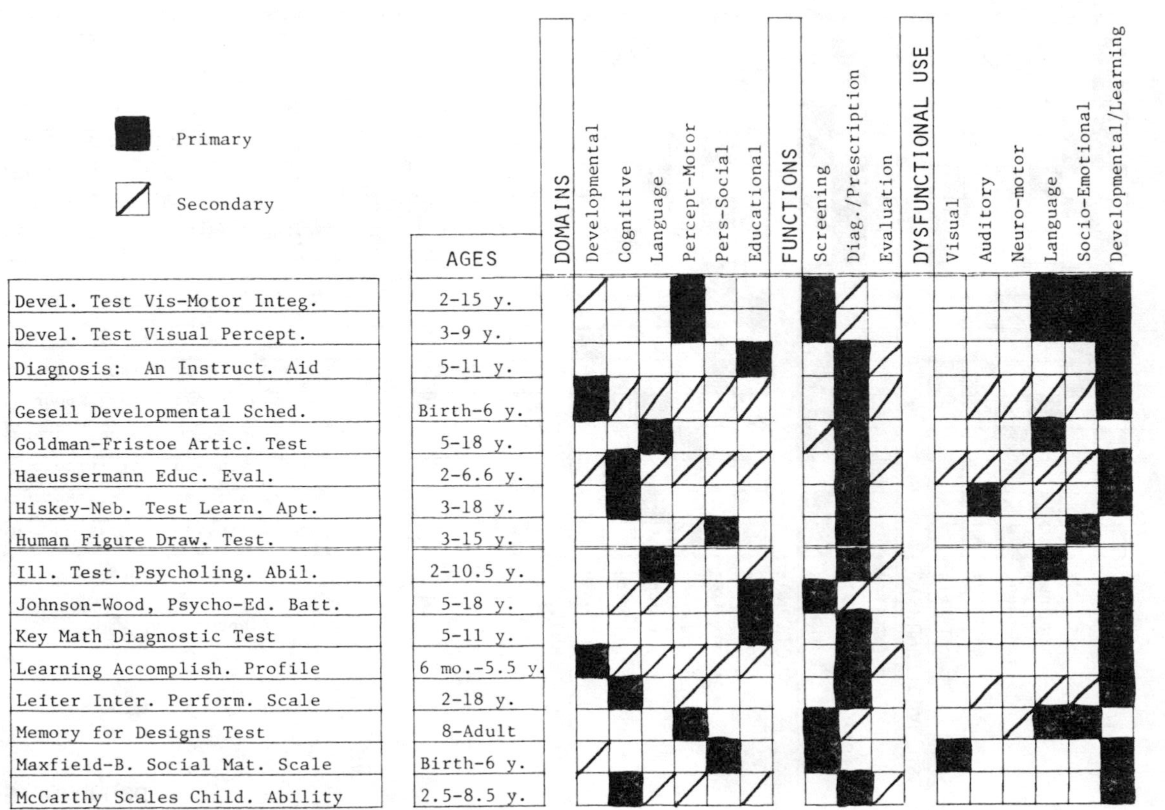

Figure 3-5 continued

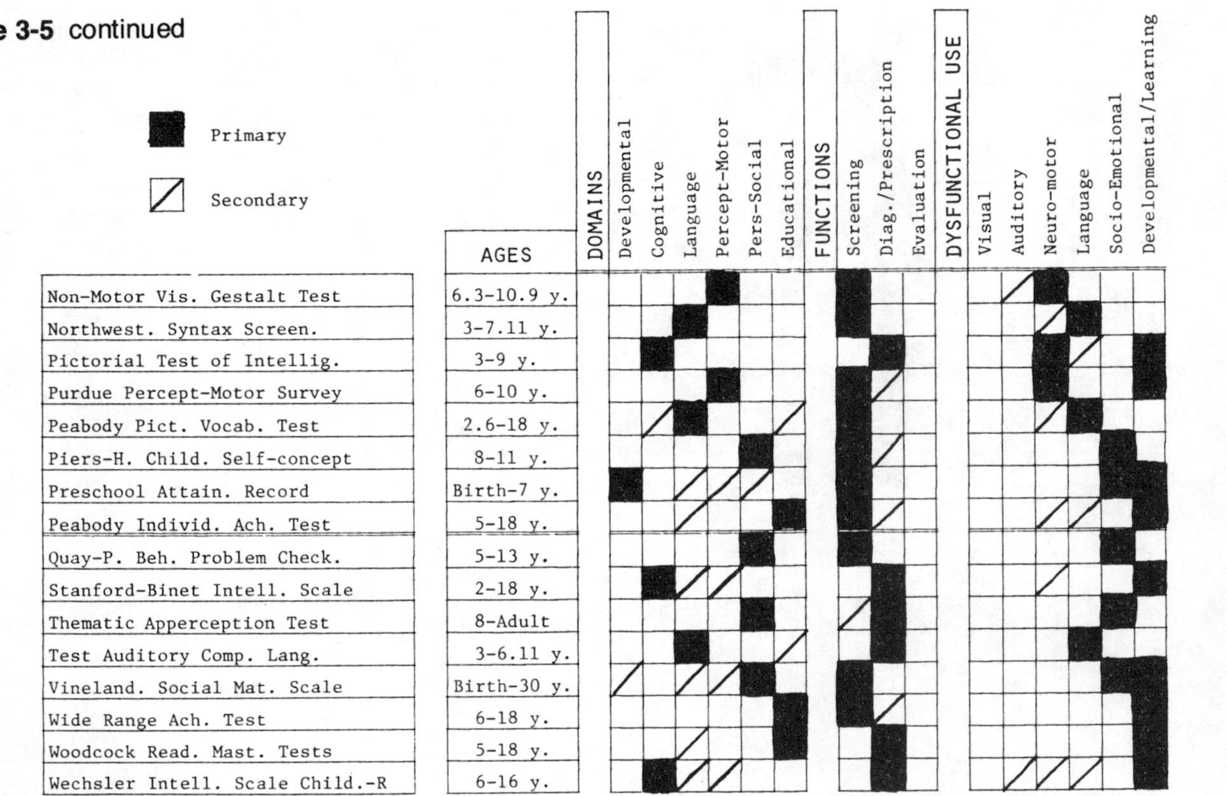

■ Primary

/ Secondary

	AGES	DOMAINS: Developmental	Cognitive	Language	Percept-Motor	Pers-Social	Educational	FUNCTIONS: Screening	Diag./Prescription	Evaluation	DYSFUNCTIONAL USE: Visual	Auditory	Neuro-motor	Language	Socio-Emotional	Developmental/Learning
Non-Motor Vis. Gestalt Test	6.3-10.9 y.				■			■				/	■			
Northwest. Syntax Screen.	3-7.11 y.			■				■					/	■		
Pictorial Test of Intellig.	3-9 y.		■						■				■	/		■
Purdue Percept-Motor Survey	6-10 y.				■			■	/				■			■
Peabody Pict. Vocab. Test	2.6-18 y.		/	■			/	■					/	■		
Piers-H. Child. Self-concept	8-11 y.					■		■	/						■	
Preschool Attain. Record	Birth-7 y.	■		/	/	/		■							■	■
Peabody Individ. Ach. Test	5-18 y.			/			■	■	/				/	/		■
Quay-P. Beh. Problem Check.	5-13 y.					■		■							■	
Stanford-Binet Intell. Scale	2-18 y.		■	/	/				■				/			■
Thematic Apperception Test	8-Adult					■		/	■						■	
Test Auditory Comp. Lang.	3-6.11 y.			■			/		■					■		
Vineland. Social Mat. Scale	Birth-30 y.	/		/	/	■		■							■	■
Wide Range Ach. Test	6-18 y.						■	■	/							■
Woodcock Read. Mast. Tests	5-18 y.			/			■		■							■
Wechsler Intell. Scale Child.-R	6-16 y.		■	/	/				■			/	/	/		■

Sources: Neisworth, J.T., Willoughby-Herb, S.J., Bagnato, S.J., Cartwright, C.A., & Laub, K.J. *Individualized education for preschool exceptional children.* Germantown, Md.: Aspen Systems Corp., 1980. Reprinted with permission.

Hatch, E., Murphy, J., & Bagnato, S.J. The comprehensive evaluation of handicapped children. *Elementary School Guidance and Counseling Journal,* February 1979, *13*(3), 179-195. Reprinted with permission.

Part II

Curricula for the Exceptional Preschooler

Chapter 4

Developmental Curricula for Young Exceptional Children: Design and Content

Perhaps the major reason for assessment is to provide help in planning programs for children. With this purpose in mind, assessment can be conducted in a way harmonious with program content and goals. As stated earlier, assessment findings and developmental objectives can be linked so that individual programs can be rather easily developed. The content of the program, especially the curriculum, becomes a crucial matter, since it partly dictates assessment activities.

THE QUESTION OF WHAT TO TEACH

Teachers are always faced with the question of what to teach. This is especially true at the preschool level. Later schooling usually becomes tilted toward academic achievement, where reading, writing, arithmetic, social studies, vocational preparation, and so forth, predominate the program content. At the preschool level, however, there is great and understandable controversy over what is appropriate and teachable content.

A curriculum is basically a set or pattern of educational objectives. The curriculum is the "what to teach" of the preschool program. The curriculum the teacher selects or develops is a pivotal consideration, since it comprises the objectives for enrolled children, influences assessment, instructional methods, the teacher's role, materials that are purchased, and parent involvement. Indeed, a program's success is often measured by how many children achieve how many curricular goals.

The preschool years are considered to be the most crucial in setting the direction and rate of many aspects of development (Horowitz & Padden, 1973). For handicapped youngsters especially, early education can help to remedy and prevent many problems (Garwood, 1979). Most experts emphasize the importance of the preschool experience but vary on what should be the "right" and appropriate content of the curriculum.

To confound matters, what is the "right" curriculum not only depends upon the developmental needs of the children but also on the professional and personal characteristics of the teacher. A curriculum that is well suited for a given child will probably not be taught effectively if the teacher disagrees with the objectives or associated teaching methods. Certainly, an optimal program is one in which there exists a good match or relationship among teacher characteristics, curriculum, materials, and children (Safford, 1978). Likewise, parents and, hopefully, the child should concur with the educational (i.e., curricular) content of the preschool program. Most curriculum developers agree on program goals when stated in general and abstract terms. That is, few experts object to program goals such as teaching self-respect, appreciation of one's culture, caring about others, problem solving, independence, and so on. These general goals, while involving some value judgments, are vague enough to be agreeable! It's when such goals are broken down into smaller parts and when specific behaviors are stated that the trouble really begins.

It should not be surprising, in view of the controversy, that many preschool curricula have been developed and promoted by various factions within early education. Indeed, hundreds of published curricula are available. Many are essentially similar and are only variations of each other. On the other hand, many curricula are quite distinct, reflecting differing philosophies concerning child development and the role of the preschool experience (see Appendix B summaries of prominent curricula).

FOUNDATIONS FOR A CURRICULUM

First of all, a curriculum must have some philosophical basis or rationale for its content and organization. Most acceptable and useful curricula do come from some identifiable position or point of view and have goals, objectives, and related methods that are consistent with the point of view (Mayer, 1971).

Curricula produced by First Chance projects (a network of government-funded early education projects for handicapped preschoolers) have been analyzed and grouped into five major clusters (Wood & Hurley, 1977). As you read about these five approaches for developing a curriculum, try to decide which one or ones best represent your view. Which approach do you think makes most sense for the children with whom you are concerned? Remember that the curricular approach you choose will influence the kind of assessment that will be appropriate. Selecting a curriculum narrows the range of instructionally relevant assessment activities.

Basic Skills Approach

Many people talk about "getting back to basics." This curricular approach emphasizes the teaching of key or fundamental skills and knowledge. What is "basic," of course, varies among experts; but most can agree on including the development of child competency in the areas of socialization, spoken language, attention, fine and gross motor capabilities, self-help, problem solving, and retention. A basic skills curriculum might include other areas but it is generally limited to a few fundamentals as targets for all children enrolled in a program (see, for example, Staats, 1968). The areas selected for inclusion are said to be basic for later development. Comprehensiveness of objectives is sacrificed in order to permit concentration on presumed foundational skills. If you employed this sort of curriculum, assessment would be focused on determining each child's attainment within each basic skill area. This information would help in selecting curricular objectives for each child and on designing group activities.

Psychological Constructs Approach

A number of psychologists have proposed particular traits or processes they believe to be important to child development. Examples of important psychological constructs that form the basis for a curriculum of this type are motivation, self-concept, locus of control, cognition, achievement motivation, and creativity. This approach to programming for children emphasizes the development of alleged psychological *processes,* whereas a basic skills curriculum focuses on building observable capabilities. Use of a curriculum emphasizing psychological constructs dictates a different kind of assessment from that of a basic skills approach. With the psychological constructs approach, assessment would be focused on finding out each child's level of development of a particular trait, such as "ego strength," "achievement motivation," and so on. Programming is then aimed at promoting each child's progress in the particular trait. A curriculum based on one or more psychological constructs is frequently developed for purposes of exploring further the utility of the construct(s) and is often part of a research-oriented project.

Preacademic Approach

Advocates of this approach are concerned with getting children ready for the academic content of the regular school. Initial training in language, reading, numbers, the arts, and science are often found in the preacademic curriculum (see, for example, Bereighter & Engleman, 1966). It seems clear that this approach is a downward extension of the curricula of most public school programs and is derived from a traditional educational model. Use of a preacademic curriculum would require assessment that provides information on a child's standing in each academic area to be taught.

The preacademic curriculum is often the subject of controversy among parents of children enrolled in a program that uses this approach exclusively. Many parents do indeed want their children to begin school-related work in the preschool. On the other hand, there are a great number of parents who strongly object to the preacademic training focus. Instead, they want their children to be part of a program that promotes more general, overall development. Such parents argue that regular schooling will come soon enough and that early education should focus on socialization, play, and general enrichment.

Remedial Approach

A curriculum based on the remedial approach focuses on a child's deficits or weaknesses. Obviously, remedial objectives cannot be prescribed until the child's problems are identified. Once assessed, the child's developmental problems or delays become the "targets" for program intervention. This approach is also referred to as the "diagnostic-prescriptive" approach (Cartwright, Cartwright, & Ysseldyke, 1973). The remedial approach is a frequent choice when working with handicapped preschoolers. With proper assessment, children's problems can be specified, remedial goals and objectives designed, and teaching can be aimed at ameliorating the deficits. Such an approach is not without criticism, however. Preoccupation with a child's problems may be at the expense of neglecting development in nondeficit areas. Thus, these areas may eventually become weak and remedial targets themselves, so that the program becomes one of constantly playing "catch-up." Nevertheless, the remedial approach can be of great service to handicapped youngsters who are in need of immediate help in specific areas. Sometimes correcting a few fundamental deficits can go a long way in improving a child's entire developmental picture.

Developmental Tasks Approach

Traditionally, nursery school authorities have advocated a "whole child" approach (Hymes, 1968). Their position is that preschool experience should foster progress within and across all important areas of development. With a whole child philosophy, the curriculum must include goals, objectives, and experiences coming from all basic developmental domains and include communication (speech and language), socialization and self-care, physical competence (fine and gross motor), and affective (emotional) and intellectual (cognitive) development.

Using a developmental tasks approach, developmental domains may include a great many objectives—sometimes hundreds. Developmental tasks or objectives within each area are arranged in a hierarchy, that is, a sequence. The hierarchies are lists of objectives that roughly correspond to sequences of skills displayed by normal children during their developmental progression. Drawing on a large body of observational research, experts have compiled lists of tasks that are ordered from easy to hard or early to later in development (Havighurst, 1956). Along with the technique of task analysis, which breaks tasks down into simpler components, a given developmental milestone might have dozens of subskills or *readiness* skills. The skill of eating with a spoon, for example, is preceded by many other skills normally developed earlier—such as chewing and swallowing, eye-hand coordination, and grasping. If a child is unable to spoon-feed, instruction can begin on tasks earlier in the hierarchy. When the preschooler still cannot perform the earlier skill, the teacher can keep moving back in the hierarchy until an objective is found that the child has mastered. Instruction can proceed forward from that point. As you can see, developmental hierarchies provide not only instructional objectives but also diagnostic profiles of a child's range of functional skills. Finding where a child is within a hierarchy is a relatively rapid way to evaluate developmental status.

The developmental task approach is used by many programs that include handicapped youngsters. Many early educators advocate using a developmental task curriculum because it is highly structured and sequenced and permits informal developmental assessment. Additionally, a comprehensive, developmentally sequenced curriculum almost invites "mainstreaming." Children of varying developmental levels can be readily accommodated. Frequently these curricula are built to include children with developmental ages of 0 to 5.

ORGANIZATION OF CURRICULUM CONTENT

As stated earlier, a curriculum is a collection of educational objectives, and the content varies according to the model or approach underlying it. The *organization* or pattern of the objectives and how to use them is yet another matter. A curriculum with excellent content may be useless if it is not put together in ways that facilitate instruction.

There are at least three common types of organization for the content of a curriculum (Wood & Hurley, 1977). Figure 4-1 displays these three modes of organization. Unfortunately, many curricula seem to have no reliable organization (see Figure 4-2). Remember, too, that a given curriculum may be a combination of types.

Figure 4-1 Schematic Illustrations of Three Styles for Organizing Curriculum Content

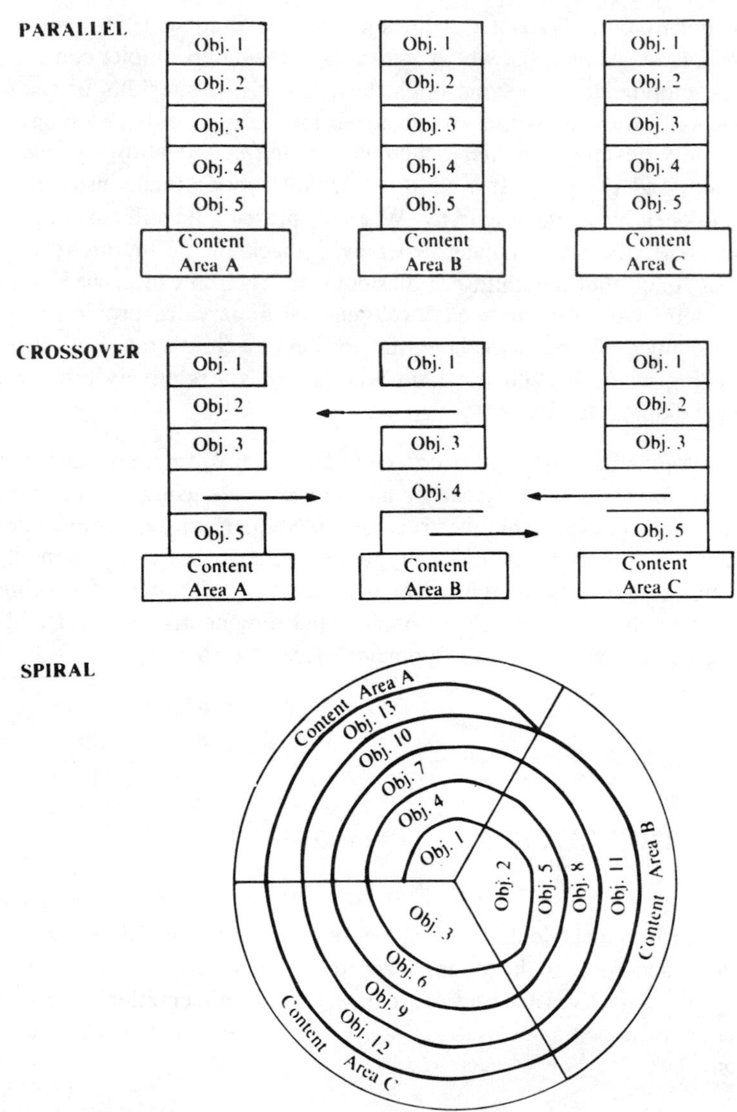

Source: Jordan, J.B., Hayden, A.H., Karnes, M.B., & Wood, M.N. *Early childhood education for exceptional children.* Reston, Va.: Council for Exceptional Children, 1977. Reprinted with permission.

Figure 4-2 Schematic Illustration of a Curriculum with No Organization

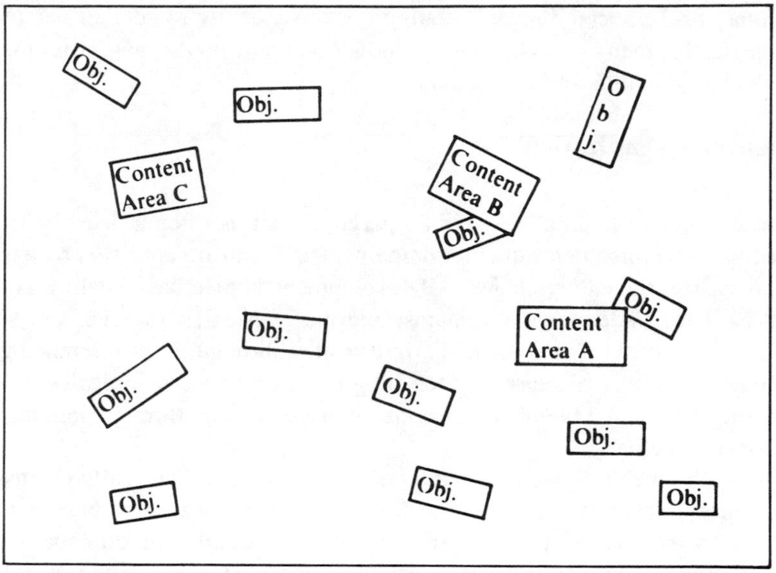

Source: Jordan, J.B., Hayden, A.H., Karnes, M.B., & Wood, M.N. *Early childhood education for exceptional children.* Reston, Va.: Council for Exceptional Children, 1977. Reprinted with permission.

Parallel Organization

Depending on the nature of the content, curricula usually involve several areas or *domains*. Typically, each domain is made up of an array of related objectives. In a developmental task curriculum, for example, there may be dozens or hundreds of objectives grouped under each of several domains. Physical, intellectual, social, emotional, and other major domains can each include an extensive list of objectives.

As noted earlier, lists of developmental objectives are usually sequences, that is, they are arranged in hierarchies. When each domain contains separate and unrelated hierarchical lists, the curriculum is using parallel organization. With this system, the teacher can proceed with instruction in a given domain even though the child may be having trouble in another domain. With parallel organization, progress in one hierarchy is not directly tied to progress in another. Each developmental skill is listed under one domain and one only. Learning to talk on the telephone, for example, might be listed under the "communication" or "language'' domain. You can see, however, that this skill might also be reasonably included under other domains, such as ''fine and gross motor'' (manipulating the telephone) or the social domain (relating conversationally to another person). It seems clear that many skills include components of other skills, and assignment to a particular domain is rather arbitrary.

Crossover Organization

In actual practice, progress within a given domain is often at least indirectly related to accomplishments in other domains. Crossover organization recognizes and emphasizes the interrelatedness of developmental objectives. Dialing a phone might be listed under several domains; and the physical, cognitive, and social aspects of using the phone might be interrelated through cross-referencing the objectives. Teachers who use unit teaching or ''experience modules'' often are attempting to teach several dimensions of development through lessons that interrelate objectives.

You will probably agree that many tasks faced by children really do involve competence across several areas. Thus, cross-referencing makes sense, since it alerts us to the interrelatedness (and artificial separation) of domains. Also, cross-referencing objectives tends to prevent ''lopsided'' programming, that is, pushing a child ahead in one or two areas at the neglect of others. Sometimes, unfortunately, teachers will promote development in whatever domain is easiest or the one for which materials are available. Moderately retarded children are all too often given extensive instruction in self-help skills while their cognitive and social growth is neglected. A cross-referenced curriculum helps to avoid this problem by promoting concurrent progress within and across several developmental areas.

Spiral Organization

Many teachers advocate a spiral curricular pattern. Similar to the crossover organization, a spiral consists of sequences of interrelated modules or units from several domains. Objectives from different domains are taught and then ''re-visited'' later in a more detailed way (Bloom, 1956). Skills can be introduced in a simple fashion. As other parts of the spiral are mastered, the skill can be learned more thoroughly and with greater elaboration. For example, children may initially learn to tell time by the hour and half-hour. Later, as time concepts, visual discrimination, and other skills are developed, minutes and then seconds can be introduced. Thus, the spiral organization teaches prerequisite skills and stresses the interrelatedness of developmental progress. Spiral curricula are more common beyond preschool where academic content lends itself to greater and greater elaboration and qualification.

CONSIDERATIONS IN SELECTING A CURRICULUM

So far, we have discussed the five basic approaches to curriculum building (basic skills, psychological constructs, preacademic, remedial, and developmental-task) and the kinds of organization that can be used (parallel, crossover, and spiral). While some curricula are somewhat pure in their approach and organization, many are "hybrid" and combine approaches and/or organizational patterns. Depending on your purposes, some curricula are better than others. In fact, for certain purposes, some curricula are almost required and others quite unacceptable. For example, you probably would not wish to use a remedial curriculum for a group of normal preschoolers. Likewise, a preacademically based curriculum would not be a wise choice for developmentally delayed youngsters.

When you are selecting a curriculum, what should you look for and what criteria can you use? This section addresses these concerns, especially with reference to the inclusion of handicapped youngsters in a program.

Theoretical or Conceptual Basis

A curriculum can be a hodgepodge of objectives or a systematic array, depending on the approach and organization used. Generally speaking, a good curriculum has a consistent conceptual basis. The base may be learning principles, developmental theory, or some other set of constructs or variables. Often, the theoretical base for the objectives within a curriculum also acts as the basis for teaching and learning strategies associated with the objectives. Curricula based on the theories of Piaget, Skinner, or Erikson usually recommend instructional strategies and room designs in harmony with the respective theory. There is real strength in having a consistent basis for the curriculum. Objectives and methods are not likely to be at odds with each other, and various portions of the curriculum will tend to interrelate and build on each other. There will be trouble, for instance, if a teacher attempts to use behavior-modification methods to facilitate the attainment of Piagetian cognitive-developmental objectives. Likewise, Piagetian derived methods are usually not appropriate for use with a task-analyzed, behaviorally based curriculum.

The question to ask is, Is there a consistent theoretical basis for the curriculum? If not, the curriculum may be a series of disconnected objectives and involve diverse, eclectic methods that may negatively interact with each other, confuse the children, and not allow the teacher to develop a consistent, thorough approach.

Data Base

Most curricula are developed through armchair speculation, logic, and the cutting and pasting of existing curricula. Usually, little empirical research is put into the actual building of the curriculum. Moreover, once developed, there are many curricula that have no data on their effectiveness. If data are available, their quality and credibility may vary greatly.

Educators must begin to demand to "see the data" before adopting instructional materials, especially a crucial thing like a curriculum. Ideally, there should be evidence concerning the effectiveness and efficiency of the curriculum with the kinds of children with whom the educator is concerned. The number of children involved in the data base should be convincing. Usually, field testing on at least several hundred children is acceptable. The "face validity" of a curriculum may be attractive, but data on its actual use by real teachers in the "real world" are much more convincing.

The kinds of data that are useful to the potential user are such things as

- the number and kinds of children with whom the curriculum has been used;
- the number and kinds of sites where it has been in effect and the length of time in use;
- child-progress information, especially criterion-referenced evidence of progress within the curriculum (e.g., number or percent of new objectives attained) and/or developmental growth detected on standardized, norm-referenced tests; and
- teacher ratings of the utility of the curriculum; a curriculum may be well designed and effective in the laboratory, but fail to meet realistic, practical demands.

Target Population

For whom is the curriculum intended? Was it tested on the intended population? A curriculum might be excellent for one group and inappropriate for another. Try to choose a curriculum that was designed and tested on the same group of youngsters with whom you wish to work.

Conditions for Use

Some curricula are built for use with individual children and some for groups, although most can be employed in either way. Of greater concern, however, are other instructional conditions, such as necessary room layout, number of staff needed to carry out the curriculum, and materials required. Sometimes a curriculum will include appropriate objectives, sequence of activities, or other features but involve materials that a program cannot feasibly obtain or afford. Also, some curricula demand a degree of structure in planning, teaching, and evaluation that goes beyond the capabilities and desires of a program's staff. If a curriculum involves more hassle in using it than it gains in benefits, it would be better to switch to another one. Perhaps a different curriculum might not be as good on paper, but it may be better in actual use—because it can be used with greater ease and reliability.

Training for Use

Closely related to the issue of conditions for use is the staff training needed to carry out a curriculum. If a curriculum is thorough, it will usually contain instructions for its use. Some curricula may require a training workshop provided by the developers or the publisher. A training workshop will usually not involve more than two days. Again, the benefits must be weighed against the training time and effort. Especially when working with handicapped children, a good curriculum often does demand staff training in its use. This training is usually quite practical and aimed at effective use of the curriculum.

Record Keeping and Assessment

A well-organized curriculum should permit easy recording of child progress. Some curricula have a progress check-off space next to each objective. When a child shows mastery of a given objective, that skill is checked or dated. A related concern in connection with mastery of a skill is the criterion for mastery. Again, some curricula will include suggestions for what defines success, while others leave the setting of mastery standards to the teacher.

More and more, preschool programs are concerned with documenting child progress. This may be due to parental wishes or funding agency demands or because the contemporary early educator knows the importance of getting information on how well instruction is going. Whatever the reason, an acceptable curriculum must provide a feasible way to assess a student's entry skills, a system for documenting student progress within the curriculum, and a way to organize and report child performance to parents and others.

There should be no mystery about how well a child is doing, and it should not take much effort or time to determine progress. Both formative and summative evaluations should be possible by simply glancing at a checklist or some other record-keeping device.

Specific Lesson Components

A good curriculum is really more than an array of objectives. As noted earlier, the organization of the objectives is crucial. The sequence and arrangement of objectives should promote good and easy instructional use. Some of the benefits that good content and organization will provide are

- specific prerequisites to instruction
- general goal statements
- specific, behaviorally stated objectives
- specific techniques for teaching each objective
- strategies for teaching retention of skills
- strategies for enhancing transfer or generalization skills to settings other than the preschool
- suggestions for accommodating various handicaps

As the provisions of P.L. 94-142 become more and more a part of the educator's professional standards, an effective and efficient curriculum becomes an essential. A curriculum that meets the standards we have described will allow the teacher to write IEPs in a relatively rapid yet precise manner. It is so much easier and better to write individual programs on the basis of a consistent and comprehensive curriculum. Random selection or invention of objectives, based on hunches or convenience, does a disservice to young children. With P.L. 94-142 as the legal mandate, professional ethics to guide us, and a suitable curriculum, every child can have an individualized set of educational and developmental objectives.

Normalization

One of our goals as educators is to help exceptional children to become more normal and adequate in their functioning and appearance. The process of normalization refers to the use of objectives and methods that are increasingly more normal or typical (Wolfensberger, 1972). Thus, a curriculum should provide objectives that progressively move a child to more normal functioning. Likewise, instructional techniques should move from highly specialized, contrived strategies toward more normal or typical ones (Smith & Neisworth, 1975; Neisworth & Madle, 1975). Thus, initially, a token economy may result from motivational techniques, but such techniques should then be modified so that, eventually, the children will work under the same motivational conditions as "regular" children. A curriculum that necessitates highly contrived materials and techniques throughout its use will not promote normalization and may in fact trap the children into remaining unnecessarily "exceptional" and dependent on artificial circumstances.

It should be pointed out that a curriculum that does not promote normalization will also inhibit mainstreaming. It is difficult and inappropriate to require nonhandicapped youngsters to integrate with handicapped children if the program does not aim toward normalized objectives and strategies.

Rather than segregating handicapped youngsters, we wish to integrate them into our classrooms and programs. If you use a curriculum that is comprehensive and broad enough in its scope, children with varying levels of development can be included. Several children of greatly differing levels of sophistication may, for example, be seated at the same table working on fine-motor activities. The tasks may vary in their difficulty level, each one suited to the child's present level of functioning. Again, an appropriate curriculum will contain hierarchies of skills that permit entry at different levels.

Product Quality

Finally, a curriculum can also be evaluated on factors like durability, format, portability, and cost. These factors should not be primary, but they can play a part in the final selection of a curriculum. Examine the Curriculum Evaluation Form in Exhibit 4-1 for more details on this and other features of a curriculum.

Exhibit 4-1 Curriculum Evaluation Form

This curriculum evaluation form is designed so that the names of up to five curricula can be entered for evaluation purposes. Each category should be marked with a check to indicate the presence of a specific attribute.

1.0 Theoretical or Conceptual Basis

- 1.1 The program has a strong theoretical/conceptual base
- 1.2 The program is based on research in experimental or applied settings

2.0 Product Data Base

- 2.1 The product was developed through a planned process
- 2.2 There is data on product effectiveness
  If 2.2 is yes, the type of data presented is:
  - 2.2.1 single subject studies
  - 2.2.2 between group comparisons
  - 2.2.3 lesson specific child performance data
  - 2.2.4 other ______________________
  - 2.2.5 The field test or data collection procedures (conditions) are specified precisely and could be replicated
  - 2.2.6 Product effectiveness data
    - 2.2.6.1 accompanies the product
    - 2.2.6.2 is referenced for easy access
    - 2.2.6.3 is inaccessible
  - 2.2.7 Product effectiveness data
    - 2.2.7.1 shows a strong effect
    - 2.2.7.2 shows a moderate effect
    - 2.2.7.3 shows a weak effect

3.0 Target Population

- 3.1 The child population the curriculum was tested on is specified
- 3.2 The suggested audience for the curriculum is the same as the population the product was tested on

Exhibit 4-1 continued

4.0 Conditions for Product Use

4.1 The conditions under which the product was designed to be used are specified
4.2 The conditions exist, or can be created in the teacher's own classroom

5.0 Teacher Training for Product Use

5.1 The product requires teacher training before use
If 5.1 is yes, training is:
5.1.1 minimal (self study)
5.1.2 moderate (demonstration)
5.1.3 extensive

6.0 General Product Components

The product contains:

6.1 a scope and sequence or other skill progression charting system
6.2 a system for assessing students' entry skills into the curriculum
6.3 a system for documenting student performance
6.4 a system for organizing and reporting student performance
6.5 child use materials for each specific lesson
6.6 supplementary charts or listing of materials needed to teach specific lessons
6.7 general directions for product use

7.0 Specific Curriculum/Lesson Plan Components

The lesson plans contain:

7.1 program specific prerequisites to instruction
7.2 general goal statements

Exhibit 4-1 continued

7.3 specific objectives, formulated to meet PL 94-142
- 7.3.1 material specified
- 7.3.2 behavior stated and objectively defined
- 7.3.3 statement of criterion performance

7.4 pre-posttest procedures defined

7.5 pre-posttest criterion specified

7.6 teaching procedures that are
- 7.6.1 written specifically ("Do this")
- 7.6.2 general strategies
- 7.6.3 general suggestions for games/activities
- 7.6.4 other ______________________

7.7 define defined instructional procedures:
- 7.7.1 reinforcement
- 7.7.2 correction
- 7.7.3 demonstration
- 7.7.4 prompting
- 7.7.5 fading

7.8 sequential skill progressions, based on task/concept analysis

7.9 defined criterion for progress to next more complex sequential task

7.10 structured program modification strategy for student who experiences difficulty

7.11 internal framework for modifying instructional procedures for attendant handicapping conditions

7.12 planned strategies for
- 7.12.2 documenting maintenance (demonstrating skill acquisitions over time)
- 7.12.2 documenting generalization (demonstrating skill acquisitions in different settings, with different materials, with different teachers, or under slightly different environmental conditions)

7.13 suggestions for demonstrating, or practicing, the skill in other activities

Exhibit 4-1 continued

8.0 Product Quality Factors

8.1 The product is durable
8.2 The layout facilitates quick scanning
8.3 The organization of the content is logical
8.4 The language is clear and comprehensible

9.0 Content Specificity Analysis

The product may be described as:

9.1 General instructional suggestions
9.2 Sets of objectives, and suggested activities
9.3 Sets of objectives, and task analyses
9.4 Task analyzed programs, containing objectives and general instructional procedures
9.5 Task analyzed, sequenced programs containing objectives, defined instructional procedures
9.6 Task analyzed, sequential programs, containing objectives, defined instructional procedures, and defined decision making strategies

10.0 Product Cost

Enter the cost in the column for each product that is being evaluated

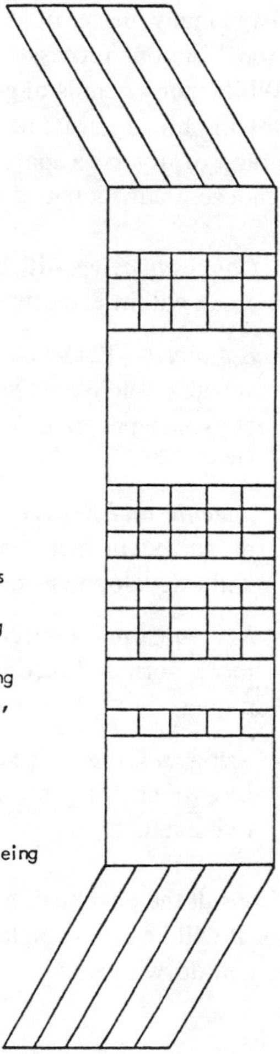

Source: From *Curricula for the Severely Developmentally Retarded: A Survey and Primer on the Curriculum Development Process* by J.W. Tawney and S.L. Deaton. USOE: Final Report, vol. 1, grant numbers OEG-0-72-5361 and OEG-0-75-00669, 1979. Reprinted by permission.

SUMMARY

The job of prescribing and teaching an individualized education program is not an easy one. With effective procedures and materials, however, the educator's job can become organized, efficient, and rewarding. An appropriate curriculum will assist in many phases of instructional planning and conduct and enable you to "be on top" in your professional activities.

While many details of good curricula have been discussed, we suggest that the following broad guidelines will be helpful in selecting a curriculum for use with children of diverse capabilities and developmental differences.

Choose a curriculum that is

- *Comprehensive*—It should include all areas of development, including subareas within each major dimension of development.
- *Balanced*—Each area of development should contain a sufficient number of subareas and objectives to permit a full instructional program. This will help to avoid a program that becomes lopsided with just one or two developmental areas.
- *Specific and Sequential*—Objectives must be phrased behaviorally and be organized in hierarchies. Hierarchies (sequences) should be derived from child development research and/or task analyses.
- *Normalizing*—Objectives should provide for development of progressively more normal functioning with progressively more normal teaching techniques.
- *Self-Assessing*—The content, organization, and format should allow for entry assessment, easy recording of individual progress, and formative and summative evaluation.

Consult the checklist in Exhibit 4-1 for details of what to look for in a curriculum. It will be up to you to decide which features must be present and which ones you can do without.

Chapter 5

Close-Ups of Prominent Preschool Curricula

This chapter is designed to provide a close-up of five early education curricula. While there are many curricula that deserve in-depth descriptions, five leading ones that link easily to norm-referenced and criterion-referenced tests were chosen. The five to be examined in detail are:

1. Learning Accomplishment Profile (LAP)
2. HICOMP
3. Portage
4. Memphis
5. Developmental Programming for Infants and Young Children

As you become more familiar with these five curricula, you will be in a better position to decide if they meet your personal style of teaching. You will also be able to decide which of these five curricula will coordinate with the educational philosophy of the organization where you are or will be employed. For example, teachers using the American Montessori techniques have also used the HICOMP curriculum because it links so well to the structured activities advocated by the Montessori method.

Before purchasing a new curriculum, it is sensible to have an actual trial period in which to study or use it. Often publishing companies will offer a trial period in which to determine if the curriculum, in fact, is suitable for your students' needs. Educational materials centers, common in larger school systems, often receive complimentary copies of curricula. Calling such centers for information should be one of your first steps when selecting curricula to preview. Local colleges and universities will also have sample copies of curricula. Colleges of education, psychology, and human development are the major centers for developing and field testing curricula. If these institutions of higher learning are not developing such materials, individual professors should know how to direct you to other sources that may help you.

You should and will also have to consider the parameters of the budgets of the institution where you are or will be employed. When it is impossible to fund the purchasing of a new curriculum, there are methods to circumvent the situation. You may wish to borrow a sample copy from another school district or educational materials center. You can use the copy with a selected number of students for a prescribed period of time to determine if the curriculum is suitable for you and your students. Publishing companies and authors are often willing to provide you with free copies of a curriculum if, in return, you collect data on the progress of your students using the curriculum. If you are in a position of having to convince parents and your supervisors about the merits of a curriculum, the collection of data from a trial group of youngsters may be necessary before a curriculum is purchased by the institution. The five curricula reviewed here are designed for the collection of such important data. Let us now take a close-up view of these five curricula.

THE LEARNING ACCOMPLISHMENT PROFILE

A very popular curriculum, the Learning Accomplishment Profile (LAP) uses a developmental task approach as its theoretical orientation. It is suitable therefore for both "normal" and developmentally delayed youngsters. The six major developmental domains designated in the curriculum are gross- and fine-motor skills, social, self-help, cognitive, and language skills.

LAP Products

The LAP is composed of seven major products to be used directly with children. These products may be ordered by writing to:

KAPLAN
600 Jonestown Road
Winston-Salem, N.C. 27103

Product		Price
Learning Accomplishment Profile	291A152	$ 2.00
A Manual on the Use of the LAP	291A154	2.50
Diagnostic Edition Kit (LAP-D)	291A100	180.00
A Planning Guide: The Preschool Curriculum	291A153	7.95
Early LAP	291A00180	4.50
Learning Activities	291A160	10.00
Planning Guide for Gifted Preschoolers	291A00151	10.00

There are other supplementary manuals and audio-visual aides, such as film strips on implementing the LAP profile, which may be ordered. A few of these additional materials are listed below:

Product		Price
Programs for Parents of Preschoolers	291A00170	$ 6.50
Working with Families	291A155	4.50
The Chapel Hill Model for Training Head Start Personnel in Mainstreaming Handicapped Children	291A157	5.00
The Carolina Developmental Profile	291A1500	.75

Product Number 1, *The Learning Accomplishment Profile,* is a paperback book designed to be used to record an individual child's progress or rate of development in the curriculum. The book is divided into three major sections. Part 1 contains the listing of the hierarchy of developmental behaviors from birth through 5 years of age for each of the six major domains addressed in the curriculum (see Table 5-1, which shows a listing in the domain of fine-motor skills).

Part 2 provides the teacher, paraprofessional, or parent with suggestions for skill-sequence development and a means for recording the child's behaviors on a specific task (see Exhibit 5-1). As you can see, Part 2 guides the teacher to plan long-term goals for the child. It is particularly helpful as a reminder that it takes many specific steps before a skill may be considered totally mastered by the child. Toilet training, for instance, should not even be considered for the 12-month-old. Many individuals have the preconceived notion that as soon as a youngster begins to stand he or she should to toddling off to the bathroom!

Part 3 contains plans for 44 weeks of curriculum units (see Exhibit 5-2). Again, notice that there is the provision for recording the child's responses to the hierarchy of tasks outlined in the units.

To implement the LAP curriculum, a paperback book, Product Number 2, *Manual for the Use of the Learning Accomplishment Profile,* specifies the criteria and demonstrable behaviors associated with the specific objectives listed in Part 1 of the *Profile*. A sample page from the *Manual* is shown in Exhibit 5-3. The *Profile* and *Manual* are the core of the LAP curriculum package.

Table 5-1 Listing of Fine-Motor Skills in LAP, Part 1

Bibliog. Source	*Behavior*	*Dev. Age*	*Credit Given If*	*Comments (Example)*
2	Pushes car	11 mos.	Child pushes the car with its wheels on the table.	Push the little car slowly across the table across the child's field of vision. Then push it to him, indicating by gestures and words (such as, "Baby, push it," or "Make it go") that he should push it. If necessary, repeat the demonstration and invitation two or three times.
2	Puts 3 or more cubes in cup	12 mos.	At least three cubes are in cup at one time.	Place a cube in the cup, then take it out and hand it to the child. By word and gesturing encourage him (with repeated demonstrations if necessary) to put it in the cup, with such words as "Baby do it," or "Put the block in the cup," "Put it in." Place eight or more cubes in front of him and say, "Let's put them all in." "Put all the blocks in the cup." If necessary, urge by gestures, and repeat the request once or twice if his attention strays.
3	Marks with pencil	12 mos.	The child makes any kind of marks on the paper. (If he makes a definite scribble, he is given credit at 14 months and if he does so without demonstration, he is credited at 18 mos.	Procedure: A piece of paper and a pencil (no longer than 3½ inches nor shorter than 2½ inches). The lead should be soft and the point blunt. Red or blue (red or blue lead is preferable to black) are placed before the child with the request "______ write." If after 5 or 10 seconds he does not scribble, the paper and pencil are taken from him and again placed before him with the same request. If there is still no response, the examiner takes the pencil and demonstrates by scribbling six to eight lines back and forth, about 3 inches in length, then places the pencil on the table before the child again.

Source: Sanford, A. *Learning accomplishment profile.* Winston-Salem, N.C.: Kaplan School Supply, 1978. Reprinted with permission.

Exhibit 5-1 Sample Sheet for Recording Skill-Sequence Development, LAP, Part 2

Bibliog. Source	Behavior	Age (Dev.)	Assessment Date	Date of Achievement	Comments (Criteria, materials, Problems, etc.
3	Manipulates egg beater	27 mos.	+ 9/18/73		Whipped soap suds. Teacher held handle.
9	Enjoys finger painting	30-35 mos.	+ 9/20/73		Finger painted on formica table. –10 min.
9	Makes mud and sand pies	30-35 mos.	+ 9/24/73		Made sand pies using tea set
13	Paints strokes, dots, and circular shapes on easel	30-35 mos.	+ 9/27/73		Imitated teacher w/ ½" brush
6	Cuts with scissors	35 mos.	+ 10/2/73		Cut ½" partially cut strips (2 whacks)
13	Picks up pins, thread, etc., with each eye separately covered	36-48 mos.	– 10/3/73		
7	Drives nails and pegs	36-48 mos.	– 10/4/73		These will
13	Builds tower of nine cubes	36-48 mos.	– 10/5/73		become
7	Holds crayon with fingers	36-48 mos.	+ 10/8/73		objectives
3	Strings 4 beads	36-48 mos.	– 10/8/73		for this child.
13	Can close fist and wiggle thumb in imitation, R & L	36-48 mos.			
11	Puts 6 round pegs in round holes on pegboard	36-48 mos.			

Note: The child has demonstrated a dev. age of 35 mos. in Fine Motor Skills. Failure on 4 of 5 items represents ceiling.

*Mark + for positive demonstration of skill
Mark - for negative demonstration of skill

Source: Sanford, A. *Learning accomplishment profile.* Winston-Salem, N.C.: Kaplan School Supply, 1978. Reprinted with permission.

Exhibit 5-2 Form for Recording Responses to Hierarchy of Tasks, LAP, Part 3

Unit 29
ANIMALS

LAP - Sanford ©
III - Curric Units

Animals	Match	Discrim. Toy Animals	Discrim. Pictures	Assoc. Sound	Classify as animal	How it moves--(walks, flies, swims)	Assoc. with land, air or water	Classify as circus farm or home animal	Verbalize (Imitate)	Verbalize "What is This?"
dog										
cat										
cow										
horse										
duck										
pig										
sheep										
turkey										
bird										
rooster										
frog										
rabbit										
turtle										
elephant										
squirrel										
tiger										
fish										
monkey										
giraffe										
lion										
bear										

Source: Sanford, A. *Learning accomplishment profile.* Winston-Salem, N.C.: Kaplan School Supply, 1978. Reprinted with permission.

Exhibit 5-3 A Sample Page from the LAP Manual

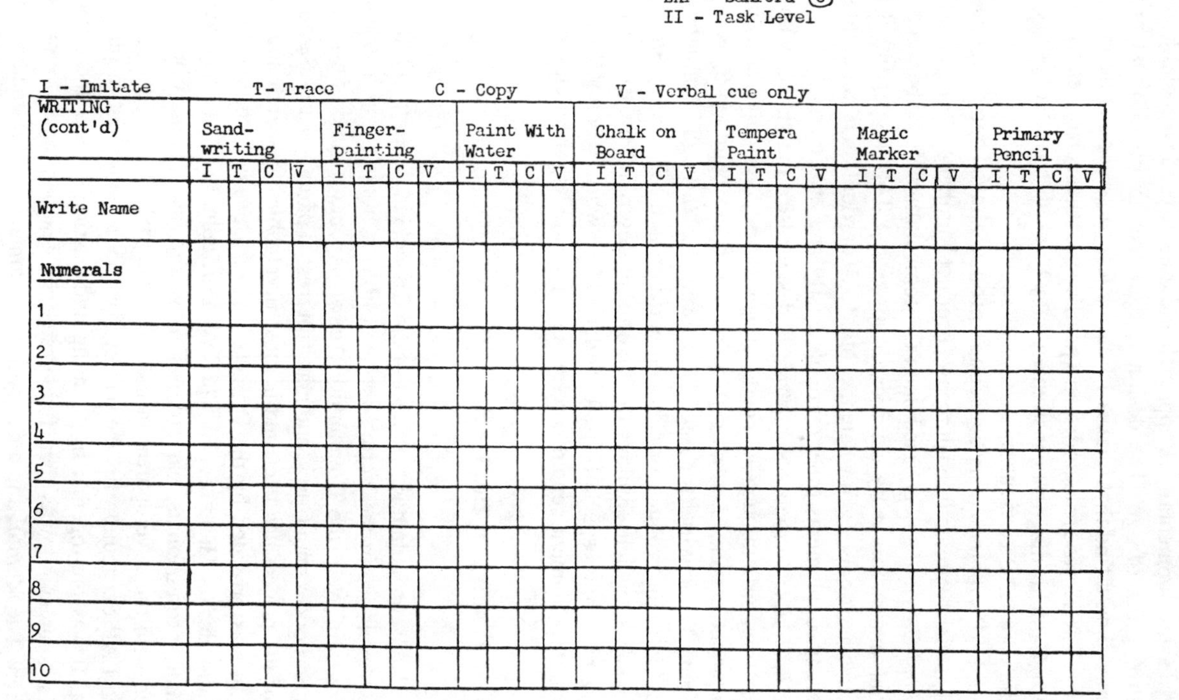

LAP - Sanford ©
II - Task Level

I - Imitate T- Trace C - Copy V - Verbal cue only

WRITING (cont'd)	Sand-writing				Finger-painting				Paint With Water				Chalk on Board				Tempera Paint				Magic Marker				Primary Pencil			
	I	T	C	V	I	T	C	V	I	T	C	V	I	T	C	V	I	T	C	V	I	T	C	V	I	T	C	V
Write Name																												
Numerals																												
1																												
2																												
3																												
4																												
5																												
6																												
7																												
8																												
9																												
10																												

Source: Sanford, A. *Learning accomplishment profile.* Winston-Salem, N.C.: Kaplan School Supply, 1978. Reprinted with permission.

The *Diagnostic Edition,* Product Number 3 of the LAP, was designed to be used for assessment purposes by the same person who uses the *Profile* and *Manual.* It employs a developmental task approach and may be used with children from birth through 6 years of age. The design is excellent. With minimal practice, the consumer should find that it takes 1 hour or less to assess a child in a one-to-one situation. The scores are recorded on a profile sheet that correlates directly with the LAP *Profile.* This diagnostic instrument may be used separately or in conjunction with the core LAP curriculum.

Other LAP supplementary curriculum products have been designed; these you may also wish to preview and purchase: Product Number 4, *A Planning Guide: The Preschool Curriculum,* is based upon the topical units described in the *Manual.* Materials and multisensory activities are suggested. This is a paperback book often found in classrooms, even where the total LAP curriculum is not employed by the teacher. It supplements other curricula easily and effectively.

The *Early LAP,* Product Number 5, is designed for individuals who work with children from birth through 36 months of age. It, too, is popular, especially in child development centers. *Learning Activities,* Product Number 6, is a paperback containing 295 activities for use with children of 12 through 72 months of age. The final LAP major product for use with children is the *Planning Guide for Gifted Preschoolers,* which employs the taxonomy described by Bloom (1956). The *Planning Guide* is especially useful with children who are being ''mainstreamed'' in child development centers, preschools, and kindergarten classrooms.

A Brief History of the LAP

The LAP curriculum is a product of the Chapel Hill Training Outreach Project. It was developed in the North Carolina public schools. Also instrumental in its development were the Community Action Agency, Junior Services Leagues, Neighborhood Youth Corps, and many interested parents. Anne Sanford's leadership of the project has been and is most invaluable. Research and development funding was provided by the Office of Child Development and the Bureau of Education for the Handicapped. The LAP curriculum reflects the diverse skills of the many professionals, paraprofessionals, and lay persons who have been involved with the development of the LAP materials.

The LAP curriculum fits the pattern for the development of outstanding curricula. It was put together by ''cutting and pasting'' goals and objectives from several sources. It was then field tested by teachers and parents with young children. The *Manual* and the *Profile* both contain careful documentation of the original sources for individual items. For instance, the specific fine-motor objective of ''fills and dumps containers with sand, 24-29 months'' (p. 11 in the *Profile*) is referenced as being found in Arnold Gesell's *The First Five Years of Life* (1940).

A majority of the specific objectives were based upon norm-referenced assessment items or objectives like those in Bayley's Scales of Infant Development (1969) or Gesell's Developmental Schedules (1949).

Characteristics of the LAP Curriculum

Organization of Content

The curriculum content in the *Profile* is arranged in a parallel mode. This, as you recall, means that individual objectives are arranged under specific domains—each domain containing separate hierarchical lists of objectives. In reality, there are many objectives that appear to cross over in the LAP. Consider the following example. The skill of lacing shoes appears in the fine-motor domain for the developmental ages of 60 to 72 months. It also appears in the self-help domain for the developmental ages of 48 to 60 months. This characteristic of crossover in preschool curricula that take a developmental task approach is inevitable, because the developmental sequences of skills are so interdependent. An example from research that supports this opinion is the longitudinal study by White, Castle, and Held (1964). The study demonstrated that infants of 1 month of age have visual perception skills that are more advanced than their motor and tactical skills. It is not for several months that the developmental ages related to these three skills mesh. At that meshing point, the teacher or parent could use curriculum objectives that cross over, as in the LAP's "lacking skills" objective.

Target Population

The LAP was field tested as part of the requirements for a First Chance project when funded by the Bureau of Education for the Handicapped. By design, the target population were children who exhibited developmental delays in one or more major domains. This population, however, also certainly included children who were considered to be developmentally on target, to comply with the spirit of Public Law 94-142 regarding the education of all children in the least restrictive environment.

Condition for Use

The LAP was designed to be used with individual or grouped children. It is ideal for infant centers, child development centers, head start classes, pre-schools and mainstreamed kindergartens, as well as parent-involvement programs.

Training Needed

The LAP curriculum was designed to require minimal training of the personnel who would be responsible for implementation of the specific objectives and suggested activities. If you are familiar with the Bayley Scales of Infant Development, the Denver Developmental Screening Test, or other norm-referenced tests, you will have absolutely no difficulty in generalizing your knowledge to the LAP's curriculum objectives. What are required of the consumer are the skills in observation and the recording of young children's specific behaviors.

Before implementing the curriculum, a two-day training workshop is recommended to ensure that there is consistency of behaviors among the staff and/or parents as they use the LAP core products. To maintain uniformity throughout the period of implementation, it is also recommended that refresher sessions be held the first 1½ years.

Record-Keeping and Assessment

Both the LAP *Diagnostic Edition* and the *Profile* are designed to individualize record-keeping. For the program to function effectively, each child should have his or her own *Profile* in which the program manager, like the teacher or paraprofessional, can record daily attempts or achievement of objectives. The writing of Individual Educational Programs (IEPs) is enhanced by use of the *Profile*'s listing of short- and long-range goals.

As the handicapped child attains specific goals, these achievements can be compared easily to a "normal" child of the same chronological age. The child may be mainstreamed for greater periods of time as the *Profile* serves as a record to justify the normalization movement.

Components for Lesson Planning

From the above discussion, it is clear that the LAP curriculum meets most of the criteria outlined in the preceding chapter, in which lesson components were examined. Specific behaviorally defined strategies for teaching objectives, however, are not stressed in the LAP curriculum. For example, the teacher is not told to use "manual prompting" when teaching handwriting. Moreover, suggestions for accommodating various handicaps are not available in the core curriculum. Thus, if you are teaching a blind child to lace, the steps on how to do this are not outlined, nor are behavioral strategies suggested. Thus, assistance from an outside consultant may be necessary to teach staff members and parents skills in these two specific areas to maximize the use of the Lap curriculum.

Practical Qualities

The LAP core curriculum products have been revised a number of times. The *Diagnostic Edition* is packed in a tool box that makes it convenient for traveling, although very heavy to carry. The materials in the kit are durable, which is certainly a plus given the rising cost of educational assessment kits. The testing manual is in a hardback three-ringed notebook that is sturdy and easy to use.

The costs of the *Profile* and *Manual* are reasonable due to the copying format, which is of medium quality. If the *Profile* were used to record a child's progress in a program for 3 years, it is probable that tape and staples would be needed to hold the book together. If both school and parents were involved in using the *Profile,* it probably would be best to order two copies per child.

The summary checklist in Exhibit 5-20 at the end of the chapter provides an overview of the LAP's salient features.

THE HICOMP CURRICULUM

A distinguished accomplishment among curricula designed for young children is the HICOMP Curriculum. HICOMP is an acronym for "higher competencies" in the four domains of *c*ommunication, *o*wn-care, *m*otor, and *p*roblem-solving. In theoretical orientation, this curriculum also takes a developmental task approach. It is suitable for use with normal, developmentally delayed, and multihandicapped children.

HICOMP Products

HICOMP is primarily composed of two core products: the *COMP Curriculum* and the *COMP Curriculum Guide*. Both are in the paperback form. The *COMP Curriculum* was designed with ample space to record a child's progress. Ideally, a copy of the *Curriculum* should be used for each child in a program. This makes it easy to develop and evaluate individualized programs. It also helps meet the requirements of an individualized educational plan as outlined by P.L. 94-142.

The HICOMP Curriculum is divided into 4 major domains—communication, own care, motor, and problem solving—that are designed by color-coded tabs to make handling more efficient. These domains are then subdivided, yielding 21 subdomains. A supplementary handout of definitions of these subdomains for teachers and parents was developed by the HICOMP Outreach staff. The following definitions of the problem-solving domain comprise 8 subdomains:

1. *Attention:* Teacher/parent focuses child's attention on object or event. For example: "Watch me," "Listen."
2. *Imitation:* Teacher/parent models behavior, words, or sequences of actions and statements for child to imitate. For example: Teacher/parent says, "Say mill," "Do this;" or teacher plays peek-a-boo with a doll, and child does so with his/her doll.
3. *Recall:* Teacher/parent provides situation where child must remember previously acquired information to solve problem or answer question. For example: Teacher covers up an object, then asks, "What is under the cup?" After

reading a story, teacher points to a picture and asks, "What was his name?" "What did you have at snack time to eat?"

4. *Concept Information:* Teacher/parent provides a situation of objects that the child must learn to respond to as representatives of the same class, or as situations or objects requiring different labels or responses. For example: When teacher calls name of aide to help a child, the child looks toward the aide named. Teacher/parent asks, "What color is this?" "Is this red?" "Find another circle like this one." "Show me the top of the box." "How many are here?" "Which group has more?"
5. *Grouping:* Teacher/parent provides objects, pictures for child to classify according to color, size, or shape. For example, "Show me all the cars." "Put the number one's in this pile, all the number two's in this pile." "Pick out all the things you can eat."
6. *Sequencing:* Teacher/parent provides objects, pictures, or words for child to arrange in a specified order. Teacher/parent focuses on teaching series, succession (number or letter sequences), consecutive orders, left to right progress. For example, "Put these in order of size or redness." "Tell me your ABCs." "Let's count to 10." "Sound out this word."
7. *Application of principles:* Teacher/parent provides problems or situation to which child must apply previously learned skills before a solution is attained. Teacher/parent encourages child to generalize material to new situation, encourage child to make deductions or to guess. For example: Teacher/parent closes a gate; child must open it to get through to the teacher/parent. Teacher/parent asks, "It has a tail, gives milk, and moos. What is it?" "If the boy in the picture sticks the balloon with a pin, what will happen?" "Here is a picture of a snowman, but he is melting. Why?" "Count from 7 to 10." "How are a football and a baseball alike?"
8. *Creativity:* Teacher/parent provides new objects for child to explore, creates new situation for the child to respond to, or asks child to use familiar object in a new way. For example, "What would you do if you lived on the moon?" "How many things can you tell me about a block?" "What would be a good name for a bird?" When looking at a child's drawing, teacher/parent says, "Tell me about your picture." Teacher/parent asks, "Can you form a letter with your whole body?"

The HICOMP curriculum has specific listings in a hierarchy of 800 developmental behaviors or objectives for children from birth through 5 years of age. Especially at the very early ages, many of these objectives include skills in more than one domain. There are also lesson plans that accompany these 800 objectives in the latest edition of the *COMP Curriculum*. A sample page from the curriculum in Exhibit 5-4 depicts how the objectives are arranged.

The *COMP Curriculum Guide* suggests behavioral strategies for implementing the 800 developmental objectives and evaluation techniques to detect child progress. The *Guide* could actually be used alone to supplement other curricula, such as the LAP, which lacks specific explanations of behavioral strategies for teaching and evaluating. For instance, the page of the *Guide* shown in Exhibit 5-5 is a portion of the section describing the strategy of "shaping."

The *Guide* also covers topics such as

- planning accelerating consequences using six methods
- planning decelerating consequences using five methods
- placing (linking) a child into the curriculum using results from an assessment scale
- planning lessons and programs that include sample lesson-plan formats and sample Individual Educational Programs (IEPs)
- examples of reinforcers including recipes for nutritious snacks

As stated earlier, evaluation of the child's progress in the curriculum is a stressed feature of HICOMP. One example of the 11 suggested evaluation methods is a "checklist with criteria for check-off," as shown in Exhibit 5-6.

The *Curriculum* and *Guide* are the core *HICOMP* products. Additional products are available for use alone or in conjunction with the core materials. The *COMP-Ident Find/Screen Planning Package* is a descriptive manual and organizational guide for planning and conducting child find/screen efforts in rural areas. The methods and procedures described may easily be adapted to urban and suburban areas. Like other HICOMP products, the *COMP-Ident* comes in paperback manual form.

The *Perceptions of Developmental Skills* (PODS Profile) is a profile that may be used by parents, teachers, or paraprofessionals to assess a child's skills in the four developmental domains. A *Home Visitors Guide* and a *Family Needs Assessment* have also been developed to promote close ties between the child's family and the agency serving the child. The *COMP-Parent* is a manual for parent trainers that stresses behavioral techniques taught in a modular format either to groups or to individual parents. A popular item is the "Jotty Giraffe." This is a hierarchical checklist of behaviors demonstrated by young children on a giraffe-like chart, like a "growing chart."

Exhibit 5-4 A Sample Page from the HICOMP Curriculum

Domain and year level are listed at the top of each page of the curriculum. The code number in column 1 indicates the domain, the year, the subdomain which is simply a "broad skill area" within each domain, and the general objective. The general objective is printed in column 2. It serves as a starting point for you to identify the specific goal(s) for your lesson plan. The child's entry level skills should be marked in column 3. In columns 4 and 5, you can record the date when instruction began and ended on a specific objective. Specific teaching strategies (column 6) are recommended for each objective. It is not essential that you use the recommended strategy, but this notation in column 6 indicates which of the strategies described in Chapter 5 have been field tested and found appropriate. Similarly, the evaluation techniques, described in Chapter 4, listed in column 7 are optional. You may supplement or substitute another means of determining whether a child has achieved a given objective. The remaining columns are self-explanatory.

COMMUNICATION - Year 1 - Page 1

Col. 1	Col. 2	Col. 3	Col. 4		Col. 5	Col. 6	Col. 7
Objective Number	General Objective	Pretest	Date Begun	Date Ended	Strategy	Evaluation Technique	Comments: Activities: Materials:
C-1-1.1	Vocalizes a pleasant sound				1,3	3	
C-1-1	Language Related Play						
C-1-1.1	Vocalizes a pleasant sound				1,3	3	
C-1-1.2	Vocalizes frequently				1,3	3	
C-1-1.3	Vocalizes varied sounds				1,3	11	
C-1-1.4	Repeats particular sounds (e.g., ah-goo)				1,3	3	
C-1-1.5	Varies loudness, pitch, and speed of sounds playfully				1,3	11	
C-1-1.6	Laughs when played with (e.g., in familiar game)				1,3	11	
C-1-1.7*	Vocalizes amusing sounds (e.g., coughs, animal sounds)				1,3	11	

C-1-1.8	Repeats syllables over and over (e.g., di-di-di, da-da-da-da)				1,3	11	
C-1-1.9	Repeats performance laughed at				1	11	
C-1-1.10	Babbles or hums along with the rhythm of a game or with music				1,3	11	
C-1-1.11	Uses jargon with toys or persons				1,3	11	
C-1-1.12	Cooperates in game (e.g., during "pat a cake")				1	11	

Source: Forsberg, S.J., Neisworth, J.T., & Laub, K. *COMP-Curriculum and manual.* University Park, Pa.: HICOMP Project, Penn State University, 1977. Reprinted with permission.

Exhibit 5-5 Page from *COMP Curriculum Guide* Describing "Shaping" Strategy

Strategy 1: Shaping

Often we are faced with teaching new, difficult behaviors to children. We cannot simply ask a two-year-old to throw a ball across the room and expect that he or she will then do it. The child will, at first, experience difficulty in aiming the ball in the correct direction and/or in throwing the ball such a great distance. Nor can we simply *wait* for the child to accomplish such a difficult task, so that we can reinforce its complete performance. We must reinforce small approximations toward the terminal performance of the task. For example, we would at first reward the child for simply throwing the ball. After the child becomes proficient at the first approximation of the task, reinforcement is withheld until the child more closely approximates the desired behavior. Thus, we might tell the child, "Good, but now throw it to *me*." Then we would only reinforce throws that came *toward* the teacher.

In shaping, *the teacher cannot always predetermine the steps in the shaping process but must watch the child closely and reinforce even slight approximations to the terminal behavior.* Some typical shaping sequences are given below:

1. In the communication curriculum we find the following terminal objective: Child repeats proper sentence when teacher says, "Mary, say this, 'Give me the pencil.' "

   The child's typical responses during shaping could proceed from
   a) "Pencil;" to
   b) "Give pencil;" to
   c) "Give me pencil;" to
   d) "Give me the pencil."

Source: Forsberg, S.J., Neisworth, J.T., & Laub, K. *COMP-Curriculum and manual.* University Park, Pa.: HICOMP Project, Penn State University, 1977. Reprinted with permission.

Exhibit 5-6 HICOMP Checklist with Criteria for Check-off

The form of this evaluation may be one of simply marking the behavior with a check. However, a plus, minus, or question mark can also provide an easy answer to whether a child can or cannot perform a specific behavior.

Example:

Scissors Cutting Checklist

Behavior Criteria	*Yes*	*No*	*Sometimes*
1. Places finger and thumb in correct scissors holes.	[ ]	[ ]	[ ]
2. Opens and shuts scissors repeatedly.	[ ]	[ ]	[ ]
3. Places scissors perpendicular to paper.	[ ]	[ ]	[ ]
4. Holds paper firmly in place when cutting (i.e., for 3 opening and shuttings of the scissors).	[ ]	[ ]	[ ]
5. Moves scissors ahead after cutting for 3 openings and shuttings.	[ ]	[ ]	[ ]
6. Cuts a line 2″ long.	[ ]	[ ]	[ ]
7. Cuts a line 4″ long.	[ ]	[ ]	[ ]

Source: Forsberg, S.J., Neisworth, J.T., & Laub, K. *COMP-Curriculum and manual.* University Park, Pa.: HICOMP Project, Penn State University, 1977. Reprinted with permission.

The latest HICOMP curriculum product is a *COMP Lesson Plan Manual,* which may be purchased separately or as part of the *COMP Curriculum.* The lessons are designed around the 800 general objectives listed in the *COMP Curriculum.* Each original lesson gives suggested strategies to employ when teaching the particular objective(s). Each lesson models one of the evaluation methods outlined in the HICOMP *Guide.* Parents and paraprofessionals have been especially pleased with the *COMP Lesson Plan Manual.*

HICOMP Products

To order the following products write to:

The HICOMP Outreach Project
Division of Special Education
and Communication Disorders
327 CEDAR Building
The Pennsylvania State University
University Park, PA 16802
Phone: (814) 863-2280

Product	Price
COMP Curriculum	$ 8.00
COMP Curriculum Guide	8.00
Curriculum Package (includes both above)	14.00
Perceptions of Developmental Skills (PODS)	2.50
PODS Scoresheet	.15
Family Needs Assessment Inventory	2.50
Home Visitor's Guide	2.50
Jotty Giraffe (1-9)	.50
(10-99)	.25
(100-up)	.10
COMP-Ident	
Assessment Format	2.50
Find/Screen Packages	2.50

Make checks payable to: The Pennsylvania State University

A Brief History of HICOMP

The HICOMP Curriculum was a product of the HICOMP Project, part of the network of First Chance projects funded by the Bureau of Education for the Handicapped. Under the directorships of John Neisworth and Carol Cartwright at

The Pennsylvania State University, it served as a model outreach project for 3 years across 25 states and in overseas preschool and child care settings.

The HICOMP Curriculum has been adopted by infant development centers, head start centers, child care centers, and private and public preschools and kindergartens. It has also been used as a supplement in several American Montessori-model preschools.

Since 1978, several U.S. Air Force Child Care Centers have employed the HICOMP Curriculum. Because the curriculum provides a built-in record keeping system, it can be hand carried from one base to another by the parent when a family is transferred. No time is lost in the child's individualized program, since the new base's child care center personnel can immediately begin working on objectives by simply glancing at the child's current attainment within the curriculum.

The HICOMP Curriculum was "cut and pasted" from goals and objectives in norm-referenced tests, such as Gesell's Developmental Schedules (1949) and criterion-referenced curricula. It was then field tested for 3 years in a model preschool at The Pennsylvania State University and by numerous other preschool and child care centers.

Characteristics of the HICOMP Curriculum

Organization of Content

The content of the *COMP Curriculum* is arranged primarily in a parallel mode. The four domains contain lists of separate hierarchical objectives. There are 800 objectives, thus making the four lists quite comprehensive of behaviors exhibited by children from birth through 5 years of age. Room is provided at the end of each domain for consumers to add their own personal special objectives.

Crossover is found throughout the curriculum. The *Guide* provides a reference list of the objectives that are identical in several domains. These items are also starred in the *Curriculum* (the sample page in Exhibit 5-4 contains an example of such an item).

Target Population and Conditions for Use

Like the LAP, the HICOMP Curriculum was designed to be used with both "normal" and developmentally delayed youngsters. The curriculum complies with the mandates outlined in P.L. 94-142. It may be used with an individual child or with groups of children. U.S. Air Force child care workers maintained updated curricula on each child who attended the center on a daily basis—for over 250 children! Parents also find the *Curriculum* and *Guide* extremely helpful, especially for keeping records of their child's development. When both the parents and the child care center and/or preschool use the HICOMP Curriculum, communication between the home and "school" is certainly strengthened.

Training Needed

It is possible to implement the HICOMP Curriculum with a thorough study of the *COMP Curriculum Guide*. The *Guide* provides clearly stated procedures for assessing and placing a child in the curriculum. It also explains how to teach the specific objectives with suggested lesson plans and strategies. Finally, it suggests how to evaluate performance to determine when a specific objective has been attained.

A popular HICOMP workshop for child care workers and teachers explains to the attendants how to "link" a child's results on a norm-referenced test like the Gesell Developmental Schedules (Gesell, 1949) or a criterion-referenced test like the LAP-D to the HICOMP Curriculum. This workshop can be covered in one day with lay personnel and in one half day with professional personnel (see chapter 8).

Record-Keeping and Assessment

One of the major selling features of the HICOMP Curriculum is its facile form for record-keeping. Exhibit 5-4 demonstrates this important point. Unlike the LAP, which has three places to record a child's progress, the HICOMP has only one. The teacher or parent, of course, may use additional records, such as individual charts or graphs of a child's progress on particular objectives in the curriculum, to record additional data. Because HICOMP's record-keeping method is designed so efficiently, it leaves more time for the parent or teacher to work with the individual child or groups of children. Time is a precious element when planning programs for young children.

Components for Lesson Planning

The HICOMP Curriculum meets the criteria described in the previous chapter as the necessary components for lesson planning. The illustrations in the present chapter from the HICOMP Curriculum depict many of these criteria, such as "specific, behaviorally stated objectives" and "specific techniques for teaching each objective."

The 11 behavioral strategies described in the *COMP Curriculum Guide* provide the teacher, paraprofessional, and parent with the means to help accommodate a child with one or more handicaps. Consultants would still be needed, however, to provide inservice on such topics as how to "sign" with a deaf child. The HICOMP Curriculum could also be used in conjunction with other programs designed by specialists, such as physical therapists.

Compared to other curricula, the HICOMP Curriculum is unique in its comprehensiveness of objectives. Teaching a child a sense of humor, for example, is an area not addressed in most curricula. In the HICOMP Curriculum, affective skills are taught using behavioral strategies.

Practical Qualities

HICOMP Curriculum materials have undergone several revisions. The manuals are paperback but have plastic bindings that enable the user to fold back pages easily to record data. The printing is of high quality and large enough to be read while in the process of working with a child. After several years of use with one child, the *COMP Curriculum* could begin to show wear and tear. With the high cost of printing, however, the present form is certainly acceptable.

The summary checklist in Exhibit 5-20 at the end of the chapter provides an overview of HICOMP's outstanding features.

THE PORTAGE CURRICULUM

When early education curricula are discussed, the Portage Project is usually mentioned. Often shortened to the Portage, this curriculum's theoretical orientation involves a developmental task approach. Parents and teachers of both normal and developmentally delayed youngsters have found this curriculum extremely helpful in planning and teaching the youngsters in their care. The curriculum is divided into six developmental areas: (a) infant stimulation, (b) socialization, (c) language, (d) self-help, (e) cognitive, and (f) motor. These divisions, which are similar to those in most early education curricula, may be easily linked to norm-referenced developmental scales, such as the Bayley Scales of Infant Development (1969) and Gesell's Developmental Schedules (1949).

Portage Products

The Portage is composed of three major components, with several products related to each of the components. The following products may be ordered by writing to:

Portage Guide to Early Education
The Portage Project
Cooperative Educational Service Agency 12
412 East Slifer Street
Portage, Wisconsin 53901

Product	Price
1. The Portage Guide Kit	
1.1 *Manual:* Instructions for kit	$32.00 (total for kit)
1.2 *Card File Box:* Cards with suggested ideas for teaching specific skills and behaviors	

1.3 *Checklist* (15 per kit): A record of an individual child's developmental progress	
—Additional checklist (15 per packet)	6.50
2. *The Portage Parent Program*	
2.1 Sets (5) of parent readings and inventories	18.00
2.2 Instructor's Set and Manual Includes: 1 Parent Reading 1 Inventory 1 Instructor's Manual	10.00
3. *Parent Guide to Early Education* A textbook to accompany the *Portage Parent Program*	12.00 (plus $1.50 shipping costs)

The Portage Guide Kit is the portion of the total project that will be described in this review. The kit is used in both school-based and home-based early education programs.

A Brief History of the Portage

The Portage curriculum is a product of the Portage Project, which began in 1969 as a program funded by the Bureau of Education for the Handicapped. The curriculum has been developed to serve children from birth through 6 years of age. The original target population was handicapped preschoolers living in rural Wisconsin. The focus of the program was the child's home setting. The parents were taught behavior management techniques to use with their handicapped child. It had been decided that the rural geographic area was too large to make it practical to transport the children to central locations. When the project was in its developmental stage, a "home teacher" visited the child's home for 1½ hours weekly over a 9½-month period. The home teacher assisted the parents in assessing their child's skills, in determining the sequence in which skills would be taught, and in teaching the specific skills employing behavioral strategies.

In 1975, the Portage model was validated for national dissemination and replication by the Joint Dissemination Panel of the U.S. Office of Education. Forms were developed to evaluate the project's success in its outreach phase of funding. The forms were designed to be used by most projects that provide training and technical assistance to other projects or organizations, such as a head start program. An agreement form or contract, for example, could be modeled on the Portage form. On other forms developed by the Portage staff, information about individual teachers, paraprofessionals, parents, and children was gathered to evaluate the impact Portage had upon the population it served. The success of the Portage Project is certainly in part due to the foresight employed in the original assessment and evaluation plan developed in the early funding stages of the project.

The Portage Project has had over 30 replications using the Portage curriculum. Portage *Card File Boxes* and *Checklists* have been purchased by over 9,000 individuals and agencies in the United States and in other countries such as Australia, Belgium, Canada, England, Israel, Jamaica, Japan, Lebanon, Mexico, New Zealand, Sweden, Uruguay, and Venezuela.

Characteristics of the Portage Curriculum

Organization of Content

The curriculum content of the Portage is arranged in parallel mode. Especially at the younger ages, crossover occurs between or among domains. The *Card File Box* is the actual curriculum. Color-coded cards for the separate domains are chosen to teach the child only after the child's skills have been assessed and recorded on the "checklist." A sample card from the infant stimulation subsection is shown in Exhibit 5-7.

Target Population and Conditions for Use

Although the Portage curriculum was designed as a First Chance project to be used with handicapped preschoolers and their parents, it now has a wider audience. The suggestions in the curriculum are useful with all young children. Parents who have organized play groups for their preschool-age children will find the Portage curriculum a good resource for stimulating ideas for additional lessons to use with the play group. Likewise, child development/care centers and preschools will find the curriculum useful. The curriculum would be useful to parents of children who are developmentally normal or advanced as well as to those with children who demonstrate developmental delays.

Training Needed

A needs assessment of the population desiring to use the Portage curriculum is recommended before implementation of the curriculum. If you are familiar with normed developmental tests, such as the Bayley Scales of Infant Development, you will find that the rationale for the sequence of skills is quite easy to understand. Minimal training of certified teachers is required to institute the Portage. When training paraprofessionals or parents in its use, a series of training workshops is suggested. Topics, such as how to use the *Checklist* and other data collection

Exhibit 5-7 A Sample Card from the Portage *Card File Box*

infant stimulation 10

TITLE: **Indicates sensitivity to body contact by quieting, crying, or body movement**

WHAT TO DO:

1. When baby cries, hold him snugly wrapped in light blanket. Walk around the room with him in your arms.
2. Gentle rocking motion of your arms may quiet baby.
3. Gentle rubbing of head may sooth.
4. It is not always necessary to pick up child. Try gently patting or stroking him while you talk quietly as child lies in crib.
5. Turn baby over and try to sooth him by rubbing his back or tummy.

PortageGuide

Source: Shearer, D. *The Portage guide to early education: The Portage project.* Portage, Wis.: Cooperative Educational Service Agency 12, 1975. Reprinted with permission.

methods, need to be introduced, then practiced, by the trainees with children in their work or home settings. Follow-up workshops are recommended to introduce the additional behavioral methods discussed in the *Manual,* such as task analysis.

Record-Keeping and Assessment

It is suggested that children be administered one of the norm-referenced developmental scales, such as Gesell's Developmental Schedules, before implementing any curriculum such as the Portage. Public Law 94-142 specifies such steps for developmentally delayed youngsters. The child's data may then be easily linked into any of the curricula reviewed in this chapter. The Portage curriculum is arranged so that the linkage from the norm-referenced test is easily accomplished using the individual checklists. The *Checklist,* like the curriculum cards, is color-coded for each of the six domains to make handling easier. A sample page from the *Checklist* is shown in Exhibit 5-8. Parents and child care givers thus have a record of the child's achievements and rate of learning for each domain. These records also serve as a source of positive reinforcement for the parent or care giver.

Components for Lesson Planning

In the preceding chapter, we described the necessary criteria for lesson plans. The Portage curriculum meets the majority of these criteria because it has a behavioral design. Evaluation procedures are not defined and numbered however, as they are in the HICOMP Curriculum, in which 11 methods are described. Evaluation is employed daily in the Portage project, mostly in the form of frequency charts, as shown in Exhibit 5-9.

Practical Qualities

The Portage Curriculum is packaged to facilitate its implementation. The individual lessons on cards makes handling quite easy. The parent or teacher may have the card nearby when working with a group of children and need only to glance occasionally at the card for visual prompts. Laminating the cards would add additional years to their use. Laminating, however, would increase the curriculum cards' bulk and would require that an additional box be purchased to hold all of the cards. The cost of the *Checklist* seems to be excessively high. Since the *Checklist* is a necessary component of the total curriculum, it might become necessary for you to design your own checklist to alleviate the added expense when implementing the Portage curriculum in a large setting, such as a child care center that serves 50 or more children daily.

The summary checklist in Exhibit 5-20 at the end of the chapter outlines the outstanding features of the Portage curriculum.

Exhibit 5-8 A Sample Page from the Portage *Checklist*

infant stimulation

Age Level	Card	Behavior	Entry Behavior	Date Achieved	Comments
Infant	1	General visual stimulation (Under six weeks)		/ /	
	2	General visual stimulation (six weeks and older)		/ /	
	3	General tactile stimulation (Under six weeks)		/ /	
	4	General tactile stimulation (six weeks and older)		/ /	
	5	General auditory stimulation (Under six weeks)		/ /	
	6	General auditory stimulation (six weeks and older)		/ /	
	7	Sucks		/ /	
	8	Moves head to side while lying on back		/ /	
	9	Opens mouth for bottle or breast when nipple touches mouth		/ /	
	10	Indicates sensiti[illegible] to body contact by quieting, crying, or body movement		/ /	
	11	Turns head [illegible]ard [illegible]le when his cheek is touched		/ /	
	12	Looks in [illegible]rection of sou[illegible]d or changes body movement in response to sound		/ /	
	13	Looks at [illegible]rson attempt[illegible]g to [illegible]is attention by talking or movement		/ /	
	14	Quiets o[illegible] [illegible] body [illegible]		/ /	
	15	Shows b[illegible] or [illegible]sat[illegible] of [illegible]ult		/ /	
	16	Lift[illegible] momentarily su[illegible]		/ /	
	17	Cries differentially due to different discomforts		/ /	
	18	Falls asleep at appropriate times		/ /	
	19	Thrusts arms about—no direction		/ /	
	20	Follows an object, visually, moved past midline of body		/ /	
	21	Smiles		/ /	
	22	Follows light with eyes, turning head		/ /	
	23	Follows sound, moving head		/ /	
	24	Regards hand		/ /	
	25	Kicks vigorously while on back		/ /	
	26	Opens mouth, begins sucking prior to nipple touching mouth		/ /	
	27	Maintains eye contact 3 seconds		/ /	

PortageGuide

Source: Shearer, D. *The Portage guide to early education: The Portage project.* Portage, Wis.: Cooperative Educational Service Agency 12, 1975. Reprinted with permission.

Exhibit 5-9 A Portage Frequency Chart

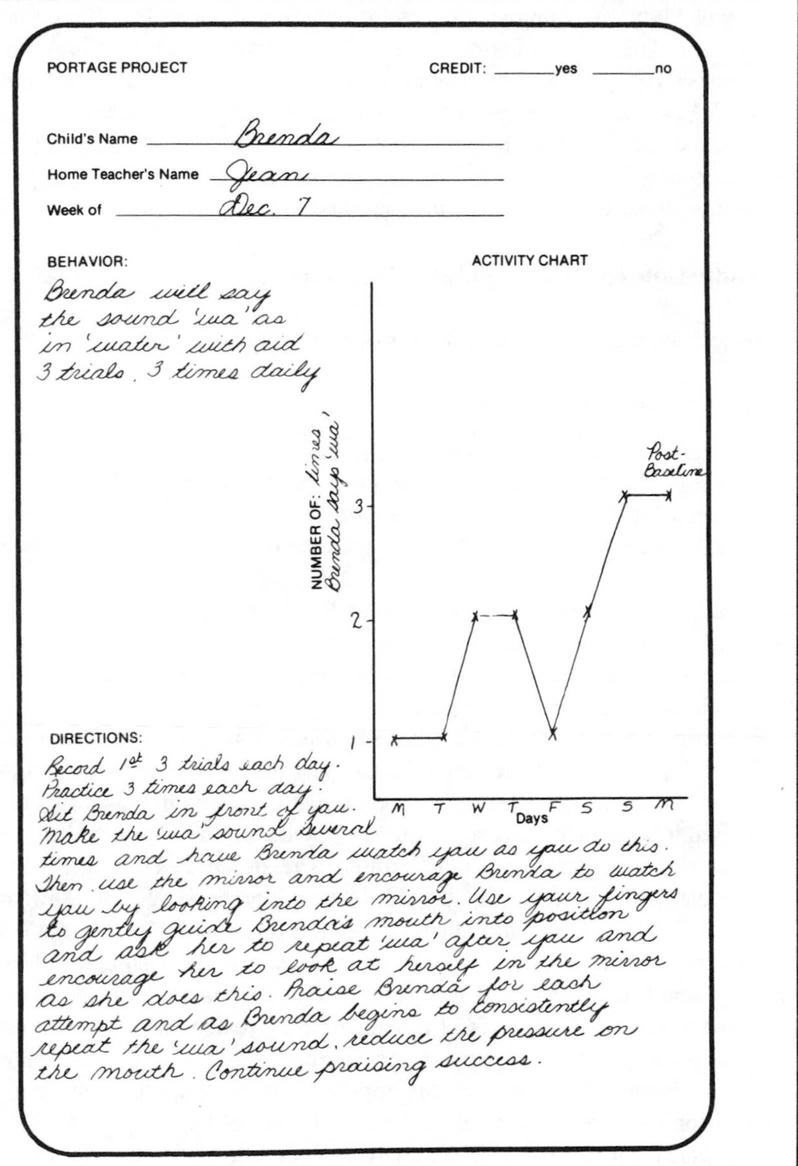

PORTAGE PROJECT

CREDIT: ______ yes ______ no

Child's Name Brenda

Home Teacher's Name Jean

Week of Dec. 7

BEHAVIOR:

Brenda will say the sound 'wa' as in 'water' with aid 3 trials, 3 times daily

ACTIVITY CHART

DIRECTIONS:

Record 1st 3 trials each day. Practice 3 times each day. Sit Brenda in front of you. Make the 'wa' sound several times and have Brenda watch you as you do this. Then use the mirror and encourage Brenda to watch you by looking into the mirror. Use your fingers to gently guide Brenda's mouth into position and ask her to repeat 'wa' after you and encourage her to look at herself in the mirror as she does this. Praise Brenda for each attempt and as Brenda begins to consistently repeat the 'wa' sound, reduce the pressure on the mouth. Continue praising success.

Source: Shearer, D. *The Portage guide to early education: The Portage project.* Portage, Wis.: Cooperative Educational Service Agency 12, 1975. Reprinted with permission.

THE PROJECT MEMPHIS CURRICULUM

Project Memphis employs a developmental task approach in the design of its curriculum. The 260-item curriculum has been developed for all preschool children, ages 0 to 5, with a particular emphasis on children who are developmentally delayed. Five major developmental domains are included in the Memphis curriculum: (a) personal-social, (b) gross-motor, (c) fine-motor, (d) language, and (e) perceptuo-cognitive. These are, of course, the major areas of development addressed by most developmental instruments.

Introduction to Using Project Memphis

Project Memphis advocates three steps in using its curriculum:

Step 1–Developmental Evaluation

It is first necessary to determine the child's entry level of developmental functioning. An assessment is completed by the teacher using the Memphis Comprehensive Developmental Scale (see Exhibit 5-10 and also Exhibit 3-4 in chapter 3). It should be noted that other scales may also be used for assessment purposes. The results of the assessment indicate what skills the child has or has not mastered. In addition to the current skill levels being provided, information is obtained that outlines what skills may be important for later development. The sequence of these skills, as well as the expected age range usually observed in young children, are outlined by the Memphis curriculum.

The scoring of the Memphis Scale is a relatively easy procedure. Raw scores for each developmental area are derived by adding the number of skills that the child "passes" for an area. A passed skill is one that is present in the child's repertoire on a regular basis or has been "mastered" by the child. For each skill, the child receives either a "pass" or "fail," which is recorded by circling P or F on the assessment form. To determine the child's developmental age for a skill area, the person administering the scale notes the monthly age point corresponding to the raw score. The raw score is matched with the corresponding ages, which are given in months and years. If a child has a raw score of 20 (passes) in the personal-social area, the developmental age is 21 months or 1.75 years. The scores for each skill area are recorded in the upper left-hand corner. When all of the developmental areas have been assessed and the developmental ages computed, the developmental ages for each area may be plotted on the Profile of Developmental Status (see Exhibit 5-11). The profile provides an overview of the child's developmental level as well as a comparison of the developmental skill areas.

Exhibit 5-10 Memphis Comprehensive Developmental Scale

Name ____________ Chronological Age ____________

Date of Birth ____________ Date of Evaluation ____________ Raw Score ____________ Developmental Age ____________

PERSONAL–SOCIAL SKILLS

	Years	Months	Pass	Fail	
60	5.00	60	P	F	Plays competitive exercise games.
59			P	F	Dresses self with attempts at tying shoes.
58			P	F	Spreads with knife, partial success.
57	4.75	57	P	F	Uses play materials constructively; builds, does not tear down.
56			P	F	Dresses self except tying shoes.
55			P	F	"Picks up" some after playing with no coaxing.
54	4.50	54	P	F	Attends well for short stories.
53			P	F	Uses paper straw appropriately without damaging.
52			P	F	Washes face well.
51	4.25	51	P	F	Separates from mother easily.
50			P	F	Distinguishes front from back of clothes.
49			P	F	Completely cares for self at toilet, including cleaning and dressing.
48	4.00	48	P	F	Plays with others with minimal friction.
47			P	F	Buttons medium-sized buttons.
46			P	F	Goes on very short distance errands outside the home.
45	3.75	45	P	F	Performs for others; i.e. performs a simple rhyme or song.
44			P	F	Washes hands well.
43			P	F	Brushes teeth adequately.
42	3.50	42	P	F	Attempts help at little household tasks; i.e. sweeping, dusting.
41			P	F	Completely undresses for bedtime.
40			P	F	Removes clothing for toileting.
39	3.25	39	P	F	Buttons large buttons.
38			P	F	Performs toilet activities by self (not dressing, cleaning).
37			P	F	Plays cooperatively, interacts with others.
36	3.00	36	P	F	Puts on shoes and socks (tying not required).
35			P	F	Feeds self with little spilling, both fork and spoon.
34			P	F	Shares upon request.
33	2.75	33	P	F	Avoids simple hazards (hot stove, etc.)
32			P	F	Puts on a coat (buttoning not required).
31			P	F	Dries hands well.
30	2.50	30	P	F	Is not overly destructive with household goods, toys, etc.
29			P	F	Gets a drink unassisted from fountain or sink.
28			P	F	Sucks from a plastic straw.
27	2.25	27	P	F	Eats with fork but spills some.
26			P	F	Recognizes self in mirror.
25			P	F	Uses single words or likenesses to show wants.
24	2.00	24	P	F	Minds–does as told generally.
23			P	F	Removes coat or dress (unbuttoning not required).
22			P	F	At least asks to go to toilet–day and night.
21	1.75	21	P	F	Does not place objects on floor in mouth.
20			P	F	Eats with spoon, spilling little.
19			P	F	Voluntarily "slows down" to take naps or rest.
18	1.50	18	P	F	Plays around other children effectively.
17			P	F	Drinks from cup or glass unassisted.
16			P	F	Pulls off socks, but not necessarily shoes.
15	1.25	15	P	F	Follows simple commands or instructions.
14			P	F	Feeds self with a spoon–some spilling allowed.
13			P	F	Holds out arms to assist with clothing.
12	1.00	12	P	F	Temporarily responds to "no," "stop."
11			P	F	Cooperates with dressing–does not resist.
10			P	F	Chews food.
9	.75	9	P	F	Places food in mouth with hands.
8			P	F	Grasps small objects with thumb and index finger.
7			P	F	Desires personal attention and contact beyond just holding.
6	.50	6	P	F	Drinks from a cup or glass with assistance.
5			P	F	Occupies self with a toy for a short period of time.
4			P	F	Grasps foot or brings hand to mouth.
3	.25	3	P	F	Pulls at clothing with hands.
2			P	F	Sucking and swallowing are present.
1			P	F	Reaches for and wants to be held by familiar persons.

Source: Quick, A.D., Little, T.L., & Campbell, A.A. *Project MEMPHIS: Enhancing developmental progress in preschool exceptional children.* Belmont, CA: Fearon, Publishers, 1974b. Reprinted with permission.

Exhibit 5-11 Memphis Profile of Developmental Status

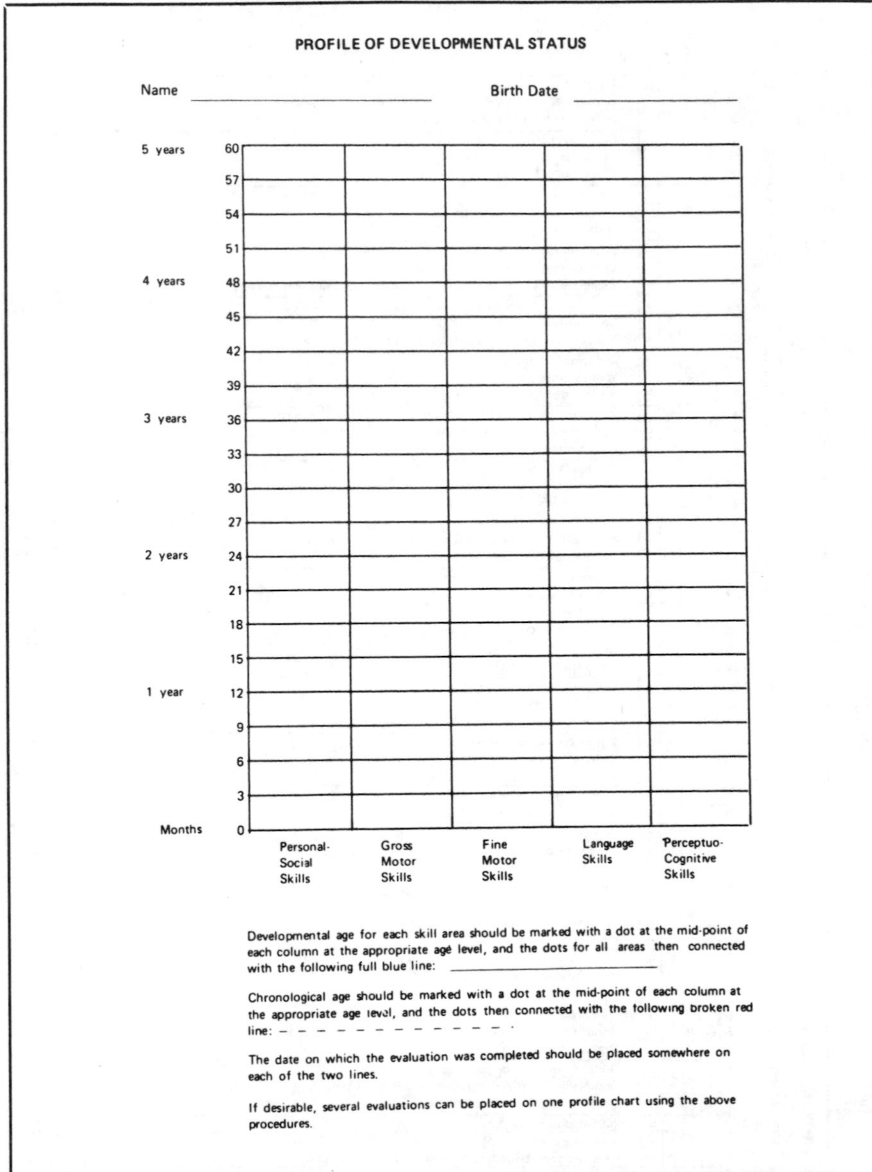

PROFILE OF DEVELOPMENTAL STATUS

Name ______________________ Birth Date ________________

	Months	Personal-Social Skills	Gross Motor Skills	Fine Motor Skills	Language Skills	Perceptuo-Cognitive Skills
5 years	60					
	57					
	54					
	51					
4 years	48					
	45					
	42					
	39					
3 years	36					
	33					
	30					
	27					
2 years	24					
	21					
	18					
	15					
1 year	12					
	9					
	6					
	3					
Months	0					

Developmental age for each skill area should be marked with a dot at the mid-point of each column at the appropriate age level, and the dots for all areas then connected with the following full blue line: ______________________

Chronological age should be marked with a dot at the mid-point of each column at the appropriate age level, and the dots then connected with the following broken red line: – – – – – – – – – – – – –

The date on which the evaluation was completed should be placed somewhere on each of the two lines.

If desirable, several evaluations can be placed on one profile chart using the above procedures.

Source: Quick, A.D., Little, T.L., & Campbell, A.A. *Project MEMPHIS: Enhancing developmental progress in preschool exceptional children.* Belmont, Calif.: Fearon, Publishers, 1974. Reprinted with permission.

Step 2–Individual Educational Program Planning

Based on the results of the Memphis Comprehensive Developmental Scale, the teacher determines which skills occur next in the developmental sequence. Skills that will be important for later success in school, such as holding a crayon or a fine-motor skill, may be emphasized in weekly plans. Specific skills to be mastered are recorded on the Assignment Record sheet as demonstrated below (see Exhibits 5-12 and 5-13).

The basic premise of the Record is that a certain percentage of the unlearned skills should be mastered in a specific amount of time. By checking how long it takes a child to learn skills in each of the five domains, the teacher will have a rough estimate of the child's rate of learning new tasks. The Record thus has a dual role: it keeps records of the child's progress in the curriculum, and it enables the teacher to predict the child's future achievements in the curriculum items.

The specific skills recorded on the Assignment Record are taken from the Memphis lesson plan guide, *Lesson Plans for Enhancing Preschool Developmental Progress*. The guide's 260-lesson-plan suggestions are sequenced by domain and developmental age. A sample page illustrating the guide's format is shown in Exhibit 5-14.

The lessons are coded to each of the skill areas, for example, "PSS—personal-social skills." A title for each plan is provided that corresponds with the wording of the related skill. In addition, each lesson plan may include suggestions for equipment to be used in teaching the skill, a procedure to be followed when teaching the skill, and extra activities and equipment that provide alternatives to help the child respond. Additionally, the lessons provide opportunities for skill generalization and include suggested criteria of mastery for use as evaluation measures to determine if and when the skill has been learned.

The lesson plans are only suggestions and are not intended to specify the only procedures for teaching a particular child. Basic lesson-plan format sheets are provided so that teachers may develop their own lessons, as in the example shown in Exhibit 5-15.

Exhibit 5-12 Memphis Assignment Record Form

Developmental Skill Assignment Record

Name ______________________ Address ______________________

Birth Date ______________________ Phone ______________________

Chronological Age ______

Handicapping Conditions ______________

Starting Date ________________ Stopping Date ________________

Source: Quick, A.D., Little, T.L., & Campbell, A.A. *Project MEMPHIS: Enhancing developmental progress in preschool exceptional children.* Belmont, Calif.: Fearon, Publishers, 1974. Reprinted with permission.

Exhibit 5-13 Specific Skills in the Memphis Assignment Record

Personal-Social Development

Skill Title:
Skill Description:

Skill Title:
Skill Description:

Skill Title:
Skill Description:

Skill Title:
Skill Description:

Language Development

Skill Title:
Skill Description:

Skill Title:
Skill Description:

Skill Title:
Skill Description:

Skill Title:
Skill Description:

Gross Motor Development

Skill Title:
Skill Description:

Skill Title:
Skill Description:

Skill Title:
Skill Description:

Skill Title:
Skill Description:

Fine Motor Development

Skill Title:
Skill Description:

Skill Title:
Skill Description:

Skill Title:
Skill Description:

Skill Title:
Skill Description:

Perceptuo-Cognitive Development

Skill Title:
Skill Description:

Skill Title:
Skill Description:

Skill Title:
Skill Description:

Skill Title:
Skill Description:

Present Personal-Social Age ____

Present Gross Motor Age ______

Present Fine Motor Age ______

Present Language Age ________

Present Perceptuo-Cognitive Age_

Name ____________________

Chronological Age __________

Starting Date ______________

Stopping Date ______________

Source: Quick, A.D., Little, T.L., & Campbell, A.A. *Project MEMPHIS: Enhancing developmental progress in preschool exceptional children.* Belmont, Calif.: Fearon, Publishers, 1974. Reprinted with permission.

Exhibit 5-14 Sample Page from the Memphis Lesson Plan Guide

PERSONAL-SOCIAL SKILL—2 **Developmental Level .25 Years**

SUCKING AND SWALLOWING

Purpose: To aid the child in learning to suck and swallow.

Equipment: Ice cube, cold cloth, nipple, pacifier, honey.

Procedure: Stimulate the child's lips with an ice cube or cold cloth. Stimulate sucking by massaging his cheeks when the nipple is in the mouth, using a forward-backward motion with your fingers. If this fails to stimulate sucking, place a small amount of honey on a pacifier and put it in the mouth. If the child still does not suck on the pacifier, move it in and out for him. Gradually let him do more for himself.

Additional Activities: Further encourage tongue movement by using pinches of jelly, placing jelly in the mouth under the tongue.

Additional Equipment: Jelly on a tongue depressor placed against the tongue; jello placed in the mouth under the tongue.

Suggested Criteria: Will make obvious sucking response five consecutive times when stimulus is presented.

Notes:

Source: Quick, A.D. & Campbell, A.A. *Lesson Plans for enhancing preschool developmental progress: Project MEMPHIS.* Dubuque, Iowa: Kendall/Hunt Publishing Co., 1976. Reprinted with permission.

Exhibit 5-15 Memphis Lesson-Plan Format

PERSONAL-SOCIAL SKILL—2 **Developmental Level .25 Years**

SUCKING AND SWALLOWING

Purpose: To aid the child in learning to suck and swallow.

Equipment:

Procedure:

Additional Activities:

Additional Equipment:

Suggested Criteria:

Source: Quick, A.D. & Campbell, A.A. *Lesson plans for enhancing preschool developmental progress: Project MEMPHIS.* Dubuque, Iowa: Kendall/Hunt Publishing Co., 1976. Reprinted with permission.

Step 3–Record-Keeping and Assessment

The Continuous Record for Educational Developmental Gain is used to record the child's performance on assigned skills, the dates of performance, and the teacher's judgment about the quality of performance and mastery of the skills. Sample pages from the Continuous Record are shown in Exhibits 5-16 and 5-17.

As indicated by the title, the Continuous Record is an ongoing record of performance and mastery of skills for the duration of the child's enrollment in the curriculum. Each of the five domains has separate recording sheets. The coding format is quite self-explanatory.

In addition to individual evaluation of program success, it is possible to determine the success of an entire program, that is, to evaluate group progress. A teacher may set a criterion for group performance on specific skills by stating that 80 percent of the students should master at least 90 percent of assigned skills in order for the lesson or lessons to be considered successful. If, for example, the teacher developed lesson plans around a unit theme of the fall season and the students did not reach the set criteria, the teacher would need to examine the teaching of the unit. Was each lesson presented in the proper manner? Were frequency, rate, and duration of presentation of each skill adjusted to meet both the individual's and the group's needs?

Memphis Products

To order the following Memphis products, write to:

Fearon Publishers
6 Davis Drive
Belmont, CA 94002

	Price
1. *Enhancing Developmental Progress in Preschool Exceptional Children* by Quick, Little, and Campbell	$5.00
2. Instruments for Individual Program Planning and Evaluation	
2.1 Comprehensive Developmental Scale	
2.2 Developmental Skill Assignment Record	
2.3 Continuous Record for Educational-Developmental Gain	5.10
3. Guide to Programming	

Exhibit 5-16 Sample Page from the Memphis Continuous Record

Continuous Record
For
Educational - Developmental Gain

Name ______________________________

Address ______________________________

Birth Date ________________ Phone ____________

Chronological Age ______________________________

Handicapping Conditions ______________________________

Starting Date ________________ Stopping Date ________

CODE FOR RECORD SHEETS:

Q = Quality of Skill

P = Pass (3 or 4 under Q)

F = Fail (1 or 2 under Q)

QUALITY CODING:

Q = 4 = **Extreme Competence** in performin the skill or behavior.

Q = 3 = **Adequate Competence** in perforn ing the skill or behavior.

Q = 2 = **Some Competence**, but not adequ in performing the skill or behavior

Q = 1 = **No Competence,** at all in performi the skill or behavior.

COMPLETION RECORD
Skills Assigned and Mastered

	NUMBER ASSIGNED	NUMBER MASTERED	PERCEN MASTERE
1. Personal-social	____	____	____
2. Gross Motor	____	____	____
3. Fine Motor	____	____	____
4. Language	____	____	____
5. Perceptuo-cognitive	____	____	____
6. Total	____	____	____

Source: Quick, A.D., Little, T.L., & Campbell, A.A. *Project MEMPHIS: Enhancing developmental progress in preschool exceptional children.* Belmont, Calif.: Fearon, Publishers, 1974. Reprinted with permission.

Exhibit 5-17 Sample Page from Memphis Continuous Record

Name ________________ Starting ______ Stopping ______

Developmental Area ______________

Skill One ________				Skill Two ________				Skill Three ________				Skill Four ________			
Date	P	F	Q	Date	P	F	Q	Date	P	F	Q	Date	P	F	Q
____	__	__	__	____	__	__	__	____	__	__	__	____	__	__	__
____	__	__	__	____	__	__	__	____	__	__	__	____	__	__	__
____	__	__	__	____	__	__	__	____	__	__	__	____	__	__	__
____	__	__	__	____	__	__	__	____	__	__	__	____	__	__	__
____	__	__	__	____	__	__	__	____	__	__	__	____	__	__	__
____	__	__	__	____	__	__	__	____	__	__	__	____	__	__	__
____	__	__	__	____	__	__	__	____	__	__	__	____	__	__	__
____	__	__	__	____	__	__	__	____	__	__	__	____	__	__	__
____	__	__	__	____	__	__	__	____	__	__	__	____	__	__	__
____	__	__	__	____	__	__	__	____	__	__	__	____	__	__	__
____	__	__	__	____	__	__	__	____	__	__	__	____	__	__	__
____	__	__	__	____	__	__	__	____	__	__	__	____	__	__	__

One of these sheets should be used for each of the five developmental areas in which skills have been assigned.

Source: Quick, A.D., Little, T.L., & Campbell, A.A. *Project MEMPHIS: Enhancing developmental progress in preschool exceptional children.* Belmont, Calif.: Fearon, Publishers, 1974. Reprinted with permission.

To order the lesson plan manual write to:

Kendall/Hunt Publishing Company
Dubuque, Iowa

Product	Price
Lesson Plans for Enhancing Preschool Developmental Progress by Quick, A., and Campbell, A.	$13.95

A Brief History of the Memphis

Project Memphis is one of many preschool projects funded by the Bureau of Education for the Handicapped and aimed at studying methods of educating preschool handicapped children and their parents. It was developed to provide a working model for training preschool handicapped foster children and their foster parents.

The child-training component of the project was intended to develop techniques for remediation of developmental deficiencies. Through this early intervention process, it was hoped that children could be placed into the regular classroom rather than in some more restrictive setting, such as a special education facility or residential setting.

The parent-training component was designed to help parents learn strategies that would enable them not only to cope with their handicapped child but to take an active part in enhancing the development of the child. The child needs an ongoing supportive environment in order to maintain and generalize acquired skills. Since the preschool child spends a major portion of time at home, it is important that the child's care giver has the knowledge and skills that will enable the child to develop, maintain, and transfer skills.

Characteristics of the Memphis Curriculum

Organization of Content

The curriculum content of Project Memphis is arranged primarily in a parallel mode. The five developmental skill areas contain a total of 260 developmental tasks sequentially ordered from 0 to 5 years of age. The 260 tasks are considered by the project's authors as functional milestones in human growth and development.

There is some crossover in Project Memphis; that is, some of the skills found in one domain may also be found in another. Although the purpose of the skill may be different in each domain in which it appears, the instructional approach remains the same. Numbers indicate those lesson plans that are cross-referenced with other domains.

Target Population and Conditions for Use

Project Memphis was developed for use with handicapped preschool children with foster parents. However, the program can also be used with children who are developmentally "normal" and reside with their natural parents. The program can be used with an individual child or groups of children.

Training Needed

Project Memphis provides a text, *Enhancing Developmental Progress in Preschool Exceptional Children* by Quick, Little, and Campbell (1974), which is intended to provide the reader with effective ways of implementing and maintaining the training programs. The text provides an overview of Project Memphis, with specific discussions of the program components as well as a description of procedures for parent training.

Components for Lesson Planning

Lesson Plans for Enhancing Preschool Developmental Progress provides the teacher with suggestions for materials or equipment to be used in teaching each skill. The teaching procedures are generally detailed enough to tell the teacher what and how to teach the skill. Although behavioral strategies, for example, manual prompting, are not stated as such, the authors do indicate that the teacher should "hold the child's hand." This is, of course, manual prompting. Suggested criteria are given. There is no mention, however, of the amount of time it should take the child to complete the task. How long should it take to string four beads for this task to be considered mastered? If the child can string four beads but it takes 25 minutes to do it, should the skill be considered mastered? Although time may not always be relevant to skill mastery, it should at least be considered.

Practical Qualities

The *Lesson Plans for Enhancing Preschool Developmental Progress* comes in a soft-covered, three-ring, loose-leaf notebook. The skills are divided into developmental sections, for example, fine-motor. Preceding each section is a page from the Memphis Comprehensive Developmental Scale corresponding to the developmental domain.

Referencing would be made easier if dividers were provided between each section. In its present form, it is necessary to guess the approximate location of a particular domain.

There also are several places to record information about the child's progress. It would certainly be easier for the teacher to have a compiled record of data about the child, considering the amount of paperwork already demanded of teachers.

For a summary of the *Project Memphis Curriculum*'s salient features, see the checklist in Exhibit 5-20 at the end of the chapter.

DEVELOPMENTAL PROGRAMMING FOR INFANTS AND YOUNG CHILDREN

If you are working with children in the developmental ages from birth through 36 months of age, the Developmental Programming for Infants and Young Children (DPI) is a good curriculum choice. As the title indicates, this curriculum's theoretical orientation involves a developmental task approach. The six domains stressed in the curriculum are perceptual/fine-motor, cognition, language, social/emotional, self-care, and gross-motor. The curriculum was designed to be used with both normal and developmentally delayed youngsters.

There are three products in the total DPI package. Part 1 is the *Assessment and Application Manual* (paperback), which may be used to enter the child at the correct starting point in the curriculum. Part 2 is the *Early Intervention Developmental Profile,* a paperback booklet for recording the child's scores on the DPI's assessment instrument. Part 3 is the paperback manual *Stimulation Activities,* which contains the actual curriculum objectives.

DPI Products

The following products may be ordered by writing to:

The Early Intervention Project for Handicapped Infants and Young Children
Institute for the Study of Mental Retardation and Related Disabilities
The University of Michigan Press, P.O. Box 1104
Ann Arbor, Michigan 48106

Products	Price
1. *DPI Assessment and Application*	$ 7.00
2. *DPI Early Developmental Profile*	.50
3. *DPI Stimulation Activities*	7.00

A Brief History of the DPI

The DPI is an outgrowth of the early intervention project at the Institute for the Study of Mental Retardation and Related Disabilities at the University of Michigan. The project was funded from a grant from the U.S. Office of Education,

Department of Health, Education and Welfare. It was classified as a First Chance project by the Bureau of Education for the Handicapped in August, 1974. The curriculum was developed by experts in the six domains. Each expert then trained the other staff members to implement the activities in their own domain of expertise. The staff thus became interdisciplinary in its approach.

Like most curricula, the DPI was "cut and pasted" from norm-referenced assessment instuments, such as Bayley's Scales of Infant Development (1969) and Cattell's Infant Intelligence Scale (1940). It was field tested throughout the project's funding period with both normal and developmentally delayed children.

Characteristics of the Curriculum

Organization of Content

The curriculum content in the DPI is arranged in a parallel mode. Each domain is broken into several subdomains under each three-month age span. Exhibit 5-18 illustrates the subdivisions.

Crossover of specific objectives occurs in this curriculum, especially since the child's developmental age is between birth and 36 months of age. In that developmental age range, children often are practicing skills in more than one domain. For example, a child shaking a rattle is building muscle strength and may also be practicing eye-hand coordination.

Target Population and Conditions for Use

The DPI was field tested with children who had developmental delays and also with children who were developing normally. After each list of activities, there are helpful suggestions to adjust the activities for a child with impairments in hearing, vision, or motor functioning. (See Exhibit 5-19.)

By referring to Exhibit 5-18, you can see that there are no provisions in the curriculum for recording the child's accomplishment of specific short-term goals. It is necessary to create such a booklet for each child in order to keep accurate records. The curriculum also does not instruct its consumer on how to use specific behavioral strategies, such as prompting or the teaching of individual activities. There is also no section outlining methods to evaluate a child's performance, such as a criteria checklist, on a specific activity. Those using the DPI's *Stimulation Activities* should be competent in applied behavioral-analysis skills to ensure that the activities are taught and evaluated properly.

Exhibit 5-18 Sample Page from *DPI Stimulation Activities*

Perceptual/Fine Motor

0-2 Months

Short-term goal

Child will focus on an object placed 10 to 12 inches in front of his eyes (midline). ***Visual Focusing***

Activities

At various times during the day, position yourself where the child can see you. Talk to the child, make interesting noises, and change your facial expression when the child indicates he can see you.

Place a mobile on the child's crib or chair so that he will have something to focus his eyes on.

Shake a colorful noisemaker in front of the child's face to gain his attention and to promote focusing of his eyes.

Encourage the child to look at his food or bottle when being fed. Reward his looking by feeding him immediately.

Cut out shapes (triangle, star, bull's eye, face) from black or red construction paper. Paste the shapes on a white background or draw shapes directly on white paper. Hang the picture where the infant can see it. Young infants are most attracted to interesting configurations which have highly contrasting components, such as a bull's eye with alternating black and white concentric rings.

Note: If the child's eyes do not focus on the object, move his head to face the object.

Hearing Impaired: *NC*

Motorically Involved: *NC*

Visually Impaired: *Give the child the opportunity to listen to a variety of sounds such as noisemakers, records, and voices. Cessation of activity or increased activity is indicative that he is hearing the sounds. Later he will begin to locate the sounds of his environment.*

Exhibit 5-18 continued

Short-term goal

Child's eyes will follow objects that are moving horizontally in front of him (horizontal tracking). ***Visual Tracking***

Activities

1. When the child is looking at you, move your face from one side of the child to the other. Encourage the child to follow you with his eyes.

2. In a darkened room, move a penlight horizontally across the child's face. (Do not shine the light directly into his eyes.) Encourage the child to follow the light visually.

3. Put thimbles on your thumb and index finger and click them together as you move your hand across the midline in front of the child's face, encouraging him to follow visually.

4. Hold a toy or finger puppet about 12 inches from the child's face. Slowly move it from side to side. Be sure the child's eyes are focusing on the object. Gradually increase the distance of the object from side to side.

5. Hang a swinging mobile above the child's crib. Hang it so it swings horizontally. Encourage the child to follow its swing.

6. When the child's eyes are focused straight ahead, present an interesting object to the side. Shake it slightly and try to attract the child's attention.

Source: Schafer, D.S. & Moersch, M.S. *Developmental programming for infants and young children.* (Vol. III) Stimulation Activities. Ann Arbor, Mich.: University of Michigan Press, 1977. Reprinted with permission.

Exhibit 5-19 Sample Page from *DPI Stimulation Activities*

Key

The following symbols are used consistently throughout the book. They describe an adaptation of the activities due to a child's handicap and the appropriate teaching methods for a given short-term goal.

O. *Omit because of handicapping condition. Use alternative activity if given (see page 13).*
NC. *No changes in activities are necessary (see page 11).*
MA. *Only minor adaptations are necessary to make the activities appropriate, for example:*

Hearing Impaired: Give oral and gestural cues consistent with the alternative communication system being used. Continue to talk to the child and to label objects for him so that any residual hearing may be tapped. Continue amplification if used. Substitute signs or symbols for words when appropriate.

Motorically Involved: Position the child in a relaxed position where he can achieve maximal use of the motor patterns he exhibits being careful not to encourage inappropriate compensation patterns. Present object at midline when possible. Encourage eye pointing if the child is unable to use his hands and arms or unable to speak.

Visually Impaired: Use bright colors and large objects to effectively tap any residual sight. Encourage the child to consistently wear his corrective glasses if prescribed. Compensate for lack of vision by substituting objects with sounds, textures, and smells.

Source: Schafer, D.S. & Moersch, M.S. *Developmental programming for infants and young children.* (Vol. III) Stimulation Activities. Ann Arbor, Mich.: University of Michigan Press, 1977. Reprinted with permission.

Training Needed

The DPI curriculum was designed to be used by teachers, paraprofessionals, and parents. Minimal training is necessary to implement the suggested activities. It is reasonable to expect that more training may be required to implement the adaptive suggestions for handicapped children. The training should probably stress performance rather than verbal skills. Thus, the workshop trainer would have the participants practice the suggested instructional tactics. Practicing behavioral strategies for teaching skills, such as modeling and evaluation techniques, could also be included in the workshop to make up for the lack of these strategies in the formal presentation of the curriculum. Initially, the participants could practice working with each other. This would help avoid adding any extra stress to a planned lesson with a youngster, especially if the child has a developmental delay.

Record-Keeping and Assessment

The DPI materials are designed to be used as a total package. The profile designed to keep records of the child's scores on the assessment instrument, the *Early Intervention Developmental Profile,* is supposed to be administered every 3 months to the child. During the 3-month intervals, it is expected that the *Stimulation Activities* will be used. As noted previously, there is no form to record the child's progress on each short-term objective. The development of such a record becomes an extra burden for the preschool teacher or parent, who is often viewed as being indefatigable.

Saving time is another argument for having a record-keeping form that may be filled in daily. This perhaps would obviate the need to give a formal reassessment to the child every 3 months. A device that permits daily and/or weekly recording of a child's achievements would be more practical and effective. Recording child progress as it occurs is more reinforcing to the individuals involved in the child's individual educational plan. They can see the growths the child makes daily as a result of their well-planned activities and consistent hard work.

Components for Lesson Planning

The DPI's manual *Stimulation Activities* meets most of the criteria as outlined in chapter 4. Strategies to implement activities, such as "verbal prompting," are not formally labeled and defined. The teacher is told, however, to say the word for the child and to encourage imitation. A curriculum guide is not included in the package. Such a guide could list strategies, criteria of performance, lesson-plan formats, and other items, such as methods for writing IEPs using the DPI curriculum. A consultant may be necessary to help implement the DPI curriculum if it is used in formulating IEPs.

Practical Qualities

The DPI curriculum is in paperback format with plastic binders to make handling easier. Because daily recording is not an attribute of the curriculum, the paperback manual should be sufficient for at least 2 or 3 years of continual use by a teacher, paraprofessional, or parent. An overview of the DPI curriculum is provided in Exhibit 5-20; this should serve as a model to help you compare curricula.

Exhibit 5-20 Curriculum Evaluation Form and Checklist

This curriculum evaluation form is designed so that the names of up to 5 curricula can be entered for evaluation purposes. Each category should be marked with a check to indicate the presence of a specific attribute.

Item	LAP	HICOMP	PORTAGE	MEMPHIS	Developmental Programming for Infants and Young Children	
1.0 Theoretical or Conceptual Basis						
1.1 The program has a strong theoretical/conceptual base	✓	✓	✓	✓	✓	
1.2 The program is based on research in experimental or applied settings	✓	✓	✓	✓	✓	
2.0 Product Data Base						
2.1 The product was developed through a planned process	✓	✓	✓	✓	✓	
2.2 There is data on product effectiveness	✓	✓	✓	✓	✓	
If 2.2 is yes, the type of data presented is:						
2.2.1 single subject studies						*
2.2.2 between group comparisons	✓	✓	✓	✓	✓	
2.2.3 lesson specific child performance data						*
2.2.4 other ____________						*
2.2.5 The field test or data collection procedures (conditions) are specified precisely and could be replicated						*
2.2.6 Product effectiveness data						
2.2.6.1 accompanies the product	✓	+	✓	✓	✓	
2.2.6.2 is referenced for easy access	✓	+	✓	✓	✓	
2.2.6.3 is inaccessible						
2.2.7 Product effectiveness data						
2.2.7.1 shows a strong effect	✓	+	✓	✓	✓	
2.2.7.2 shows a moderate effect						
2.2.7.3 shows a weak effect						
3.0 Target Population						
3.1 The child population the curriculum was tested on is specified	✓	✓	✓	✓	✓	
3.2 The suggested audience for the curriculum is the same as the population the product was tested on	✓	✓	✓	✓	✓	

From Tawney, J. W., & Deaton, S. L. Curricula for the Severely Developmentally Retarded: A Survey and Primer on the Curriculum Development Process. USOE: Final Report, Volume 1. Grant Numbers OEG-0-72-5361 and OEG-0-75-00669, 1979.

*Request information, if available, from project director(s).
+Information on file with project director(s).

Exhibit 5-20 continued

		LAP	HICOMP	PORTAGE	MEMPHIS	Developmental Programming for Infants and Young Children
4.0	**Conditions for Product Use**					
4.1	The conditions under which the product was designed to be used are specified	√	√	√	√	√
4.2	The conditions exist, or can be created in the teacher's own classroom	√	√	√	√	√
5.0	**Teacher Training for Product Use**					
5.1	The product requires teacher training before use	√	√	√	√	√
	If 5.1 is yes, training is:					
5.1.1	minimal (self study)					
5.1.2	moderate (demonstration)	√	√	√	√	√
5.1.3	extensive					
6.0	**General Product Components**					
	The product contains:					
6.1	a scope and sequence or other skill progression charting system	√	√	√	√	√
6.2	a system for assessing students' entry skills into the curriculum	√	√	√	√	√
6.3	a system for documenting student performance	√	√	√	√	√
6.4	a system for organizing and reporting student performance	√	√	√	√	√
6.5	child use materials for each specific lesson	√	√	√	√	√
6.6	supplementary charts or listing of materials needed to teach specific lessons	√	√	√	√	√
6.7	general directions for product use	√	√	√	√	√
7.0	**Specific Curriculum/Lesson Plan Components**					
	The lesson plans contain:					
7.1	program specific prerequisites to instruction	√	√	√	√	√
7.2	general goal statements	√	√	√	√	√

Exhibit 5-20 continued

	LAP	HICOMP	PORTAGE	MEMPHIS	Developmental Programming for Infants and Young Children	
7.3 specific objectives, formulated to meet PL 94-142						
7.3.1 material specified	✓	✓	✓	✓	✓	
7.3.2 behavior stated and objectively defined	✓	✓	✓	✓	✓	
7.3.3 statement of criterion performance	C	C	C	C	C	
7.4 pre-posttest procedures defined	✓	✓	✓	✓	✓	
7.5 pre-posttest criterion specified	C	C	C	C	C	
7.6 teaching procedures that are						
7.6.1 written specifically ("Do this")	✓	✓	✓		✓	
7.6.2 general strategies				✓		
7.6.3 general suggestions for games/activities	✓	✓	✓	✓	✓	
7.6.4 other ____________						
7.7 define defined instructional procedures:						
7.7.1 reinforcement		✓				
7.7.2 correction		✓				
7.7.3 demonstration		✓				
7.7.4 prompting		✓				
7.7.5 fading		✓				
7.8 sequential skill progressions, based on task/concept analysis	✓	✓	✓	✓	✓	
7.9 defined criterion for progress to next more complex sequential task	C	C	C	C	C	
7.10 structured program modification strategy for student who experiences difficulty	✓	✓	✓	✓	✓	
7.11 internal framework for modifying instructional procedures for attendant handicapping conditions					✓	
7.12 planned strategies for						
7.12.2 documenting maintenance (demonstrating skill acquisitions over time)	✓	✓	✓	✓		
7.12.2 documenting generalization (demonstrating skill acquisitions in different settings, with different materials, with different teachers, or under slightly different environmental conditions)						*
7.13 suggestions for demonstrating, or practicing, the skill in other activities		✓				*

[C]Teacher/parent instructed to set criteria.

*Request information, if available, from project director(s).

Exhibit 5-20 continued

		LAP	HICOMP	PORTAGE	MEMPHIS	Developmental Programming for Infants and Young Children
8.0	Product Quality Factors					
8.1	The product is durable	√	√	√	√	√
8.2	The layout facilitates quick scanning		√	√		√
8.3	The organization of the content is logical	√	√	√	√	√
8.4	The language is clear and comprehensible	√	√	√	√	√
9.0	Content Specificity Analysis					
	The product may be described as:					
9.1	General instructional suggestions					
9.2	Sets of objectives, and suggested activities					
9.3	Sets of objectives, and task analyses					
9.4	Task analyzed programs, containing objectives and general instructional procedures					
9.5	Task analyzed, sequenced programs containing objectives, defined instructional procedures					
9.6	Task analyzed, sequential programs, containing objectives, defined instructional procedures, and defined decision making strategies	√	√	√	√	√
10.0	Product Cost					
	Enter the cost in the column for each product that is being evaluated	See detailed report in preceeding pages of this chapter.				

Source: From *Curricula for the Severely Developmentally Retarded: A Survey and Primer on the Curriculum Development Process* by J.W. Towney and S.L. Deaton. USOE: Final Report, vol. 1, grant numbers OEG-0-72-5361 and OEG-0-75-00669, 1979. Reprinted by permission.

Part III

Closing the Gap between Assessment and Curriculum

Chapter 6

Approaches to Linking Assessment and Curriculum

Psychologists have long realized that the optimal result of the assessment of a handicapped child should be more than a number. Early attempts at linking assessment and curriculum can be seen in the pioneering work of Elizabeth Lord in the 1920s and Else Haeussermann in the early 1950s, both psychologists working with physically handicapped children. They realized that developmental assessment and curriculum planning are interdependent operations in enhancing the progress of young handicapped children. Assessment has little purpose or practical value unless it leads to individualized programming. Programming without assessment is an imprecise and wasteful activity. Thus, assessment should be a functional "baseline" or starting point for programming, as well as a vehicle for program evaluation.

Despite the critical importance of assessment-intervention linkage and the popularity of the diagnostic/prescriptive approach, relatively little information has been available for unifying assessment and the curriculum for the young exceptional child, since most educational innovations and mandates center on the school-age population. This section highlights, discusses, and illustrates several linkage methods that can be of great use to the early childhood specialist in planning systematic intervention for young handicapped children. Several models will be briefly surveyed; these vary in their application to young children but form a brief backdrop to the topic of assessment-curriculum linkages. In chapters 7 and 8, a developmental task model with direct application to early childhood special education will be presented.

THE NEED FOR ASSESSMENT-CURRICULUM LINKAGES

In order to be effective and purposeful, the assessment-intervention process must be viewed as consisting of interdependent phases, each with distinct purposes but merging with the purposes of the next: screening → identification →

comprehensive assessment → individualized programming → monitoring child progress and program effectiveness (see Figure 3-1). This critical need is highlighted by Kamii and Elliott's call (1971) for designing and using developmental measures that will more effectively match the objectives of new curricula for handicapped infants and preschoolers. Expanding the linkage concept further, Jordan et al. (1977) and Mayer (1971) emphasize the "internal consistency" that should exist between rationale, goals, objectives, materials, instructional techniques, and assessment methods.

Individualized Education Program (IEP)

The development of the Individualized Education Program (IEP) concept has intensified the need for devising reliable and effective methods of basing programming decisions on comprehensive assessment outcomes. The early childhood specialist who is basing programming on a criterion-referenced, skill-sequenced curriculum will find IEP writing relatively easy. In fact, periodic assessment of progression through a curriculum should be a natural occurrence. Skill acquisition can be informally monitored in the classroom by observing the child's day-to-day progress. Periodically, a formal skill-level assessment can be conducted to pinpoint current levels, measure retention of previously mastered skills, and allow for comparisons of growth across several functional domains. These domains might include gross- and fine-motor ability, language development, cognitive skills, social development, and adaptive behavior. Pertaining to handicapped preschoolers, the IEP format is a method for ensuring that comprehensive developmental assessment strategies function as a "profile and base for curriculum planning" (Meier, 1976, p. 190). It is truly less than optimal if the result of diagnostic assessment is merely a global developmental quotient. Actually, many of the classic assessment techniques—such as the Gesell Developmental Schedules, the Bayley Scales, and the Cattell Infant Intelligence Scale—are based on the normal progression of abilities in the nonhandicapped child. This raises two problems. First, handicapped children were excluded from the norm groups of these techniques; this makes comparisons psychometrically inappropriate. Second, handicapped children are sometimes physically unable to perform the test tasks. Scoring as failures those items that the child can not physically do—for example, items whose materials the child can not manipulate—is more a measure of the child's disability than ability. This could possibly result in an underestimation of the child's mental and functional capabilities. What is required in this case is adaptive assessment techniques. With such techniques, developmental diagnosis involves choosing adaptive assessment methods that circumvent the child's impairment as much as possible so as to obtain a functional evaluation of the child's capabilities. The outcome of this assessment then suggests individualized goals and strategies for intervention.

THE DIAGNOSTIC-PRESCRIPTIVE METHOD

The diagnostic-prescriptive approach is the most prominent assessment-curriculum linkage model. It is a method for identifying the most appropriate goals and effective instructional strategies for children as an outcome of their performance on a variety of assessment instruments.

The initial outcome of performance on assessment instruments is an index of relative standing compared with normal age peers. This is perhaps useful placement information, but not what educators need to formulate systematic intervention programs or IEPs. Optimally, assessment is just one interrelated stage of a continuum. This includes finding and precisely identifying developmental and educational delays, intervening to facilitate progress, and evaluating the effectiveness of that intervention. If any stage of this continuum is omitted, full service delivery has not been achieved. Different outcomes can be expected depending on which stages are omitted.

According to the model presented by Cromwell, Blashfield, and Strauss (1975) if the intervention stage is omitted, the continuum can function merely as a valid diagnostic appraisal and be useful only for prognosis. However, to estimate prognosis without regard to intervention is assuming the most nonnurturing environmental circumstances. Today, in light of mandated education for all handicapped children, the most nurturant environment should be assumed. If the evaluation of the intervention stage is omitted, full service delivery is not guaranteed because the continuum is utilizing an intervention with no known or specifically expected outcome. In this case, reasonable progress is only subjectively gauged. If the continuum includes only etiological information or assessment results or only the intervention and prognosis, the full-service flag is flying at half mast. A full four-stage continuum is in the interest of learners, psychologists, educators, and administrators alike.

According to Salvia and Ysseldyke (1978), the steps involved in diagnostic-prescriptive teaching include finding students with learning difficulties, specifying their strengths and weaknesses, and using this information to choose programmatic goals, methods, materials, and so on. It is implicit in this process that four critical assumptions be met:

1. Students enter a teaching situation with strengths and weaknesses.
2. These strengths and weaknesses are causally related to the acquisition of academic skills.
3. These strengths and weaknesses can be reliably and validly assessed.
4. There are well identified links between student strengths and weaknesses and the relative effectiveness of instruction (p. 445).

Much criticism has been directed at the integrity of the diagnostic-prescriptive model regarding the reliability of the assessment instruments used, the types of behaviors assessed, and the efficacy of the interventions employed (Ysseldyke & Salvia, 1974). The use of classic assessment instruments with children under 2 years of age is not very reliable in predicting later intelligence. However, the probable source of error in this correlation is worthy of hypothesis. Two groups will be considered.

For the most part, very young children who score in the average range of intelligence will continue to progress normally and will function in that range years later. A small percentage of this group might be subject to environmental influences that will cause their development to be retarded. These influences might include traumatic injury, disease, situational hearing impairment (serous otitis media), or a deprived environment. Also, a small percentage of this group might improve in their intellectual functioning. This could be due to the removal of negative environmental influences or the provision of a very stimulating environment.

Very young children who score in the mildly retarded range of intelligence stand a chance of making significant improvements. Of course, the lowest quarter of this population, such as those with severe neurological damage, can be expected to make gains at a much slower rate than their normal peers and to reach their intellectual ceilings at an earlier age. Children in this group can be expected to remain significantly retarded in their development years later. It is among the upper ¾ of the mentally retarded group that substantial gains can occur and indeed should be facilitated. One causative factor might be the adaptability of the brain in very young children. This "plasticity" theory states that the function of some damaged neural structures can be learned and carried out by other parts of the brain. This, of course, takes time and sustained educational efforts. A more general causative factor of developmental and intellectual improvements might be the combined presence of a very stimulating environment, a loving family group, and effective educational intervention. In such situations, it may be hypothesized that there is the greatest source of error in the correlation between the measured intelligence of the children when they are very young and when they are older. This, however, is a desirable consequence and not the psychometric shortcoming that it appears to be at first glance. With increasing mandated educational services for several handicapped populations, it is conceivable that in the future all developmentally disabled infants and toddlers will be entitled to a free public education. Currently, some services are available for this population, but service could be vastly expanded. Needless to say, this would be costly.

The types of behaviors assessed in developmental diagnosis have also been the center of some critical debate. It is impossible to assess all behaviors that are indicative of developmental status or intelligence. Norm-referenced measures tap a limited sample of behaviors. These measures compare a learner's performance with the performance expected from others. This results in ease of standardized administration but sets the stage for the possibility of reduced reliability on repeated testings. In general, the more items a test has, the more reliable it tends to be. Criterion-referenced measures typically sample many more behaviors. While not providing an index of relative standing, these measures test a thorough and sequenced schema of skills in a variety of areas. By clearly identifying what skills a learner does and does not have, these types of measures can provide more useful information to aid in formulating a particular student's educational program than the knowledge of how that learner compares to other students.

The efficacy of the interventions employed is perhaps the crucial determinant in the success of the diagnostic-prescriptive approach. Educational interventions must be carefully monitored to determine how well they work. If they are not successful, their continued use is a disservice to the learners.

The crux of the diagnostic-prescriptive debate centers on two different approaches to assessing and programming for children with developmental-learning disabilities: ability training and task analysis.

Ability Training

Proponents of the ability-training approach to assessment and intervention believe that the learning of academic skills, such as reading, depend upon the intact development of specific, underlying abilities or psychological "processes" that are inferred from behavior, such as figure-ground problems, auditory-perceptual deficits, and visual-sequential memory difficulties. Once dysfunctions in those underlying processes have been identified through the administration of batteries of psychoeducational tests, remedial treatment programs are prescribed under the assumption that they will enhance the deficit psychological processes and thus enable a child to learn. The training of abilities or processes is viewed as a prerequisite to academic success. However, relatively little research supports the effectiveness of methods that purport to train underlying abilities. Children are often placed in such experimental programs but excluded from programs that have been demonstrated to increase observable skill development.

The ability-training approach directs remedial intervention to areas that are not the immediately relevant educational problem. After successful ability training, the student must still learn the deficit academic skills.

Task Analysis

Specialists who advocate a task-analytic viewpoint generally reject the belief that dysfunction in underlying abilities can be accurately identified and effectively trained. Instead, developmental learning problems are seen as caused by the absence of specific observable skills and enabling strategies for completing complex tasks although developmental processes encompass these skills. In this approach, assessment strategies focus on identifying each child's range of functional skills (strengths and weaknesses) so that instructional strategies can be implemented to develop those functional behaviors that are necessary prerequisites to learning. Thus, instruction is designed to develop specific behavioral skills rather than "unseen" abilities or processes. The task-analytic model has been characterized as the "test-teach-test" concept. First, the teacher analyzes the particular skills a child has or has not acquired within the developmental sequence. This breakdown of skills is known as task analysis. Once the assessment is completed, the specialist then teaches mastery of the undeveloped skills. After a period of instruction, criterion-referenced tests again evaluate mastery of the developmental tasks and, thus, of educational and developmental progress.

Despite the controversy surrounding diagnostic-prescriptive teaching, the general approach is widely used and supported in work with school-age children. The task-analytic method appears to offer the most reliable, practical, and justifiable alternative to linking assessment and programming. Developmental task analysis applies the diagnostic-prescriptive method most effectively in work with handicapped infants and preschoolers.

THE DEVELOPMENTAL TASK CONCEPT: CLOSING THE GAP

The diagnostic-prescriptive model views assessment as the vehicle for profiling a child's pattern of strengths and weaknesses across multiple functional areas. The profile then serves as a "blueprint" for individualized instructional planning. Observable skills and measurable objectives are the keys to the accuracy and efficacy of this approach. However, one of the major problems with the diagnostic-prescriptive model is the lack of similarity between the behaviors assessed and the skills taught. Most often, the assessment and programming approaches are not based on a common framework.

Both to provide a "unifying bridge" and to make the diagnostic-prescriptive approach much more relevant to intervention with infants and preschoolers, successful early intervention programs operate from what is commonly called a developmental task approach. In fact, preschool programs that combine comprehensive skill analysis with a normal developmental approach have been called "developmental prescriptive" (Anastasiow & Mansergh, 1975).

Although there are wide variations of this model, in general the developmental task approach assumes that development is a process consisting of a series of invariantly sequenced, increasingly more sophisticated operations or tasks in all functional areas that arise at certain developmental stages when "readiness" is most sensitive to stimulation and experience. Success in acquiring each developmental skill or mastering each operation is a vital prerequisite for the attainment of more complex capabilities later in the developmental process. The application of this philosophy to curriculum planning can be summarized in the following manner:

> The *developmental tasks* approach begins with sequences of normal development. Curricula provide hierarchical sequences of tasks, skills, or content that are derived from normative information about the ways children develop or from developmental analysis of task complexity, usually related to chronological age or sequence of skills. Content areas selected in this approach tend to be broad categories of child development that are subsequently sequenced into objectives representing hierarchical steps in maturation or in task analysis. (Jordan et al., 1977, p. 135)

In effect, the developmental task concept is extremely useful for generating educational objectives, providing a framework for broad-spectrum curriculum development, timing structured stimulation and learning experiences, and monitoring child progress. However, its major practical contribution becomes evident in providing a common frame of reference for developmental assessment and developmental programming, that is, the sequence of developmental tasks. In work with handicapped infants and preschoolers, the developmental task framework provides a structured sequence of goals and activities that are age-related and functionally important for effective growth and learning. In addition, by enabling specialists to determine what functional skills children have in their repertoires and what skills need to be developed through planned learning experiences, the developmental tasks provide a common reference point for diagnosis and intervention. Finally, the sequence of developmental tasks provides a series of functional goals that provide cues to enable teachers to design individualized, adaptive learning activities for various dysfunctions, that is, language, neuro-motor, cognitive, and personal-social.

LINKING DEVELOPMENTAL ASSESSMENT AND INTERVENTION: A REVIEW OF MODELS

The growing cooperative involvement of parents, teachers, psychologists, and teams of other specialists in planning treatment programs for young handicapped children underscores the pressing need for devising practical methods of linking developmental diagnosis and curriculum planning. The more precise the match between a child's pattern of capabilities and the plan and method of instruction, the more effective the total learning experience will be.

The IEP highlights and describes each child's range of "individual differences" or needs and then suggests curricular goals and instructional strategies that most effectively match those needs so that development and learning can be enhanced. In effect, the IEP is a vehicle that effectively links assessment and intervention. Specifically, it matches the needs of the handicapped child as reflected in current levels of developmental functioning with appropriate objectives and teaching strategies (see Exhibit 6-1). The following points characterize the process and content of the IEP development in early special education:

- Use comprehensive, adaptive, and nondiscriminatory methods of assessing current developmental progress; such methods should cover multiple functional areas and derive from varied sources of information.
- Design an IEP as a direct outcome of the assessment procedures that detail annual and short-term developmental objectives, as well as specific instructional strategies, materials, and services required for each child's developmental needs.
- Devise functional criteria common to both assessment and teaching for effectively monitoring both child progress and program effectiveness.

Person-Environment Interaction Models

The attitude that different children develop best when treatment and instruction are matched to their individual developmental differences—that is, in a *person-environment interaction model*—is crucial in work with young handicapped children. Although research over several years has failed to demonstrate the effectiveness of any one instructional approach, *structured* educational methods using well-defined goals and strategies have the best track record with both normal and handicapped children.

The Aptitude-Treatment Interaction Model

Diagnostic-prescriptive methods that seek to match assessed child needs with differential methods of treatment and to evaluate their effectiveness in promoting development have been labelled aptitude-treatment interaction (ATI) models. The ATI concept is primarily a research and evaluative method that seeks to identify relationships or interactions between a person's range of individual differences and the most effective method of instruction for that person's needs (Hunt & Sullivan, 1974). Most often, this process takes the form of administering assessment measures to delineate a child's developmental skills and personal technique of approaching problems, called *cognitive style*.

Exhibit 6-1 An Example of a Single-Domain IEP for a Child

DEVELOPMENTAL AREA: *Cognitive/Readiness*
DEVELOPMENTAL LEVEL: *42-48 months*

CHILD *Paul E.*
MEASURES: *Gesell and LAP Scales*

DEVELOPMENTAL OBJECTIVE	INSTRUCTIONAL METHODS	CHILD PROGRESS EVALUATION			
		ASSESSMENT METHODS	PRE	POST	GAIN
1. Attends & listens during focused tasks	Physical-verbal prompts in low distraction, structured setting with simlified activities	Time-sampling anecdotal records			
2. Scans activities in an organized way before responding	self-instructional steps with teacher guidance & prompts in simple tasks	Duration measures Anecdotal records			
3. Copies & traces increasingly complex geometric forms	Large colorful form cards and templates	LAP Profile			
4. Names, identifies & matches a variety of shapes	one-one setting DLM materials	LAP Profile			
5. Names, identifies & matches primary & secondary colors	one-one setting DLM materials	LAP Profile			
6. Names & identifies & classifies pictured & concrete objects	one-one setting DLM materials	teacher developmental checklist			
7. Explains action & relationships in stories	one-one and small group (2-5) settings; Peabody Lang. Kit	Gesell Agent-actions Anecdotal records			
8. Demonstrates understanding of positional & comparative concepts	one-one and small group settings	CSAB Battery teacher checklist			
9. Counts objects 1-10	one-one setting; pair verbal and motor behaviors	CSAB Battery teacher checklist			
10. Identifies missing parts in pictured situations	one-one setting structure attention	Binet Missing Parts			
11. Defines objects in terms of use	one-one setting small group	CSAB; Peabody Lang. Kit			
12. Draws basic man form and places parts on incomplete man	one-one setting use models & prompts	Gesell & Binet tasks			

Once a pattern of skills, needs, or problem solving is identified, a teaching approach or plan is designed to instruct the child in the most effective manner to accomplish various individualized objectives. For example, some children who are highly impulsive and distractible in approaching a task often are unsuccessful because the instructional environment is too distracting or the task itself is too complex. On the other hand, many children who are independent learners and who naturally approach a task carefully and systematically might be restricted in learning if the educational approach is too highly structured. Therefore, psychologists and educators often recommend that impulsive and distractible learners should be taught through a highly structured and directive approach while independent, reflective learners might progress better with a student-centered, open-classroom method. If a learner with a particular set of needs or characteristics develops better under one instructional method compared to a different approach, an aptitude-treatment interaction has occurred. Figure 6-1 provides a hypothetical illustration of an ATI showing the high and low performance of impulsive and reflective learners under two instructional methods.

The BPE Model

A more practical version of the ATI or person-environment interaction model is the BPE approach (Hunt & Sullivan, 1974). The concept $B = P \times E$ summarizes the statement that behavior (B) is the result of the person (P) and the environment (E). In educational terms, Learning (B) results from matching child needs, skills, and characteristics (P) to the instructional approach (E). This statement reminds us that learning can occur only when we tailor instruction to the current developmental levels of children. In work with young handicapped children, this model directs us to use adaptive materials and an individualized approach that are appropriate to the developmental skills in the child's repertoire.

It is no coincidence that a written IEP incorporates each of the factors included in the BPE model. For example, effective IEP development is based upon a comprehensive assessment of a child's capabilities across multiple fields of behavior (P). Then, short-term and annual objectives are generated that match the child's functional levels and represent sequential behavior or tasks to be mastered (B). Finally, individualized instructional strategies and special services are arranged so that effective learning can occur (E).

Thus, the BPE model is really a useful conceptual framework for the initial stages of planning educational programs that link assessed needs with individualized goals and strategies.

Table 6-1 shows how the BPE model could be employed to design differential methods for facilitating the same behavior in two children functioning at different developmental levels. Thus, a 1½-year-old normal infant could be effectively encouraged to play independently with objects in the child's world if the teacher or

Figure 6-1 Aptitude-Treatment Interaction Model (ATI)

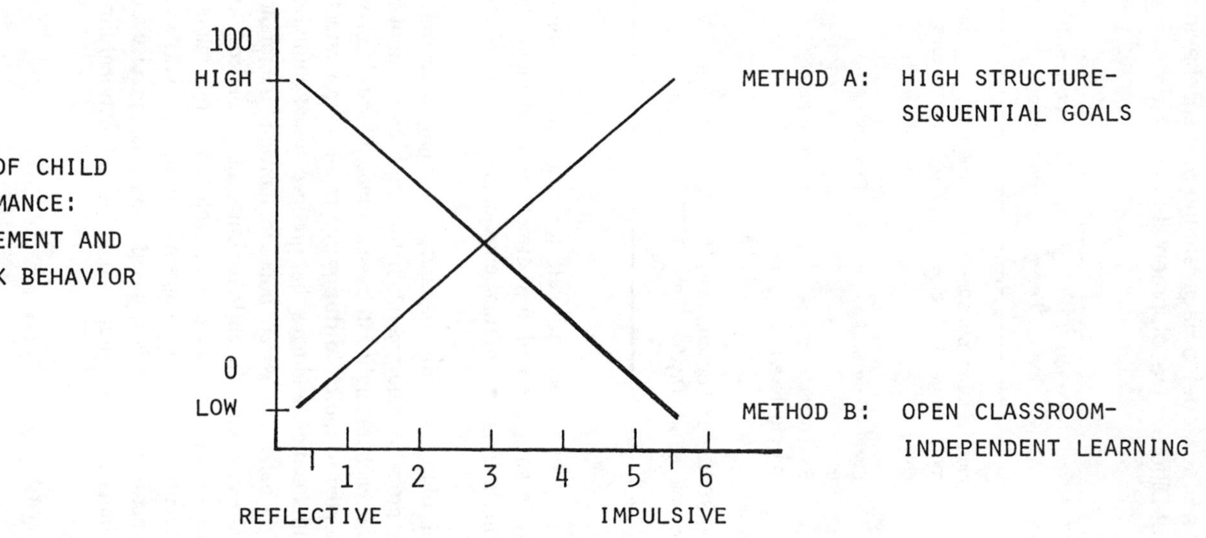

1. Student standing low on individual difference dimension learns better by method B.
2. Student standing high on individual difference dimension learns better under method A.

Table 6-1 Design of a BPE Model to Facilitate the Same Behavior in Two Children at Different Developmental Levels

Behavior (B) *(Goals)*	*Person (P)* *(Developmental Level)*	*Environment (E)* *(Instructional Method)*
Independent play in exploring objects in the environment	Normal infant sensorimotor stage (21 mo. level)	Free play High-interest toys Low structure
	Cerebral palsied infant Sensorimotor stage (11 mo. level)	Planned play Adaptive toys High structure

Source: Adapted from the BPE model described by Hunt, D.E. & Sullivan, E.V. *Between psychology and education.* New York: Dryden Press, 1974.

parent establishes a free play period with selected colorful, high-interest, and movable toys. Very little structure and few directions or demands would be required to encourage the development of this behavior and thus to promote natural learning experiences.

In contrast, a 3-year-old, physically handicapped infant functioning at the 1-year level would most probably require a much more highly structured approach. For instance, parents and teachers might establish planned periods of play wherein adaptive toys are presented to the child during the one-to-one interaction. Enlarged toys, objects with handles, and toys that produce sound could be deliberately placed in the child's hand. The parent could then prompt the infant to shake the bell or rattle and praise or reward the child for imitating the desired action. Eye contact and attention to the task could also be developed in this manner.

Finally, by using a BPE-type model in program planning, specialists can ensure that educational treatment is goal-directed; based upon clear, precise analyses of the child's needs; and individually adapted to the child's functional limitations.

The Structure of the Intellect Model

Focusing on the specific rather than the general nature of intelligence, Guilford (1967) formulated the Structure of the Intellect (SOI) model, a theoretical model of cognitive abilities consisting of more than 120 different factors. The SOI model presented three structural dimensions of the thinking process: content, operations, and products. For example, one type of cognitive operation might involve analyzing a scrambled set of letters in order to determine how many words could be formed from them. In this task, the person would use convergent thinking (operation) to analyze figural and semantic information (content) to produce different words (products).

Although complex and somewhat cumbersome, the SOI model presents a useful way of analyzing and visualizing the subcomponents of thinking. Guilford asserts that the levels of cognitive skills and operations can be assessed and developed through structured thinking. Thus, Meeker (1969) devised a method of analyzing tasks from traditional intelligence tests and determining how each matched the components of the SOI model. Then, by profiling the strengths and weaknesses of children on the matched test activities and SOI factors, specific goals and lesson plans were generated to remedy and enhance deficits in cognitive operations like memory and convergent thinking involving abstract and concrete information.

Exhibit 6-2 illustrates one such remedial plan involving letter-number memory deficits. In this plan, performance on traditional intelligence test items is related to a model of cognitive process. This assessment-curriculum linkage forms the basis for prescriptive teaching activities.

The Functional Education Evaluation Model

As described in chapter 3, Haeussermann (1958) and Jedrysek et al. (1972) have developed a functional educational evaluation format that permits one to adapt assessment to the young child's impairments in order to survey intact developmental functioning across several sensory and cognitive areas. The results of this "adaptive-capacity" evaluation serve as a curriculum guide, that is, a developmental profile that displays strengths and weaknesses and suggests instructional goals and strategies. In effect, one assesses the qualitative aspects of a child's capabilities and delineates the levels that represent the child's current stages of developmental functioning. Tasks are arranged sequentially along a developmental continuum. A child's performance is evaluated both upward and downward along the sequence until a level is reached that represents the child's current level of maturity or operation given the disabilities. This level then establishes a target for curriculum planning and instruction. The educational evaluation is "a systematic sampling strategy across the child's functional skills and problem areas with the primary objective of . . . determining the kinds of training and experience that will best promote his own adaptive functional abilities . . . and . . . the special circumstances which are needed to create conditions for learning in the handicapped child" (Haeussermann, 1958, p. ix). Simply put, the functional evaluation determines the instructional plan.

Exhibit 6-2 A Simulated Goal-Linkage Using Stanford-Binet Tasks and Structure of the Intellect Factors (Meeker, 1969)

Child Michelle C.A. 8-3 M.A. 7-2

Problems: Short attention span; impulsivity; incomplete work; low reading comprehension

Assessment-Based Deficits:

PROCESS	*BINET-SOI FACTOR*
1. Visual analysis of pictures and designs	MA VI 3 (CFU-MSI)
2. Analyze and reproduce figural designs	MA V, VII 4 (EFS-NFU)
3. Identifying pictorial differences	MA V 5 (CFC-EFU)
4. Identify and state generic categories	MA VII-2; VIII 4 (CMT)

Instructional Goals and Strategies:

A. Develop selective attention and scanning for relevant features in pictures and designs; use physical, verbal and manual prompts to promote on task attention. Employ social praise and tokens for correct work.

B. Reproduce figural designs using a fading procedure which first employs a "tracing" activity then a free reproduction (VMI materials).

C. Use training activities to develop visual analysis of pictures; use a stimulus card and a multiple-choice format of selecting a design from an array which matches the stimulus design. (Motor-free visual perception tests and MFFT materials.)

D. Use pictures and objects to enhance the ability to group concepts into generic categories and to state the reasoning behind the grouping.

Source: Adaptation based upon Meeker's SOI model. Meeker, M.N. *The structure of the intellect.* Columbus, OH: Charles Merrill Publishing Company, 1969.

The Developmental Task Analysis Model

Valett (1967, 1972, 1978) has taken the developmental task concept and formulated a practical plan of operation for developmentally disabled children that pragmatically integrates assessment and programming. In this approach, the tasks, skills, and processes sampled on traditional performance tests are arranged in a developmental sequence or task analysis. This developmental task analysis contains skills that are viewed as prerequisites for subsequent, more complex learning. The sequencing of skills covers multiple developmental domains to facilitate comprehensive, whole-child assessment, that is, motor skills, perceptual skills, language skills, personal-social skills, and thinking skills. Thus, the approach presents a very clear and functional process for determining which skills are currently intact, which skills need to be learned next, and what are the differential strategies and instructional conditions necessary for learning to occur. Most successful early intervention programs now incorporate some form of developmental task analysis within their operations.

In Valett's (1972) view,

> The task analyst is concerned with making a systematic observation of the pupil's behavior in a specific learning situation. His emphasis is on determining what it is that the child is to learn and just how well he is doing. He must then decide whether the task expected of the child is an appropriate one, considering his total stage of development and environmental circumstances . . . on the basis of this evaluation the task analyst then proceeds to suggest or design interventions which will enhance the pupil's learning and human development. (p. 129)

Specifically, developmental task analysis is a process of identifying and analyzing children's ranges of acquired (+), absent (−), and emerging (±) developmental skills within multiple functional areas for the purpose of establishing "developmental targets" or goals for individualized curriculum planning. Exhibit 6-3 provides an example of how, in Valett's approach, an observed deficit in visual integration skills becomes an individualized goal for instructional planning.

A Developmental Task Analysis Model for Infant Stimulation

In order to formulate an infant curriculum, Meier (1976) suggested a practical format of sequencing the tasks included in the Bayley Scales of Infant Development or the Gesell Developmental Schedules to create a task analysis. Landmark or global tasks along the sequence are viewed as entry, intermediate, or terminal objectives. Teachers can add developmental behaviors between the entry or terminal objectives to extend the task analysis. This method assumes that tra-

Exhibit 6-3 Form Illustrating Use of Developmental Task Analysis Model

Skill 12
VISUAL INTEGRATION

Pupil's name ______________

Organizing and meaningfully integrating visual stimuli, parts, and impressions; providing visual closure and generalizations (common objects: clothes, tools, utensils, symbols)

EDUCATIONAL DOMAIN: Figural RLD TAXONOMY: Visual memory

Test criterion scores

	Pretest		Posttest	
	Date	Score	Date	Score
ITPA--visual association				
WISC--picture completion				
ITPA--visual closure				
Other				

	Evaluation	
	Plus	Minus
DA 5 Draw a line from the picture of the spoon to the thing that goes best with a spoon. Tell me why it goes best.		
Developmental learning tasks EASY: The first object above is a nail. Tell me what the other pictures are. The spoon does not go with the nail. What does it go with? Why?		
MODERATE:		
DIFFICULT:		
DA 7 Something is missing in this picture of a door. What is it?		
Developmental learning tasks EASY: Look at the door in this room where we are sitting. Tell me the parts you see. What does the door have that is missing in the picture above?		

Source: Valett, R.E. *Developing cognitive abilities.* St. Louis, Mo.: C.V. Mosby Co., 1978. Reprinted with permission.

Table 6-2 An Example of Meier's Sequencing of Behaviors from the Gesell and Bayley Scales to Form a Developmental Task Analysis of Infant Language Skills

---

Entry behaviors:

1. Differentiation of vocalization from cry
2. Excites, breathes heavily, strains
3. Laughs
4. Turns head to sound

1. Responds with mouth movements, smile, or vocalization to familiar sounds
2. Squeals
3. Vocalizes to toys, mirror images
4. Vocalizes attitudes—pleasure, satisfaction, etc.

1. Uses sound to localize in turning head after falling object
2. Grunts and growls
3. Bangs objects in play
4. Reflects a facial mimic

1. Interest in sound production (object)
2. Vocalizes four syllables
3. Lip closure; vocalizes—m-m-m cry
4. Polysyllabic sounds—vowels

Terminal behaviors:

1. Vocalizes similar sounds in response to familiar sounds
2. Attends without distractibility to unfamiliar sounds—may vocalize
3. Says da-da or equivalent (ba-ba, ma-ma)
4. Listens selectively to familiar words (name, baby, bottle, etc.)

Source: Meier, J.H. *Developmental and learning disabilities.* Baltimore, Md.: University Park Press, 1976. Reprinted with permission.

ditional norm-referenced scales like those of Bayley and Gesell can serve as a "profile and base for curriculum planning" (Meier, 1976, p. 190). Thus, the series of developmental behaviors included in traditional scales becomes both a profile of strengths and weaknesses and a curriculum framework (see Table 6-2).

Meier's infant assessment-curriculum linkage concept has been operationalized in many commercially available developmental curricula, such as the Infant Learning Accomplishment Profile (Sanford, 1978) and Developmental Programming for Infants and Young Children (Schafer et al., 1976).

SUMMARY

Effective education for handicapped infants and preschoolers rests upon common assessment and curriculum practices. The diagnostic-prescriptive approach is widely used, but the information derived often has been of limited use to the special educator. Yet, the demands of P.L. 94-142 require a more precise and educationally relevant merger of these two operations for IEP development.

Various approaches—such as the person-environment interaction models, the structure of the intellect model, and the functional educational evaluation model—provide useful guidelines for linking assessment and intervention. However, the developmental task analysis model advances a common framework for testing and teaching, that is, developmental sequencing and task analysis. Thus, the developmental task model provides the most reliable and practical basis for prescribing preschool programs.

Chapter 7

A Developmental Model for Prescriptive Linkage

Assessment of infants and young children is known as developmental diagnosis. This operation is a comprehensive, specific process of analyzing, describing, and profiling each child's range of developmental skills across multiple behavioral areas. Like the Haeussermann Educational Evaluation (1958), it is qualitative and seeks to identify current levels of developmental functioning to provide a baseline for curriculum planning.

Similarly, structured early intervention is a continuous process of developmental curriculum goal-planning based on continuous developmental diagnosis. Most successful handicapped preschool programs (Jordan et al., 1977) operate from a developmental task model and stress the importance of assessment-curriculum linkages as the foundation for effective individualized educational programming. Once again, the sequence of developmental stages or tasks provides the unifying "bridge" for assessment and intervention.

One of the major differences among approaches regarding assessment and programming concerns the use of curriculum-imbedded scales versus traditional norm-referenced developmental measures. Both approaches are useful and have advantages, depending on the particular assessment purpose. For example, traditional measures such as the Bayley (1969) and Gesell (1949) scales are relatively reliable instruments that provide a comprehensive assessment of the child's developmental status. However, the behavioral sequences and tasks within the scales are often not completely appropriate for severely handicapped children. Thus, they do not, by themselves, provide an adequate basis for individualized programming.

In the same manner, curriculum-imbedded scales, like the Developmental Programming Materials (Schafer, 1976), contain task-analyzed sequences of developmental skills. They are more detailed in scope and, therefore, appropriate for infants and lower-functioning children. The major problem with these scales, however, is their undetermined reliability and validity and the fact that most psychologists and diagnostic specialists are relatively unfamiliar with them.

The most reasonable and effective solution to this dilemma seems to be the use of a multimeasure, multisource approach to assessing and programming for young children. This means combining traditional scales, curriculum measures, behavior ratings and subjective judgments of adults in order to ensure adequate sampling of behaviors, reliable estimates, and precise and useful child programming data. In fact, the results of behavior ratings, actual child performance, and curriculum estimates are often in close agreement for handicapped children if similar developmental behaviors are assessed (Bagnato & Neisworth, in press; MacTurk & Neisworth, 1978; Diebold et al., 1978). Thus, it is proposed that traditional developmental scales, when matched with developmentally sequenced curricula, can help to forge practical assessment-curriculum linkages for young handicapped children. This method reflects the influences of Valett (1972) and Haeussermann (1958) regarding developmental task analysis and adaptive-process assessment.

THE PURPOSE OF ASSESSMENT

Assessment occurs in instructional situations for various purposes, but mainly for making decisions about a child's capabilities as they affect the nature of the child's educational program. The particular decision determines the types of behaviors assessed and the kinds of tests used. Tests are generally administered for four major purposes:

1. screening and identification
2. assessing child capabilities comprehensively
3. designing individualized instructional plans
4. monitoring child progress and program effectiveness

It is clear that these purposes of assessment are sequenced and that each serves as a prerequisite for the succeeding one. Thus, they are interdependent operations. For example, screening procedures aid in the identification of suspected developmental problems and serve to focus more comprehensive diagnostic measures on the nature of the specific dysfunctions. Once profiled, these more comprehensive assessments across multiple areas function as baselines to guide individualized goal-planning. Finally, both child progress and program effectiveness are evaluated according to the gains made in deficit areas as well as improvements in the quality of adaptive functioning. In establishing linkage to programming, the choice of measures for diagnostic-prescriptive purposes should be guided by practical considerations related to the nature, content, and goals of the curriculum of a particular program.

A PRACTICAL SYSTEM FOR DESIGNING DEVELOPMENTAL LINKAGES

Criterion-based developmental assessment and intervention exemplifies the view that evaluation should be imbedded in the process of educational planning. "Criterion-referenced tests have been suggested as more effective measuring instruments . . . for situations in which it is desirable to give teachers information that will help them in their teaching. This permits input for educational planning since the results indicate at what level and in what area the student is performing" (Vane, 1976, p. 39).

As in the educational evaluation model examined previously, the elements of "level" and "area" are fundamental to the assessment-curriculum linkage system called *developmental linkages*. In this system, developmental assessment is systematic, flexible, and qualitative in nature. Specifically, once the child's probable range of functioning has been determined, tasks are presented to probe more completely the skills that have or have not been acquired along the developmental sequence. Adaptive modifications of ways to administer certain tasks to children with language, visual, hearing, and neuro-motor impairments are employed to further individualize the process (Haeussermann, 1958; Chase, 1975; Dubose et al., 1979).

The assessment proceeds until sequences of fully acquired (+), absent (−), and emerging (±) skills are determined across major functional areas: language, motor, cognitive, and personal-social. From the "profile" of capabilities, developmental deficits or *targets* requiring structured intervention are detailed. These targets form the basis of the preschool child's Individualized Educational Program (IEP); structured programming is designed to enhance deficit areas by tailoring instruction to the child's current developmental style and capitalizing on the child's individual strengths. Several measures should be used (performance, interview, and ratings) to increase the reliability of these estimates of developmental functioning.

Traditional Scales as Criterion Measures

In this approach, comprehensive developmental scales like those of Bayley (1969) and Gesell (1949) are conceptualized and administered as criterion-based measures that sample a range of sequenced, prerequisite skills in language, personal-social, motor, and cognitive areas. Similarly, many preschool curricula (Quick et al., 1974a, 1974b; Forsberg, Neisworth, & Laub, 1977a, 1977b; Shearer, Billingsley, Frohman, Hilliard, & Johnson, 1971) contain developmentally sequenced behaviors comparable to those appearing in existing scales (see Table 7-1). Thus, a child's pattern of deficits on a series of standardized developmental tasks reflects that child's individual pattern and range of functional

Table 7-1 Correspondence between Developmental Areas Common to Both Traditional Scales and Commonly Employed Preschool Curricula

	DEVELOPMENTAL SCALES				DEVELOPMENTAL PRESCHOOL CURRICULA			
AREA	GESELL	LAP	GRIFFITHS	BAYLEY	HICOMP	MEMPHIS	PORTAGE	DEVELOPMENTAL PROGRAMMING
LANGUAGE	Language	Language	Hearing and Speech	Mental	Communication	Language	Language	Language
PERSONAL/ SOCIAL	Personal/ Social	Social Self-help	Personal/ Social	Infant Behavior Record	Own-care	Personal/ Social	Self-help Socialization	Social/ Emotional Self-help
MOTOR	Gross & Fine Motor	Gross & Fine Motor	Eye-hand Coordination Locomotor	Mental/ Motor	Motor	Gross & Fine Motor	Motor	Perceptual/ Fine Motor Gross Motor
COGNITIVE	Adaptive	Cognitive	Performance Skills	Mental	Problem-solving	Perceptuo-Cognitive	Cognitive	Cognition

Source: Bagnato, S.J., & Neisworth, J.T. Between assessment and intervention: Forging an assessment/curriculum linkage for the handicapped preschooler. *Child Care Quarterly,* 1979, *8*(3), 179-195. Reprinted with permission.

skills. These deficits can be considered as "curriculum-entry objectives" that are developmentally appropriate for emphasis in program planning. In this way, developmental assessment guides and supplements the preschool teacher's formulation of individualized goals and strategies.

Again, it should be noted that traditional developmental scales are not as task-specific as the developmental curricula employed. However, by using these familiar scales, developmental school psychologists can provide preschool teachers and infant stimulation specialists with a range of general targets for individual child programming. These targets make curriculum planning more precise and can be adjusted or modified as needed by the teacher when the child is entered into the curriculum.

Table 7-2 presents an outline illustration of the sequence of steps involved in creating developmental assessment-curriculum linkages in terms of a sequence of goals.

Goal 1—Select Developmental Scales According to Curriculum Content

As a starting point for curriculum planning, developmental scales must be selected on the basis of their congruence with tasks in the curriculum employed in the preschool program. If the developmental task sequence and the functional domains that are covered are similar, then more useful assessment-curriculum linkages can be generated. In practice, the psychologist and special educator "test to the teaching."

In addition, it is helpful if there is a match between assessment content and instructional content at each level of the curriculum. Thus, scales should be selected that ensure comprehensive sampling of all behaviors at each level of the curriculum. This practice implements the multimeasure, multisource approach, which is vital for a reliable appraisal of young handicapped children.

Table 7-3 briefly illustrates how combinations of child performance, teacher judgment, parent judgment, and curriculum measures can provide comprehensive coverage of developmental functioning at both general and specific levels of a curriculum. This practice of selecting multiple measure batteries that sample congruent developmental skills should not be neglected. In this manner, a more complete and accurate appraisal of the handicapped preschooler is possible, taking into account various skills that are situation-specific and therefore not necessarily evident in structured assessment situations. Parents, teachers, psychologists, and other specialists thus become valuable allies in the developmental diagnostic-prescriptive process.

Table 7-2 Outline Illustration of the Sequence of Steps in Creating Developmental Linkages

Goal 1. Select Developmental Scales According to Curriculum Content

Goal 2. Determine Developmental Levels Across Functional Areas

C.A. = 43 months		
	MOTOR	= 18-21 mo.
	ADAPTIVE	= 11-15 mo.
	LANGUAGE	= 9-12 mo.
	PERSONAL-SOCIAL	= 12 mo.

Goal 3. Identify "Developmental Ceilings" in Each Functional Area

Imitates common words	±
Speaks 3-4 words	-
Drinks cup-no spilling	±
Indicates wet pants	-
Jumps both feet	-
Attempts cube tower	-
Finds hidden objects	±
Goes to location	±

Goal 4. Match Developmental Ceiling Tasks to Curriculum Target-Objectives in Each Functional Area

TEST	CURRICULUM
Imitates common words	Imitates familiar words
Speaks 3-4 words	Uses words in speech
Drinks cup-no spilling	Drinks from cup-unassisted
Indicates wet pants	Gestures for wet pants and toilet
Jumps both feet	Jumps off floor/both feet
Attempts cube tower	Stacks two cubes
Finds hidden objects	Looks for object out of sight
Goes to location	Follows direction to go to location

Source: Bagnato, S.J. & Neisworth, J.T. Between assessment and intervention: Forging an assessment/curriculum linkage for the handicapped preschooler. *Child Care Quarterly*, 1979, *8*(3), 179-195. Reprinted with permission.

Table 7-3 An Example of Assessment Coverage at All Curriculum Levels via a Multimeasure, Multisource Approach

Suitable Tests	*HICOMP Curriculum Sequence*	
PODS, Rating Scales	Motor Domain (year level 2-3)	(Domain Level)
PODS, PAR, DDST	M-3-2 Fine Motor	(Subdomain Level)
	M3-2.1 Draws circle, imitating adult	(Target Level)
	M3-2.2 Draws vertical line from model	
BSID, BDS, LAP	M3-2.3 Draws horizontal line from model	
Competency-based	M3-2.4 Draws recognizable face	
curriculum checklists	M3-2.5 Builds bridge—3 cubes—imitated	
	M3-2.6 Builds tower 9-10 cubes	

PODS: Perceptions of Developmental Skills Profile—teacher judgments
PAR: Preschool Attainment Record—parent judgments
DDST: Denver Developmental Screening Test—general child performance
BSID: Bayley Scales of Infant Development—comprehensive child performance
GDS: Gesell Developmental Schedules—comprehensive child performance
LAP: Learning Accomplishment Profile—curriculum performance

Source: Bagnato, S.J. & Neisworth, J.T. Between assessment and intervention: Forging an assessment/curriculum linkage for the handicapped preschooler. *Child Care Quarterly*, 1979, *8*(3), 179-195. Reprinted with permission.

Goal 2—Determine Developmental Levels Across Functional Areas

After an appropriate multisource assessment battery has been selected in congruence with curriculum content, a comprehensive developmental analysis can be achieved for each child. Most developmental scales sample both general developmental domains and various specific tasks comparable to those included in most preschool curricula. Thus, administration of norm-referenced developmental scales is useful for specifying a general developmental range or level. This analysis identifies the handicapped child's range and pattern of current capabilities across all functional areas. As a result, each child can be entered at an individually appropriate level of the curriculum in each developmental area. Tables 7-4 and 7-5 illustrate how norm-referenced developmental diagnosis operates when it is curriculum-based and multisource in nature. Thus, the child's entrance into appropriate curriculum levels can proceed from general to specific. This general developmental analysis reflects the norm-referenced nature and purpose of the developmental scales.

Table 7-4 An Example of Developmental Diagnosis Reflected in Congruent Assessment and Curriculum Domains

Child—C.A. = 43 mo. Disability = Down's Syndrome

Gesell Developmental Schedules (Ames et al., 1979)		*Project Memphis Curriculum*	
Personal-Social	15 mo.	Personal-Social	15 mo.
Gross-Motor	18-21 mo.	Gross-Motor	18 mo.
Fine-Motor	11-15 mo.	Fine-Motor	15 mo.
Language	9-12 mo.	Language	12 mo.
Adaptive	12 mo.	Perceptive-Cognitive	9 mo.

Table 7-5 An Example of Multimeasure Multisource Developmental Diagnosis

Child—C.A. = 43 mo. Disability—Down's Syndrome

Developmental Measures	*Level*	*Source*
Gesell Developmental Schedules (Ames et al., 1979)	12-15 months	Child Performance
Developmental Profile (Alpern & Boll, 1972)	18 months	Parent Judgment
Comp-Curriculum (Neisworth et al., 1980)	12 months	Curriculum Progress
Perceptions of Developmental Skills (Bagnato et al., 1977)	15 months	Teacher Judgment

Goal 3—Identify Developmental Ceilings in Each Functional Area

Norm-referenced developmental assessment described in Goal 2 is a vital step in the process of individualized curriculum planning. However, the creation of sets of curriculum target objectives depends on the criterion-based use of traditional developmental scales. This is one of many points at which the expertise of a developmental school psychologist can be invaluable to the early special educator in initial IEP planning. The criterion-based utility of most developmental scales, i.e., the sequence of prerequisite tasks across the age range within each functional area, is frequently overlooked.

Capitalizing on the developmental sequence for prescriptive purposes, the psychologist next identifies a child's individual "developmental ceilings" in each area of functioning, that is, the child's highest point of developed skills (± on specific tasks) or *transitional level* occurring within the developmental ranges determined in Goal 2. Specifically, those developmental tasks that the child marginally completes (±) or fails to complete (−) within the child's developmental range are identified. This sequence of ceilings then specifies a range of absent or emerging functional skills that are practically viewed as prerequisite, curriculum-entry targets that need to be emphasized in programming and instruction. In essence, a kind of item analysis is conducted on each child's developmental performance on the scales. Thus, handicap-appropriate developmental targets are provided by the developmental linkage process (see Exhibit 7-1).

Goal 4—Match Developmental Ceiling Tasks to Curriculum Objectives in Each Functional Area

The linking of the developmental diagnostic "targets" to similar curriculum-entry objectives is an important final step. Since traditional scales were not designed primarily as prescriptive instruments, no clear one-to-one relationship is apparent between all assessment ceilings and all objectives in a curriculum. Despite this shortcoming, the developmental basis of similar test and curriculum tasks across all areas allows many entry linkages to be selected at some point in the developmental task analysis. Once instruction has begun, certain targets may be modified at the teacher's discretion if they are too easy or difficult.

Developmental linkages are accomplished simply by matching those test tasks that were failed (−) or partially completed (±) to congruent curriculum objectives that are included within the child's current developmental range of functioning. This match is determined in a semisubjective manner according to the relative difficulty of the matching tasks, their similar wording, and which behaviors the child has to demonstrate to complete each task. For example, completing a three-hole formboard task (○ □ Δ) is basically the same as a "match to sample" activity involving circle, square, and triangle shapes.

Thus, the outcome of this developmental linkage procedure is the creation of a set of individually appropriate, curriculum-entry objectives across all functional areas for each child. These instructional targets are congruent with the child's current functional levels and adapted to the child's disabilities. Thus, they form the developmental basis of the young exceptional child's IEP. See chapter 8 for a child case study illustrating the entire developmental assessment-curriculum linkage process.

Exhibit 7-1 Assessment-Based Curriculum-Entry Targets

Child Michelle Curriculum

Test Gesell Developmental Schedules C.A. 34 months

DEVELOPMENTAL CEILINGS		LINK INDEX	CURRICULUM-TARGET OBJECTIVES
D.A. = 24(21-30) Mo.		COMMUNICATION	
±	Follows 2-4 simple directions		
±	Uses 20+ vocab. in speech		
−	Names pictures & Objs 8-12		
±	Uses I, me, you & plurals		
±	Identifies objs & pictures		
−	Imitates 5-6 word phrase		
−	Gives full name-requested		
±	Answers personal/factual questions		
−	Combines 3-4 words in sent.		
±	Tells action & experiences		
±	Asks for food, toilet, drink		
−	Attends & listens to a story		
D.A. = 21(18-24) Mo.		PROBLEM-SOLVING	
−	Matches ○□△ shapes in puzzle		
−	Ident., match, sort colors		
±	Understands concept of "one"		
±	" prepositions & positions		
±	Imit. fine motor beh-drawing		
±	Names & ident. objects & pictures		
−	Imitates a sequence of blocks		
−	Repeats 2 digits imit. adult		
−	Folds paper imitates adult		
±	Identifies "big" & "small"		
−	Follows 2 simple directions		
−	Gives use of objects		

Source: Adapted in part from Neisworth, J.T., Willoughby-Herb, S.J., Bagnato, S.J., Cartwright, C.A., & Laub, K.A. *Individualized education for preschool exceptional children.* Germantown, Md.: Aspen Systems Corp., 1980.

SUMMARY

The developmental linkages system attempts to offer a practical, reliable, and relatively systematic method of constructing individualized educational plans for young exceptional children. The method extends the value of traditional developmental scales by using the information provided for criterion-based curriculum planning. Thus, it provides a common ground for the roles of school psychologist and preschool teacher and makes their skills interdependent.

In terms of formative and summative evaluation, such an approach establishes functional, behavioral criteria common to both assessment and instruction that increases the reliability of results. Thus, the approach is competency-based and enables both teachers and school psychologists to monitor the progressive acquisition of developmental skills as well as program effectiveness. For example, after the linkage has been completed and instructional targets and strategies have been formulated and implemented, the child's progress in acquiring deficient developmental skills can be monitored primarily by curriculum-imbedded checklists and behavioral analysis. The developmental scales subsequently provide concurrent, summative evidence of developmental progress.

In addition, the linkage concept offers a practical vehicle for translating diagnostic results into observable curriculum goals so that parents are aware of prerequisite skills that require stimulation. It is important to compare parent perceptions of developmental progress with the child's actual situational performance so that the parent remains a vital resource in the programming and teaching process (Bagnato, Neisworth, & Eaves, 1978).

This format thus establishes behavioral and developmental criteria upon which both teaching lessons and progress assessments can be mutually based. Five major objectives are accomplished by this process:

1. Assessment is imbedded within instructional planning.
2. Similarity is ensured among behaviors assessed and behaviors taught.
3. Functional analyses of each child's range of developmental capabilities are provided, adapted to the child's handicap.
4. Multiple sources for monitoring skill acquisition are provided.
5. Both formative and summative evaluation of developmental progress is facilitated.

Chapter 8

From Assessment to Individualized Programming: A Case Study Exercise

This final chapter illustrates the entire process involved in going from initial screening and assessment to developmental linkages and individualized educational programming. The extended case study that is presented will give you practice in rehearsing the steps involved in carrying out the assessment-curriculum linkage procedure.

You will want to refer frequently to the Teacher's Sequence Record provided in this chapter (see Exhibit 8-1). It is an outline of the major sequenced steps in the diagnostic-prescriptive model and has been carefully designed to follow the guidelines of P.L. 94-142. The numbered steps in the outline will help you remember where the described activities appear in the sequence of events in the case study. Frequent reference to the outline will help you keep the global picture of the diagnostic-prescriptive process in focus. We are asking you, therefore, to read this chapter *actively*. Reading this chapter can be something like practicing for a play. The more repetitions you have, the more effective will be your performance when it is your turn to screen and identify a child and then prescribe a preschool program. You are now rehearsing what will be a major role in your career as an educator: to prescribe, efficiently and effectively, the best educational program to enhance or remediate specific behaviors demonstrated by every child for whom you are responsible.

Every time you apply this assessment-curriculum linkage model to a real child, it will most likely differ in some places. Each child's diagnostic profile will demand that you adjust this model to meet the individual needs of the child. Thus, your generalization of the skills you have learned in this text will be tested. To ensure that you "pass" each test, repeated rehearsals of the specific diagnostic-prescriptive skills should be your goal. For example, if you have determined that your skills in administering the assessment instrument Learning Accomplishment Profile-D (LAP-D) are weak, then practice the required performance skills until you reach the appropriate criteria of performance. With repeated practice, the

Exhibit 8-1 Teacher's Sequence Record

_______________ Preschool/Child Care Center

Child's name ____________________ Birthdate _________________

Activities	Date	Person(s) Involved
1.0 IDENTIFICATION PROCESS		
1.1 Initial data collection		
1.1.1 Charting and graphing		
1.1.2 Compare data to other records (e.g., The Denver Developmental Screening Test administered when child entered center)		
1.2 Home visit arranged		
1.3 Home visit conducted		
1.4 Parent(s) completes "Permission Form for Diagnostic Testing" and "Release of Information" Forms (e.g., Learning accomplish profile-diagnostic edition (LAP-D)		
1.5 Request to outside agency records if appropriate		
1.6 Diagnostic test administered		
1.7 Diagnostic test scores summarized (e.g., graph scores)		
1.8 Comparing screening and diagnostic test results:		
1.9 Outside agency information compiled		
2.0 DECISION MODULE I		
2.1 Staffing held to determine recommendations to parent(s)		
2.2 Parent conference arranged		
2.2.1 Who will attend		
2.2.2 Time/place		
2.3 Decision conference with parent(s)		
2.3.1 Data presented/discussed		
2.3.2 Options outlined		
☐ Continue in regular program with no remediations necessary: Link diagnostic test results (e.g., LAP-D) to curriculum (e.g., HICOMP)		
☐ Request norm-referenced developmental evaluation--parent signs permission form(s)		

Exhibit 8-1 continued

Activities	Date	Person(s) Involved
3.0 DEVELOPMENTAL NORM-REFERENCED EVALUATION		
3.1 Evaluation date/place arranged		
3.2 Evaluation conducted (e.g., *Gesell Developmental Schedules*)		
3.3 Team placement meeting: present:________ ________ ________		
3.3.1 Placement discussed/ suggestions recorded		
3.3.2 Further referrals discussed/ suggestions recorded		
3.3.3 Prescriptions discussed/ suggestions recorded--ex.: Link test (e.g., *Gesell*) scores to curriculum e.g., HICOMP		
3.3.4 I.E.P. Conference arranged with staff and parent(s)		
4.0 DECISION MODULE II		
4.1 Prescriptions decided		
4.1.1 I.E.P. completed		
4.1.2 School/home Information exchange		
4.1.3 Re-evaluation date(s) determined (e.g., repeated testing of *Gesell*, *LAP-D*		
4.2 Program placement decided		

individual steps described in the Teacher's Sequence Record will become almost automatic behaviors for you. Use the Teacher's Sequence Record both as an outline for this chapter and as a model for the steps involved in the diagnostic-prescriptive process.

As you read through the Teacher's Sequence Record, do not become overwhelmed by the numerous steps. Each step will be described in detail in the case study. After you have read the complete case study, then reread the Record a few times. You will, by then, have attached meaning to each step, and the logic of the task-analyzed steps will be evident to you. Learning is accomplished by rehearsal. Learning is change in behaviors. You will have acquired new behaviors in your repertoire of skills in prescribing preschool programs as you complete the text with this final chapter.

THE COMMUNITY SETTING

The Baroon Shoe factory is the major source of employment in the town of Julian. Approximately one-half of the working population is employed by Baroon. Since many of the employees of Baroon have small children, the Garment Workers Union (GWU) has established, in cooperation with the local special education unit of the county, a child care/preschool for their employee families.

The Julian Preschool Day Care Center is located in the basement of the factory and operates during the hours of 7:00 A.M. to 6:00 P.M. Various work and play areas are defined by colorful room dividers and area rugs. Financial support for teacher salaries, materials, supplies, and children's meals are provided by the GWU and local special education unit effort. Support services, such as those of a speech/hearing therapist, psychologist, social worker, and special education teacher, are also provided by the local special education unit.

Since the Baroon factory is located in a Spanish-speaking neighborhood, the preschool offers a bilingual program, with English as the first language. The curriculum is structured. It follows a developmental task approach. The teaching program is well-defined by teacher lesson plans and schedules. The Julian Preschool employs three teachers certified in early childhood education. One teacher is bilingual. Each teacher has 15 preschool children ages 3-5 who are either English-speaking or bilingual.

THE IDENTIFICATION PROCESS

Initial Data Collection

Alberto entered the Julian preschool class about 2½ months ago. In the first few weeks, he did not interact much with his peers. The teacher, Ms. Gibson, noticed that Alberto would stand near a child and watch him or her play with a toy. Once the child was finished and returned the toy to the shelf, Alberto would go to the shelf, take the toy, and imitate the same play as his peer. Although Alberto seemed interested in the toy, he stopped playing almost immediately when he saw another toy that interested him. Unfortunately, a behavior pattern began developing that consisted of going to the shelf, taking the toy, dropping the toy on the floor, and getting another toy from the shelf. At the end of a free play time, if the teachers and children did not remind Alberto to put the toys back on the shelf, all the toys from the shelf would be on the floor.

Alberto was bilingual. He rarely initiated verbal conversation in either English or Spanish to other bilingual children or adults. He did have some knowledge of English because he followed directions and responded in English to questions.

Verbal communication and playing with peers seemed consistent problems. In the area of dressing, it was difficult to identify if a problem existed. There were times when Alberto would independently unsnap and unzipper his pants to use the toilet, but there were just as many times when he stood there waiting for assistance from a teacher.

Although these three problems occurred frequently, no real data were available. We decided, therefore, to count how often each problem occurred during the day to estimate the seriousness of the problems.

Behavior Charting and Graphing

The teacher, Ms. Gibson, set up three 15-minute observation periods during the times when interactions among children were at their highest. These periods were free play time on the playground and group instruction time. Exhibit 8-2 presents a copy of the teacher's graphs of the baseline data on Alberto's verbal expression.

In the area of dressing, Ms. Gibson counted the number of times Alberto needed assistance with his pants in the bathroom. The teacher had four scheduled A.M. bathroom breaks and four P.M. bathroom breaks. If Alberto entered the bathroom area and unsnapped and unzippered his pants without delay, the behavior was not counted. However, if Alberto entered the bathroom area and made no attempt to unsnap his pants, assistance was given and the behavior was counted and recorded as shown in Exhibit 8-3.

Data Comparison

During the time baseline data were collected on Alberto, similar data were also collected by the teacher on another Spanish-speaking child who was approximately the same age as Alberto. This child had been enrolled in the preschool approximately the same length of time as Alberto. As Ms. Gibson charted the data, she was concerned that Alberto, compared to his peer, had specific behaviors that required further investigation. Charts of the data on this matched-peer are shown in Exhibits 8-4 and 8-5.

Exhibit 8-2 Baseline Data for Alberto's Verbal Expression

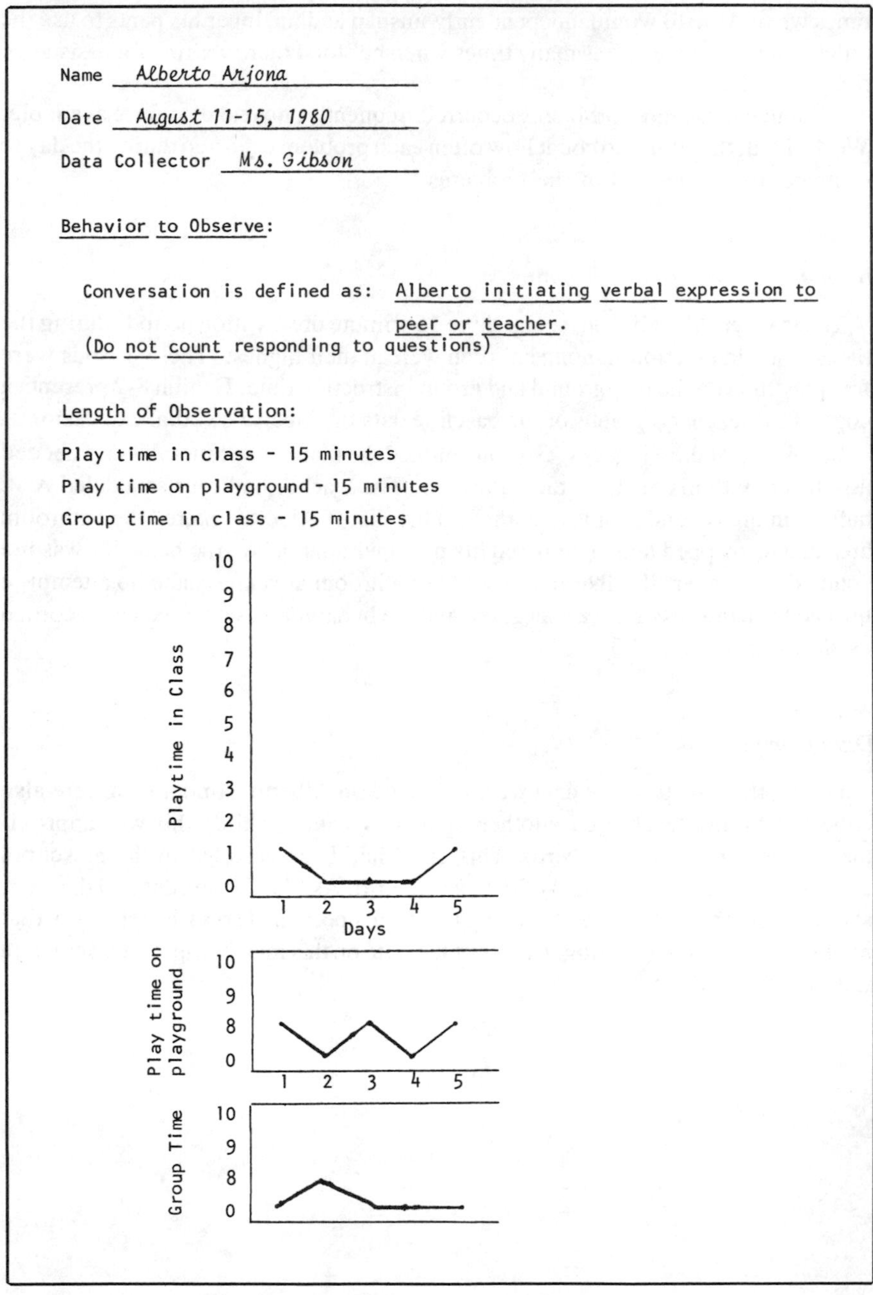

Name *Alberto Arjona*

Date *August 11-15, 1980*

Data Collector *Ms. Gibson*

Behavior to Observe:

Conversation is defined as: Alberto initiating verbal expression to peer or teacher.

(Do not count responding to questions)

Length of Observation:

Play time in class - 15 minutes

Play time on playground - 15 minutes

Group time in class - 15 minutes

Exhibit 8-3 Baseline Data on Alberto's Undressing/Dressing in the Bathroom

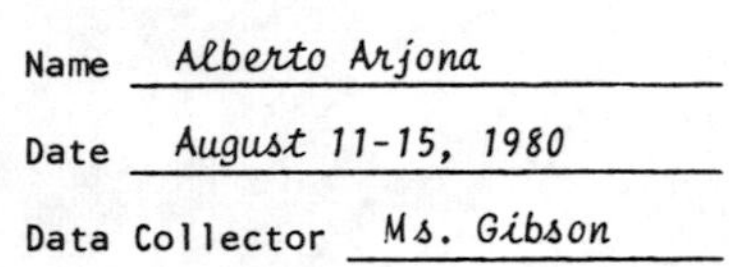
Name Alberto Arjona
Date August 11-15, 1980
Data Collector Ms. Gibson

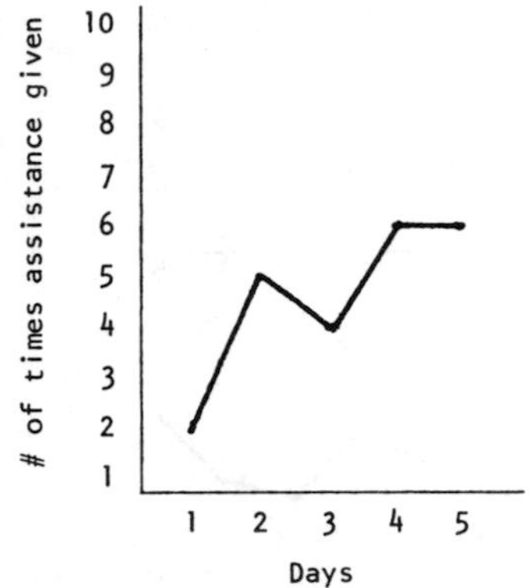

Exhibit 8-4 Peer Comparison Baseline Data

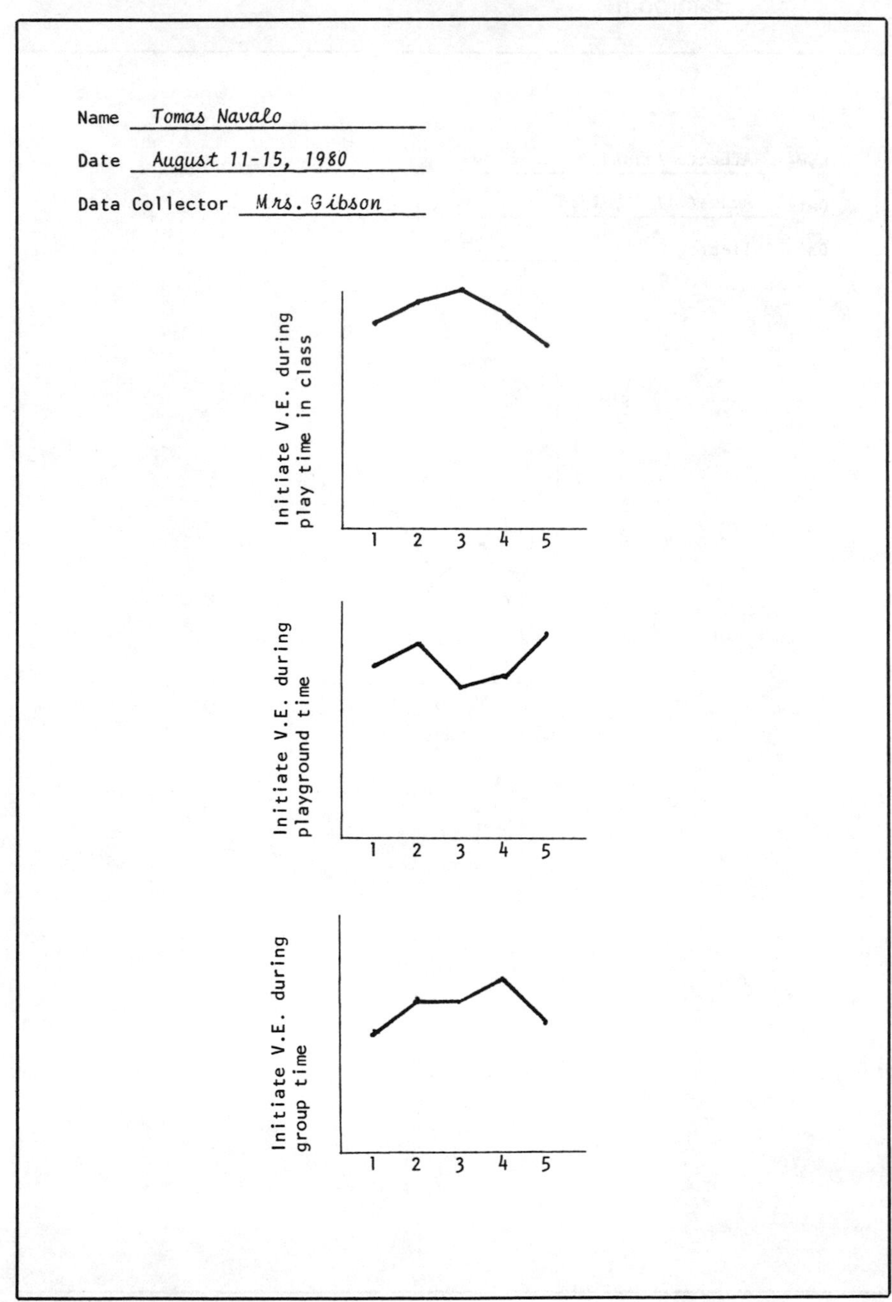

Name Tomas Navalo

Date August 11-15, 1980

Data Collector Mrs. Gibson

Exhibit 8-5 Peer Comparison Baseline Data Dressing/Undressing

Name *Tomas Navalo*

Date *August 11-15, 1980*

Data Collector *Mrs. Gibson*

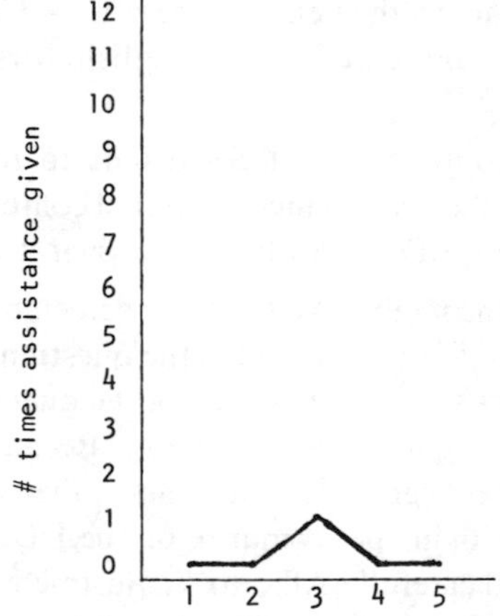

The Home Visit Arranged and Completed

An hour-long home visit was arranged with Alberto's mother, Mrs. Arjona. Due to the mother's working schedule, the teacher suggested that they meet in the evening when they both were not as rushed.

During the conference, Ms. Gibson explained the data she had recently collected on Alberto's verbal expression and dressing skills. She related these recent observations to Alberto's performance on the Denver Developmental Screening Test (DDST) (Frankenburg, Dodds, & Fandal, 1975). This is a popular screening test that is routinely administered to a child before entering the Julian center. Alberto was given the DDST by Mrs. Escovar, the bilingual preschool teacher, when he entered the center in June. Mrs. Escovar determined that Alberto's test results remained the same whether the items were presented in English or Spanish. When Alberto missed an item presented first in English, Mrs. Escovar readministered the item in Spanish.

Ms. Gibson brought a copy of the DDST results to refresh Mrs. Arjona's memory, as she had not seen the results since her initial conference with the teacher in June. A copy of Alberto's DDST results is shown in Exhibit 8-6.

The teacher explained to the mother the goal of a screening test like the DDST. Alberto's performance on the test was scored in the questionable range as defined by the test instructions. This was because one sector, language, had two delays that gave the overall screening a "questionable" rating. Because this was Alberto's first experience in a child care center and preschool, the two teachers were not initially overly concerned with his performance on the DDST. The teacher, Ms. Gibson, had agreed to record carefully Alberto's adjustment to the center and had collected data on his verbal expression skills. This initial administration of the DDST was the basis for the further investigation conducted by the teacher about one month after Alberto entered the Julian center.

Ms. Gibson also stressed in the conference that a child's skill development in the four major developmental domains—communication, own-care, motor, and problem solving—does not usually graph in a smooth upward line. The teacher was very interested in the mother's present knowledge of Alberto's development as compared to her reports given for the DDST in June. You will notice that in the Exhibit 8-6 results of Alberto's DDST many items begin with "R." "R" stands for "reported" by parent or care giver. Ms. Gibson wanted to determine if the mother was aware that Alberto's dressing skills, for instance, were weak. She also wanted to know if the mother considered that her son should be able to demonstrate more dressing skills for his age.

Alberto's mother agreed to answer the questions on the PODS Profile (Bagnato et al., 1977). The teacher quickly went over the items with her. The mother's report in the own-care domain (self-help skills) indicated that Alberto had only a "slight problem in this area"—a score of 2. From this report and further conversation with the parent, the teacher deduced that the mother was not aware that a 38-month-old child could be expected to have more skills in the self-help area, especially in self-dressing.

The parent stated that she was extremely eager for Alberto to receive any help that his teacher thought he required. She requested that the teacher give her suggestions of activities to do at home with her son. The teacher then said she would be pleased to outline an initial home prescription, a program to help the parent teach Alberto to dress himself. She gave a written outline to the mother after school the next day. The parent and teacher then decided to spend 10 minutes every afternoon after work for a week to discuss the task-analyzed program for improving Alberto's dressing skills. During those brief sessions with the parent, the teacher's goal was to teach the mother behavioral strategies such as modeling, manual prompting, and shaping of behaviors.

The teacher invited the mother to visit the preschool on her coffee break or lunch hour so she could observe the teaching strategies employed in the classroom. Ms. Gibson also offered to visit the home and observe Mrs. Arjona working with Alberto on his dressing skills. She would then be able to give the mother immediate feedback on her use of teaching strategies. Ms. Gibson was interested in observing Alberto in his home environment (the mother was a single parent and Alberto had no siblings). Ms. Gibson particularly wanted to observe Alberto's verbal expressive skills in his home setting.

Permission for Diagnostic Testing

The teacher requested the parent to consent to diagnostic testing of Alberto's developmental skills. Further testing was appropriate, based on the DDST, PODS, and interview information. A copy of the permission form signed by Alberto's mother is shown in Exhibit 8-7.

Requests to Outside Agencies

During the home visit, Ms. Gibson requested permission from Alberto's mother to gather information from agencies that were serving the family, such as the state health center. In Exhibit 8-8 is a sample of the permission form used to request such information. A copy of this form should be provided to (a) the parent, (b) the person requesting the information, and (c) the agency from whom the information is being requested.

Exhibit 8-6 Alberto's Test Results on the Denver Developmental Screening Test

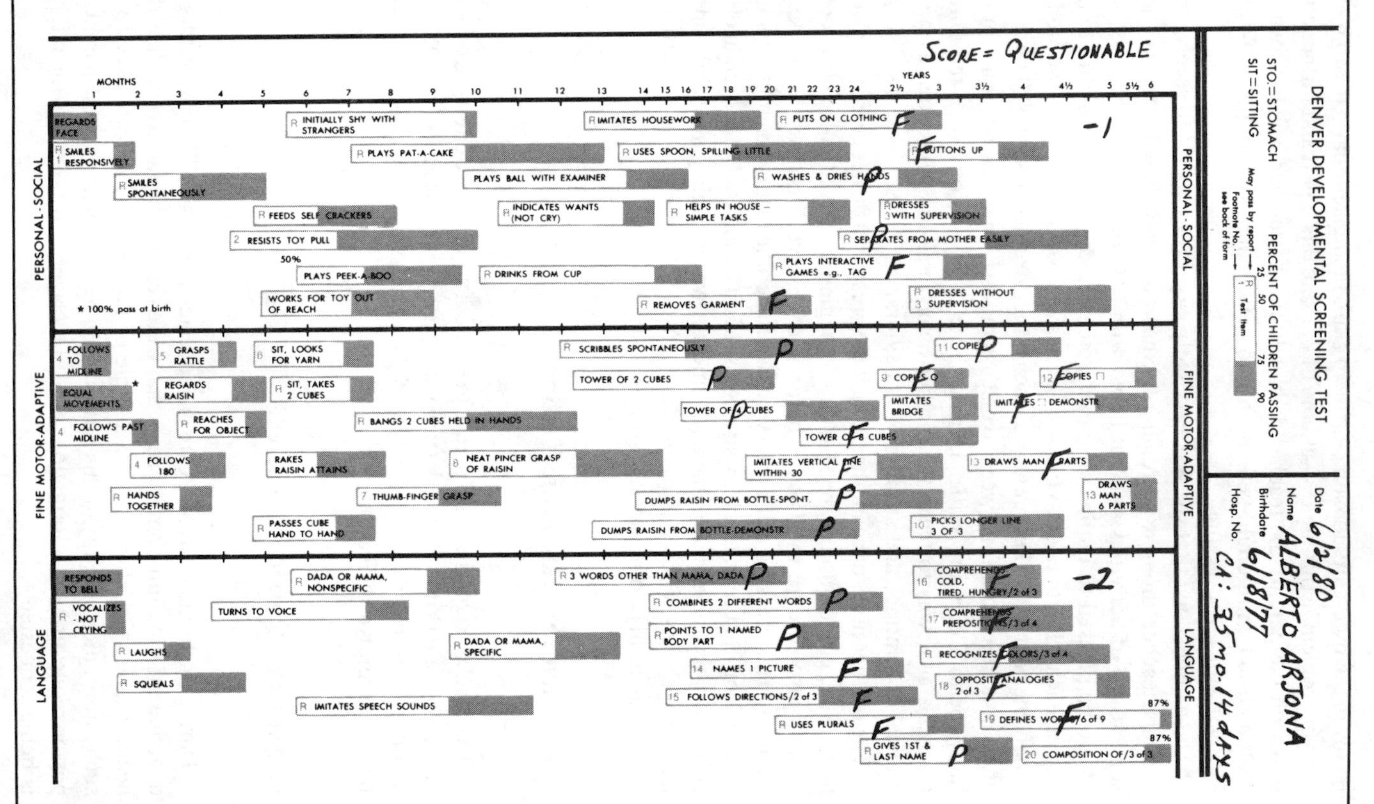

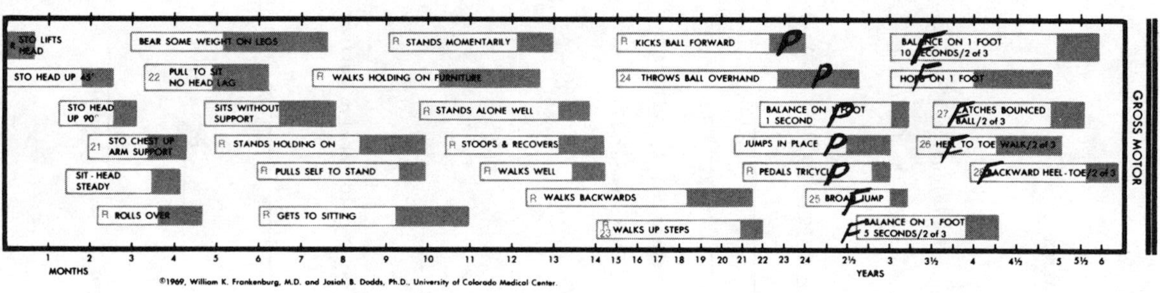

Source: Frankenburg, W., Dodds, J., & Fandal, A. *Denver developmental screening test.* Boulder, Colorado: Ladora Publishing Co., 1975.

Exhibit 8-7 Permission Form for Diagnostic Testing of Alberto

Julian Preschool

Julian, PA

PERMISSION FOR INDIVIDUAL EVALUATION

Dear Mrs. Arjona :

We are requesting your permission to do an individual evaluation on your son/daughter Alberto . We intend to use the following test(s):

The Learning Accomplishment Profile Diagnostic Test (LAP-D)

____

____

The results of the test(s) will help us determine if Alberto is in need of any further evaluations. A parent conference will be scheduled to discuss the test(s) results.

Sincerely,

Mrs. Gibson
Teacher's Name

☑ I give permission for my child *Alberto Arjona* to receive further evaluation.

Mrs. Velma Arjona — Parent or Guardian Name
8/18/80 — Date

☑ I do not give permission for my child __________ to receive further evaluation.

__________ Parent or Guardian Name
__________ Date

Exhibit 8-8 Permission Form for Requesting Other Agency Information about Alberto

Julian Preschool
Pennsylvania
August 18, 1980

Release of Information

Child's Name Alberto Arjona Birthdate June 18, 1977

Parent's Velma Arjona

Address 333 3rd Street

The Julian Preschool and Child Care Center have my permission to exchange information with the following persons and/or agencies concerning the above-named child. It is understood that this information will be used in the best interests of the child and will be held confidential.

Mrs. Velma Arjona
Parent/Guardian Signature

Mother
Relationship

8/18/80
Date

Note: Please include the name and address of any doctor/clinic, hospital, school, intermediate unit, or agency that could provide us with information concerning your child. Thank you.

Mrs. Gibson
Julian Preschool Representative

Exhibit 8-8 continued

Name ______________ Address ______________ ______________ Phone ______________	Name ______________ Address ______________ ______________ Phone ______________
Name ______________ Address ______________ ______________ Phone ______________	Name ______________ Address ______________ ______________ Phone ______________
Name ______________ Address ______________ ______________ Phone ______________	Name ______________ Address ______________ ______________ Phone ______________

Diagnostic Testing

The day after Ms. Gibson made her visit to Mrs. Arjona's home, she began to make arrangements to have the Learning Accomplishment Profile-Diagnostic Edition (LAP-D) administered to Alberto. Because Ms. Gibson was not fluent in Spanish, she asked Mrs. Escovar to administer the LAP-D in Spanish. Ms. Gibson offered to take both preschool classes during free play and snack time in order to release Mrs. Escovar to do the testing. Flexibility and cooperation among the staff at Julian were responsible in part for the high job satisfaction among the staff.

Evaluations of bilingual children at the Julian center were always conducted by a bilingual examiner. The mother had stressed in the home visit that primarily English was spoken in the home. Alberto did understand and speak Spanish, however. His grandmother, who visited often, spoke only Spanish. The neighborhood had many bilingual families, and often the children spoke both English and Spanish when playing together. When Mrs. Escovar administered the LAP-D, she needed this background information about language usage. Mrs. Escovar recorded on the testing booklet each time she administered items in Spanish. Exhibit 8-9 shows Alberto's performance recorded in a subdomain in the LAP-D scoring booklet.

As you can see, Alberto did not do any better on the missed items when they were readministered in Spanish by Mrs. Escovar. This indicated that there was not a significant language barrier that was depressing his scores.

Diagnostic Test Scores Summarized

Alberto was 38 months of age when he was given the LAP-D. The *LAP's Examiner Manual* (LeMay, Griffin, & Sanford, 1977) suggests that in a conference with parents

> raw scores give the appearance of being accurate and reliable indicators of a test subject's ability. Raw scores, however, are misleading, for while they imply a high degree of accuracy and precision, they in fact, are only interpretable in light of the age and background of the child, the total number of items on the test, the numbers of items the child might be expected to pass, the level of difficulty of the items, the variability of individual differences and so forth. . . . Rather, it is suggested to provide the parent with clearly written behavioral descriptions of observed performance. Verbal descriptions of test results always enhance the meaningfulness of the report. (p. 51)

It should be stressed here that the Public Law 94-142 ensures that the parent(s) or guardian(s) have the right of access to any written information a public institution may have concerning their child. Ms. Gibson took Mrs. Escovar's report and compiled a written summary of Alberto's results for the next parent conference, scheduled for 1 week after the administration of the LAP-D.

Exhibit 8-10 shows the graph of Alberto's scores that Mrs. Escovar gave to Ms. Gibson to maintain in Alberto's school file. When he is reevaluated using the LAP-D the following spring, the new scores will be placed on the graph so that a comparison may easily be made between pre- and post-test scores in each developmental domain.

Exhibit 8-9 Alberto's Performance in a LAP-D Subdomain

Language/Cognitive: Naming

Developmental Age	Item	Behavior	1st +/−	2nd +/−	Comments
15	LN1	Imitates names			
15	LN2	Names 3 objects	+		BASAL Achieved
24	LN3	Names 3 body parts	+		
24	LN4	Names 3 pictures	+		
30	LN5	Names 6 body parts	-		
33	LN6	Names use of objects	-		
36	LN7	Names objects by use	-		STARTED HERE
42	LN8	Names 3 actions			
42	LN9	Names 10 objects			*GAVE ALL "-'s" 1st IN
48	LN10	Names missing part			ENGLISH--READMINISTERED
48	LN11	Names 8 actions			IN SPANISH--NO CHANGE
54	LN12	Names 18 objects			
54	LN13	Names activities recently performed			
54	LN14	Names cause of event			
54	LN15	Names consequence of action			
54	LN16	Names activities he might soon perform			
60	LN17	Names differences among pictures			
60	LN18	Names picture removed from group			
66	LN19	Names source of actions			
66	LN20	Names who, what, where, why of story			
66	LN21	Names things needed for activity			
66	LN22	Names parts of items			
72	LN23	Uses analogies			
72	LN24	Names materials objects are made of			
72	LN25	Names opposites			
72	LN26	Names numerals/letters			
72	LN27	Names items in category			
72	LN28	Names category			
72+	LN29	Names printed words			
		Last Item Administered	7		
		Less Errors	- 3	-	
		Naming Score	4		

Source: LeMay, D.W., Griffin, P.M., & Sanford, A.R. *Learning accomplishment profile-diagnostic edition* (Rev. ed.). Winston-Salem, N.C.: Kaplan School Supply, 1978. Reprinted with permission.

Exhibit 8-10 Graph of Alberto's LAP-D Scores

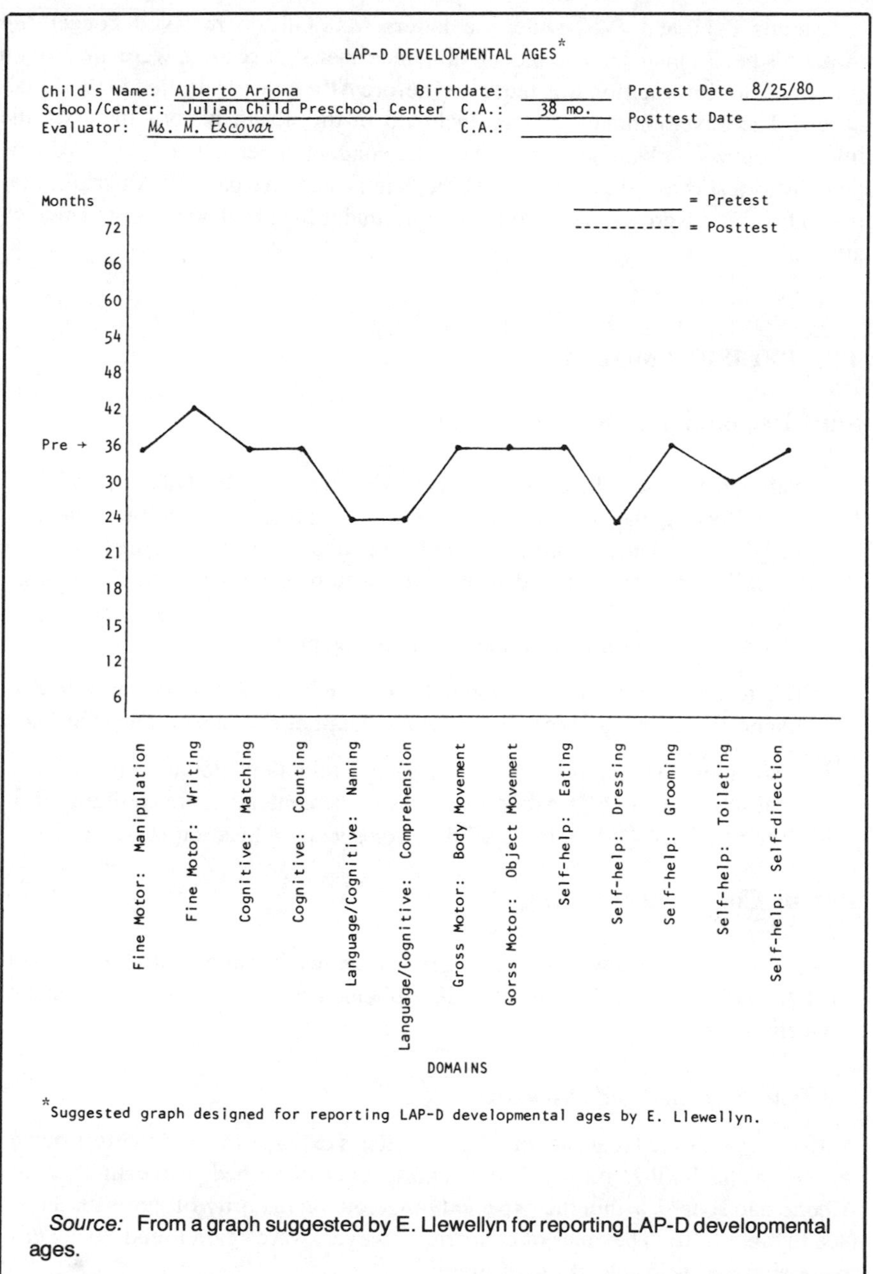

Source: From a graph suggested by E. Llewellyn for reporting LAP-D developmental ages.

Outside-Agency Information Compiled

Exhibits 8-11 and 8-12 show the letters Ms. Gibson received concerning Alberto's health history. The inoculation and other shot records were already on file, since this information was requested before Alberto was enrolled in the Julian center. The developmental history included in the health history matched the information Ms. Gibson gathered when she conducted her home visit before the diagnostic test was administered. These letters became part of Alberto's permanent file and were available to the parent (under the provisions of the Buckley amendment).

THE DECISION MODULE I

Staff Recommendations to Parents

A staff meeting was held with the center's director, Ms. Gibson, and Mrs. Escovar following the administration of the diagnostic evaluation. The staff reviewed the formal and informal data collected about Alberto. On the basis of all the data collected, they concluded that they would recommend the following:

- Alberto should continue in the Julian center program.
- The teachers and parents should (a) design remedial activities based on diagnostic results, and (b) determine the data-collection methods to employ.
- A complete developmental/psychological evaluation should be made by the local school district. If Alberto's scores in the evaluation are similar to those on the LAP-D, he would be eligible for special education services.

Parent Conference Arranged

A parent conference was then arranged for the teacher to explain the results of the LAP-D evaluation. The teacher also planned to discuss the staff's recommendations.

The Data Presented and Discussed

Mrs. Arjona stated that she found the teacher's explanation of Alberto's performance on the LAP-D most helpful. The teacher described to the mother how Alberto had scored within the expected range on the majority of items on the test (see Exhibit 8-10). The areas of concern, however, were again found to be verbal expression and self-help skills of dressing.

Exhibit 8-11 Letter from the State Health Center Regarding Alberto's Health History

State Health Center
101 North School Street
Pennsylvania 16210
August 22, 1980

Julian Preschool
Julian
Pennsylvania

Dear Ms. *Gibson*:

Alberto Arjona (birthdate 6/8/77) has attended our Child Health Conference (CHC) from September 19, 1977 for well-child check-ups and immunizations.

Alberto has received the following immunizations and tests through clinics:

DPT 10/1/77, 12/3/77, 2/4/78

Polio 10/1/77, 12/3/77, 2/4/78

Measles 6/26/78

Rubella 6/26/78

Tuberculin Test (Monovac) 5/5/78 neg.

Hematocrit 5/5/78 neg.

The following are the developmental milestones which you reported for Alberto's first eighteen months:

Eyes follow moving objects--attained at 2 months
Holds head erect--3 months
Reaches for a rattel--3 1/2 months
First tooth erupts--6 months
Rolls over--3 1/2 months
Sits alone--8 months
Creeps and pulls self to feet--11 months
Walks with support--11 months
Waves good-by (reported by mother)--18 months
Attempts self-feeding--12 months
Stands and walks alone--12 months

Exhibit 8-11 continued

The following are Alberto's height, weight, and head circumference taken his first 18 months during CHC visits.

		WT.	HT.	Head circumference
06-18-77	Birth	7 lb. 6 oz.	19 in.	
10-01-77	3 1/2 mos.	13 lb. 14 oz.	23 in.	16 1/8 in.
11-05-77	5 mos.	15 lb. 6 1/4 oz.	24 1/4 in.	16 1/4 in.
12-03-77	6 mos.	16 lb. 1 1/2 oz.	25 1/4 in.	16 1/2 in.
02-04-78	8 mos.	18 lb.	26 in.	17 in.
05-05-78	11 mos.	19 lb. 8 oz.	27 1/2 in.	17 3/4 in.
06-02-78	12 mos.	20 lb. 6 1/2 oz.	29 in.	
12-01-79	18 mos.	22 lb. 12 oz.	30 in.	18 1/8 in.

Mr. Arjona has kept regular appointments with Alberto. With every CHC visit he seemed to have a medical problam (i.e., diarrhea and fever at 10/1/77 visit, rhinitis at 12/3/77, ear infections occurred frequently, a strept throat 11/3/78, 2/10/79 and 4/12/80.

Alberto will continue to be seen at CHC until he enters first grade. If we can be of further assistance, please call.

Sincerely,

Mary Mancuso

Mary Mancuso
Public Health Nurse

Exhibit 8-12 Letter from Julian Area Medical Center Regarding Alberto's Health History

Julian Area Medical Center
Julian, Pennsylvania

August 20, 1980

Julian Preschool/Day Care Center
Preschool Staff: Ms. Gibson

Dear Ms. Gibson:

We received your request for information about Alberto Arjona who is being considered for possible inclusion by the Special Education Unit in Julian, Pennsylvania.

We have information mostly about acute illnesses such as colds, ear infections, sore throats, etc.

Alberto receives his well child care through the State Health Center. The Center's phone number is 535-3515.

Also, Gail Raisch, a social worker who is involved with the Home Health Service of Grove County, 512 High Street, Venice, Pennsylvania, phone 535-0012 would undoubtedly be of service to you for further information concerning the Arjona family.

If we could be of any further service to you, please feel free to contact us.

Very truly yours,

Diana Buckham

Diana Buckham
Nurse Practitioner

DB/jl

The teacher identified the items Alberto missed on the LAP-D and linked them into the center's curriculum, the HICOMP curriculum. She needed to do this so she could outline an individualized program for Alberto. The teacher's goals, she explained to the parent, were to increase the frequency of Alberto's voluntary verbal expressions, his attention span to tasks such as playing with toys in free-play time, and his skills in dressing himself.

The Linkage Described

The teacher linked items from the LAP-D to the HICOMP curriculum. This linkage process was not time-consuming because she had previously compiled a list of the items on the LAP-D that linked to specific items in the HICOMP curriculum. An example of this list is:

LAP-D Task	*HICOMP Curriculum Target*
FM 23 Imitates Bridge	M-3-2.5—Builds bridge of 3 cubes, imitating model

The total linkage of Alberto's scores on the LAP-D to the HICOMP curriculum is shown in Exhibit 8-13.

The teacher explained to the parent that they could use the Exhibit 8-13 linkage report to determine directly the daily teaching objectives to use in Alberto's educational program. Mrs. Arjona agreed that all the objectives were congruent with her own goals for her son. Ms. Gibson noted that the LAP-D did not evaluate as many skills or subdomains as the HICOMP curriculum. Because she wanted to provide Alberto with a very comprehensive program, she preferred to use the HICOMP Lesson Plan Chart (see Exhibit 8-14). This chart was to be posted in the classroom to serve as a reminder to the teacher and her aide to work on specific objectives from the 21 subdomains of the HICOMP curriculum. Many of the curriculum objectives would take many, many teaching trials before the criteria are achieved. Again, it should be stressed that this chart should serve as a reminder that a developing child requires a balanced ''diet'' of objectives to ensure development across all major domains and subdomains.

Exhibit 8-13 Linkage of Alberto's LAP-D Scores with the HICOMP Curriculum

ASSESSMENT/CURRICULUM DEVELOPMENTAL LINKAGES

PRETEST 8/25/80

CHILD *Alberto Arjona* C.A. 38 months

TEST Learning Accomplishment Profile, LAP CURRICULUM HICOMP

DEVELOPMENTAL CEILINGS		LINK INDEX	CURRICULUM TARGETS	
D.A. = *36 mo.*		Fine Motor--Manipulation		
FM23	*Imitates Bridge*	*M-3 - 2.5*	*Builds bridge of three cubes, imitating*	
FM26	*Weaves through sewing board*	*M-4 - 2.3*	*Strings small beads*	✓
FM27	*Puts pegs in pegboard*	*M-3 - 2.9*	*Places round object in round hole*	
D.A. = *42 mo.*		Fine Motor--Writing		
FW11	*Imitates H stroke*	*M-3 - 2.3*	*Draws horizontal line from model*	
FW12	*Imitates V stroke*	*M-3 - 2.2*	*Draws vertical line from model*	
FW13	*Copies circle*	*M-3 - 2.1*	*Draws circle, imitating adult*	
D.A. = *36 mo.*		Cognitive: Matching		
CM9	*Matches animals*	*P-3 - 4.4*	*Solves match-to-sample problems*	✓
CM10	*Matches complex patterns*	*M-4 - 2.2*	*Imitates a sequence of two behaviors where one involves a discrimination problem*	
CM11	*Matches object pictures*	*P-3 - 4.7*	*Solves match-to-sample position problems*	
D.A. = *36 mo.*		Cognitive: Counting		
CC2	*Counts three cubes*	*P-3 - 6.1*	*Following a model, reproduces a sequence of three objects*	✓
CC3	*Counts six beads*	*P-3 - 6.2*	*Following a model, reproduces a sequence of more than three objects*	
CC4	*1-10 by rote*	*P-4 - 6.6*	*Counts by rote in correct sequence up to 10*	

✓We will be working on this objective immediately.

Source: Designed by S. Bagnato and E. Llewellyn.

Exhibit 8-13 continued

ASSESSMENT/CURRICULUM DEVELOPMENTAL LINKAGES
Page 2

DEVELOPMENTAL CEILINGS		LINK INDEX	CURRICULUM TARGETS	
D.A. = 24 mo.		Language: Naming		
LN5	Names six body parts	C-2 - 2.12	Uses 50 words	✓
LN6	Names use of objects	C-3 - 3.7	Responds with a verb when asked, "What are you doing: e.g., I'm washing dishes."	✓
LN7	Names objects by use	C-4 - 2.9	Uses both generic and specific names for objects and events	
D.A. = 24 mo.		Language: Comprehension		
LC6	Follows three (related) commands	C-2 - 3.13	Remembers and correctly completes two simple related directions	
LC10	Responds to two prepositions	P-3 - 4.8	Repeats position names after a model	
LC11	Follows two-step command	P-2 - 3.10	Remembers and correctly completes two simple related directions	✓
D.A. = 36 mo.		Motor: Body Movement		
GB19	Balances one foot, 5 seconds	M-3 - 1.9	Stands on one foot, momentarily	
GB22	Walks on a line	M-3 - 1.7	Walks on line on floor	
GB23	Squats	M-2 - 1.9	Squats in play two-three minutes	✓
D.A. = 36 mo.		Motor: Object Movement		
GO16	Catches bounced ball with arms	M-4 - 1.6	Catches bouncing ball, holding it against body	

Exhibit 8-13 continued

ASSESSMENT/CURRICULUM DEVELOPMENTAL LINKAGES
Page 3

DEVELOPMENTAL CEILINGS		LINK INDEX	CURRICULUM TARGETS	
D.A. = 38 mo.		Self-Help: Eating		
	Over age for the items in	0-3 - 4.5	Blows in a controlled stream of air	✓
	this subdomain as range is	0-3 - 4.6	Removes food from spoon with upper lip	
	only 18 months. Begin at			
	38 month level.			
D.A. = 24 mo.		Self-Help: Dressing		
SD9	Pulls on T-shirt	0-2 - 5.7	Finds garment holes and puts limb in (e.g., arms)	✓
SD10	Unbuttons large button	0-3 - 5.2	Attempts unbuttoning a button	
SD11	Zips zipper	0-4 - 5.7	Independently zips a zipper	
D.A. = 42 mo.		Self-Help: Grooming		
	Completed all items in this	0-3 - 2.9	Attempts to brush teeth	✓
	subdomain which has a range	0-3 - 2.10	Brushes and combs hair	
	of 42 months. Begin at	0-3 - 2.11	Attempts to use hankerchief when coughing or sneezing	
	42 month level.			
D.A. = 36 mo.		Self-Help: Toileting		
ST7	Pulls down pants unassited	0-3 - 5.7	Puts on and removes elasticized pants with assistance	
D.A. = 38 mo.		Self-Help: Self-Direction		
	Completed all items in this	0-3 - 1.4	Follows a simple rule concerning eating behavior: saying "please"	✓
	subdomain in which has a	0-3 - 1.7	Enjoys demonstrating and practicing newly learned skills, e.g., will zip others' coat zipper.	
	range of 42 months.			

Exhibit 8-14 HICOMP Lesson Plan Chart Showing 21 Teaching Objectives

HICOMP LESSON PLAN CHART*

HICOMP 21 SUBDOMAINS	CODE	HICOMP 21 OBJECTIVES
LANGUAGE RELATED PLAY	C-[2]-1.[2]	*Initiates a game (e.g., starts "pat-a-cake").*
✓SELF EXPRESSION	C-[2]-2.[12]	*Uses 50 words.*
✓LANGUAGE RESPONDING	C-[3]-3.[7]	*Responds with a verb when asked, "What are you doing?" e.g., "I'm washing the dishes."*
IMITATION RELATED TO LANGUAGE	C-[2]-4.[6]	*Imitates speech reliably.*
LANGUAGE RELATED ATTENTION	C-[2]-5.[7]	*Attends to longer verbalizations when they are accompanied by frequent descriptive actions.*
✓MEETING SOCIAL CONVENTIONS AND DEVELOPING VALUES	O-[3]-1.[4]	*Follows a simple rule concerning eating behavior: e.g., saying "please, more milk."*
✓HEALTH, SAFETY, AND PERSONAL CLEANLINESS	O-[3]-2.[9]	*Attempts to brush teeth.*
AFFECTIVE REACTIONS TO ENVIRONMENT	O-[2]-3.[5]	*Approaches other children.*
✓EATING AND DRINKING	O-[3]-4.[5]	*Blows in a controlled stream of air.*
✓DRESSING/UNDRESSING	O-[2]-5.[7]	*Finds garment holes and puts limb in (e.g., arms).*
✓GROSS MOTOR	M-[2]-1.[9]	*Squats in play 2-3 minutes.*
FINE MOTOR	M-[3]-2.[4]	*Draws recognizable face.*
ORAL	M-[3]-3.[5]	*Blows in controlled stream of air (e.g., blows bubbles).*

ATTENTION	P-[3]-1.[5]	Engages in play or games for increasing lengths of time (or number of tasks) prior to reinforcement.
IMITATION	P-[2]-2.[3]	Imitates a combination of a motor and speech when given the signal "(child's name), do this."
✓ RECALL	P-[2]-3.[10]	Remembers and correctly completes two simple related directions.
✓ CONCEPT FORMATION	P-[3]-4.[4]	Solves match-to-sample problems.
GROUPING	P-[2]-5.[3]	Shares divisible items (e.g., gives 1/2 cracker to peer during snacktime).
✓ SEQUENCING	P-[3]-6.[1]	Following a model, reproduces a sequence of three items.
APPLICATION OF PRINCIPLES	P-[3]-7.[1]	Labels objects based on verbal information given.
CREATIVITY	P-[2]-8.[3]	Demonstrates a sense of humor.

✓ = Specific objectives from Assessment–Curriculum Developmental Linkages

*Chart Designed by Frances Hunt

Evaluation Conducted

The school psychologist, Dr. McGlynn, who was bilingual in Spanish and English, administered the Gesell Developmental Schedules to Alberto. She found that Alberto responded to English and Spanish in a similar manner. A copy of the Gesell results for Alberto is shown in Exhibit 8-15.

Request for a Psychoeducational Evaluation

The teacher described to the parent the staff's desire to have a complete psychoeducational evaluation by the local school psychologist. The LAP-D scores showed fairly conclusively that Alberto had a language delay in the verbal expression area. However, the administration of a norm-referenced test, such as the Gesell Developmental Schedules by the county Special Education Department was required before a child could receive services. Ms. Gibson predicted that the Gesell scores would be similar to the LAP-D results, indicating language therapy would be recommended for the weakness in verbal-expression skills. Ms. Gibson again reassured the parent by stating that developmental delays when identified and remediated early in a child's life are often no longer observed in the child by the time the child enters elementary school. The mother strongly desired that her son receive the additional services from the special education unit. She signed another permission form for the psychoeducational evaluation, similar to the form in Exhibit 8-7.

DEVELOPMENTAL NORM-REFERENCED EVALUATION

Evaluation Date and Place Arranged

The school psychologist arranged with the classroom teacher to visit her classroom to observe Alberto. She also wanted to have an opportunity to meet Alberto in an informal setting before administering the Gesell Developmental Schedules. The psychologist reviewed the teacher's observation charts (Exhibits 8-2 and 8-3) and added that there was a need to determine if Alberto qualified for services provided by the special education unit. It would be interesting, the psychologist said, to compare the results she obtained on the Gesell with the LAP-D scores. In order to control for a demand characteristic in the evaluation, the psychologist did not wish to review Alberto's scores on the LAP-D until she administered the Gesell.

The classroom teacher questioned if similar items on the LAP-D and the Gesell schedules would invalidate the scores obtained. The school psychologist assured Ms. Gibson that the final decision as to whether Alberto would receive service did not depend solely on the Gesell scores. In addition, similar performance on the Gesell would provide evidence of the consistency and stability of Alberto's skills and deficits.

Team Placement Meeting

Once the Gesell evaluation was completed, the teacher arranged for the psychologist, the language specialist, Mr. Zook, the bilingual teacher, Mrs. Escovar, and herself to meet and discuss the test results.

The psychologist gave each team member the Exhibit 8-16 summary of the Gesell results.

The team agreed that Alberto was eligible for a special program—language therapy. A date was set for a parent conference. At that time, Mrs. Arjona, the parent, would be informed that Alberto was eligible for special education services. The language therapy would be offered four times per week for 20-minute sessions. In addition, the language therapist would serve as a consultant to the teacher and parent for additional programming and materials. The special education unit would also lend Ms. Gibson a Distar Language Kit to use with Alberto and several other children who demonstrated delays in language development.

DECISION MODULE II

Prescriptions Decided

On Thursday afternoon, Mrs. Arjona met with team members for an IEP conference. Ms. Gibson began the meeting by reiterating the purpose of an individual educational program and the components of the program, and she also explained the due-process procedure. Mrs. Arjona was at first a bit confused by the details of the information but agreed to proceed with the meeting to see if her questions would be resolved.

The IEP Completed

The psychologist summarized the formal assessment results from the Gesell schedules. Mr. Zook, the language therapist, explained Alberto's strengths and weaknesses in language development. Mrs. Arjona agreed that language development was an important goal for Alberto. Mr. Zook, with the assistance of the team, then wrote an annual goal for Alberto in the language development area. The major focus of this goal was to help Alberto verbally interact with his peers and teachers. Using the HICOMP curriculum, the team generated several subobjectives and strategies for teaching these objectives and developed an evaluation plan to measure completion of the objections. It should be noted that Individual Educational Plans only describe remedial prescriptions. Objectives are not included in areas where the child exhibits developmentally predicted or above-predicted behaviors. The HICOMP Lesson Plan Chart thus is more comprehensive than an IEP for actual use by the school and home (see Exhibit 8-17 regarding IEP language development).

Exhibit 8-15 Alberto's Test Results from the Gesell Developmental Schedules

Gesell Developmental Schedules ALBERTO ARJONA

DOT 9/10/80
DOB 6/18/77
CA 3/2/22

Age	Motor	Adaptive	Language	Personal-Social
2	Walks: runs well, no falling Stairs: walks up and down alone Large ball: (no dem.) kicks Cubes: tower of 6-7 Book: turns pages singly	Cubes: tower of 6-7 Drawing: imitates V stroke Formboard: places blocks on separately (G) Formboard: adapts after 4 trials Color Forms: does not identify any	Speech: jargon discarded Speech: 3 word sentence Speech: uses *I, me, you* Picture Vocabulary: 2 + correct	Toilet: may verbalize needs fairly consistently Play: domestic mimicry Play: hands cup full of cubes Play: parallel play predominates Feeding: inhibits turning spoon Dressing: pulls on simple garment Commun: verbalizes immed. experiences Commun: refers to self by name Comm: comprehends & asks for "another" Temperament: gentle, easy
2½	Stands: tries, on 1 foot Cubes: tower of 10 Drawing: holds crayon by fingers	Cubes: tower of 10 Cubes: aligns 2 or more, train Drawing: imitates V & H strokes Drawing: scribbles to circular stroke Inc. Man: adds 1 part Formboard: inserts 3 blocks on presentation Formboard: adapts repeatedly, error Color Forms: places 1	Interview: gives first name Interview: tells sex (G) Prepositions: obeys 1-2 Picture Vocab: 7 correct Action Agent: 3 correct	Play: pushes toy with good steering Play: helps put things away Commun: refers to self by pronoun "me" rather than by name Commun: repetition in speech and other activity Self help: can put on own coat (not necessarily fasten) Temperament: opposite extremes
3	Walks on tiptoe, 2 or more steps Stands on 1 foot, momentary balance Skips: tries Rides tricycle using pedals Stairs: alternates feet going up Jumps down: lands on feet (G) Broad jump: distance 12" Pellets: 10 into bottle in 26" (G); 24" (B)	Cubes: adds chimney to train Cubes: imitates bridge Copy Forms: copies circle Copy Forms: imitates cross Inc. Man: adds 3 parts Formboard: adapts, no errors or immediate correction of error Color Forms: places 3 Counts with correct pointing, 3 objs. Pellets: 10 into bottle in 26" (G); 24" (B)	Speech: uses plurals ~~Interview: tells age (G)~~ Interview: tells sex (B) Prepositions: obeys 3 Digits: repeats 3 (1 of 3 trials) Picture Vocab: 11 correct Comprehension Question A: answers 1 Action Agent: 6-7 correct Picture Vocab.: 11 correct	Feeding: feeds self, little spilling Feeding: pours well from pitcher Dressing: puts on shoes Dressing: unbuttons front and side buttons Commun.: asks questions rhetorically Commun: understands taking turns Commun: knows a few rhymes Temperament: cooperative

3½	+	Stands on 1 foot 2" or more	−	Cubes: builds bridge from model	−	Interview: gives no. of siblings	+	Dressing: washes, dries, hands, face
	+	Jumps: both feet leave floor	+	Copy Forms: copies cross	−	Prepositions: 4 correct	+	Play: associate play replaces parallel
	−	Broad jump: distance 19"	−	Inc. Man: adds 4 parts	−	Digits: repeats 3 (2 of 3 trials)	−	Commun: calls self "I"
	+	Jumps down, lands on feet (B)	+	Inc. Man: eyes better than a scribble	−	Picture Vocab: 12 correct	−	Commun: asks "How" questions
	+	Hops on one foot: succeeds (G)	−	Pellets: 10 into bottle in 23"	−	Compehension Quest. A: answers 2	+	Toileting: seldom has "accidents"
	−	Pellets: 10 into bottle in 23"			−	Action Agent: 12 correct		Temperament: vulnerable
4	−	Stands on 1 foot 2-7"	−	Cubes: imitates gate or better (G)	−	Interview: gives own age (B)	−	Dressing: buttons clothing
	−	Stairs: walks down, foot to a step	⊕	Copy Forms; imitates square or better	−	Prepositions: 5 correct	+	Dressing: washes & dries face & hands, brushes teeth
	−	Skips: on one foot	−	Inc. Man: adds 5 parts	−	Digits: repeats 3 (3 of 3 trials)	−	Dresses: dresses & undresses, supervised
	−	Jumps: run. or standing broad jump	±	Inc. Man: arm straight out from body or better	−	Digits: repeats 4 (1 of 3 trials)	−	Dressing: laces shoes
		Broad jump: 20"	−	Pellets: 10 into bottle in 23"	−	Picture Vocab: 14 correct	−	Dressing: distinguishes front & back
		Bean bag catch: any method		Counts: 4 objects	−	Comprehension Quest. B: 1 correct		
		Pellets: 10 into bottle in 23"			−	Action Agent: 14 correct		

Source: Ames, L.B., Gillespie, C., Haines, J., & Ilg, F. *Gesell developmental schedules* (Revised). Lumberville, Pa.: Gesell Institute for Human Development Book Service and Programs for Education, 1980. Reprinted with permission.

Exhibit 8-16 Summary of Test Results for Alberto on the Gesell Developmental Schedules

Name: Alberto Arjona

DOT 9/10/80
DOB 6/18/77
CA 3 yr. 3 mo.

Assessment Instrument: Gesell Developmental Schedules

Alberto, age 39 months, was assessed for the dual purpose of determining his developmental capabilities and specifying an appropriate educational placement and educational objectives for him in the present school year.

Throughout the testing sessions within this evaluation, Alberto was cooperative but did not initiate any conversations with the examiner. Alberto was administered the items first in English and then in Spanish. The addition of the Spanish translation did not affect his scores on the individual items.

Results and Analysis

In the gross motor subdomain, Alberto demonstrated the ability to walk on tiptoe two or more steps, attempted to skip, stood on one foot over two minutes, jumped down from a small chair and landed on both feet, and hopped on one foot. Alberto was unable to walk up stairs with alternating feet. In the gross motor subdomain, Alberto was within the expected range for his chronological age.

In the fine motor subdomain, Alberto built a tower with ten cubes, drew pictures while holding a crayon by his fingers. He was unable to place ten pellets into a small bottle in the prescribed time of 23 seconds. Alberto's overall development in the motor domain lies between the 36 and 52 month maturity levels and is within chronological age expectations.

In the communication domain, Alberto is reported to typically not initiate conversation in either English or Spanish. Alberto gave his first name and sex when requested in English, he also correctly named seven pictured vocabulary cards. To all other requests which required

Exhibit 8-16 continued

a verbal response Alberto gave no answer. His development in the communication domain lies between the 24 and 30 month maturity levels and is significantly below chronological age expectations.

In the own care domain, Alberto is reported to feed himself with little spilling and to be toilet trained. Alberto consistently, by report of his teacher, and his examiner's observations could not undress or dress himself when he needed to use the toilet. On all items which tested dressing skills, Alberto refused to attempt except putting on his coat. His development in this domain lies between 36 and 42 months maturity levels. Albert's performance is only below his expected chronological age in the self dressing area.

In the problem solving domain, Alberto demonstrated the ability to complete the formboard inserting three blocks on presentation and in different positions, copied a cross with a crayon, and drew a man including three parts. Alberto did not perform any task which required verbal responses such as counting objects. This resulted in his level of development in the problem solving domain to be approximately at the 30 month maturity level which is below chronological age expectations.

Alberto appears to be developing normally in the motor and own care domain. Alberto's lack of skills in dressing himself should be explored further with his mother to determine if he is expected to take any responsibility in dressing himself in the home setting. Alberto's main delay at this time lies in the communication domain which also affects negatively his overall scores in the problem-solving domain. Specific language stimulation for use in the classroom is recommended. A structured preschool placement for the 1980-1981 school year is warranted for the specific purpose of developing his speech and language skills.

Melissa Moller
Special Education Unit School Psychologist

Exhibit 8-17 Follow-Up Recommendations for Home Language Development for Alberto

FOLLOW UP RECOMMENDATIONS FOR HOME LANGUAGE DEVELOPMENT

1. Encourage Alberto to make verbal requests rather than gestures when he wants something.
2. Model the verbal request and then ask Alberto to repeat it. Please don't expect perfection the first trial, but do listen carefully that each trial is better than the previous.

   E.G.: Alberto points to cookie
   Mother: "Do you want a cookie?"
   Alberto shakes head, yes.
   Mother: say "cookie"
   Alberto says "cookie"
   Mother smiles, gives Alberto the cookie

   At the second trial . . .
   Alberto says "cookie"
   Mother says "Do you want a cookie?"
   Alberto says "cookie"
   Mother: "Alberto, say, 'want a cookie.'"
   Alberto says "Want a cookie."
   Mother smiles and gives Alberto the cookie
3. Spend ten minutes a day looking at children's books, magazines, or at items in and around the house, or community. Identify and describe the items and then ask Alberto to do it.

   E.g.: Mother: "Look at this tree."
   "say 'tree."
   Alberto says "tree."
   Mother: "See the pretty green leaves."
   Alberto: "leaves"

   Begin with objects or items that Alberto is very familiar with and then gradually bring in items that are not readily available in the environment.

School-Home Exchange and Reevaluation

Mrs. Arjona began to understand the IEP development process much better and asked how she might help Alberto's language development at home. Mrs. Escovar and Mr. Zook made several recommendations for home use (see Exhibit 8-17).

Mrs. Arjona was very enthusiastic about the recommendations from the language therapist and bilingual teacher. She then asked about his dressing and undressing skills. Ms. Gibson agreed that Alberto needed particular skill development in the areas of fasteners (zippers, snaps, buckles, buttons). Another annual goal was thus written in the area of "dressing/undressing without assistance to use the toilet." Again, Ms. Gibson divided the annual goal into subobjectives, with teaching strategies for each subobjective and an evaluation plan (see Alberto's own-care instructional area in the Exhibit 8-19 IEP).

Ms. Gibson and Mrs. Arjona agreed to work together on this skill. They decided that Ms. Gibson should send a weekly report home to Mrs. Arjona describing what fastener was being taught. Mrs. Arjona could then allow Alberto to practice the skill at home (see the sample notes in Exhibit 8-18).

The final area of concern in Alberto's skill development was expressed by Ms. Gibson. She wanted to increase Alberto's attention during activity time. Mrs. Arjona agreed with Ms. Gibson's concern. The team developed an annual goal to increase "on-task" behavior during play and activity time. Following the sequence in the HICOMP curriculum, several subobjectives were written that would permit a gradual increase in Alberto's attention span (see the problem-solving instructional area in the Exhibit 8-19 IEP).

Program Placement Decided

Ms. Gibson then summarized the IEP (Exhibit 8-19) for Mrs. Arjona and the other members of the team for additions or corrections. Mrs. Arjona expressed pleasure with the goals.

As the team discussed the annual goals, a placement decision was reached. Alberto would remain at the Julian preschool and receive itinerant language therapy from the unit's special education department. Ms. Gibson would carry out the remaining annual goals and reinforce the language development goals within her class. The team agreed that Ms. Gibson would periodically receive special technical assistance from the special education consultant whenever she needed resource support.

Mrs. Arjona said she was relieved with the placement decision. The team then agreed to reevaluate the goals at the end of May. Mrs. Arjona consented to the reevaluation date and signed Alberto's Individual Education Plan.

Exhibit 8-18 Sample Notes to the Home Regarding Alberto's Progress

Wk 1 Alberto is working on zipping and unzipping. This week, please unbuckle and unsnap Al's pants, take his hand, place it on the zipper and guide the zipper down. Then allow him to pull his pants down and later up. Place your hand on his, grasp the zipper catch and zip the zipper. Then snap and buckle without Alberto.

Wk 2 Dear Mrs. Arjona:

fastener - ZIPPER

Alberto's task - UNZIP-ZIP without assistance

Your task - unbuckle-buckle (belt)

unsnap-snap (pants)

verbal prompt ("put your hand on the zipper." etc.)

Exhibit 8-19 Alberto's Individual Educational Plan

INDIVIDUAL EDUCATIONAL PLAN

09 Case Number — PROGRAM ELIGIBILITY — 1980-81 School Year

Present Developmental Levels

Cover Sheet

IU 3209

Name: Alberto Arjona — Birthdate: 6/18/77

Preschool Teacher: Ms. Gibson — Date Prepared: 10/28/80

Itinerent Teacher: Mr. Zook — Prepared by: Ms. Gibson, Mr. Zook, Mrs. Escovar, Dr. McGlynn, and Mrs. Arjona

I. Individual Psychological Examination

Gesell--A normed-referenced developmental evaluation

II. Parental Input

Home Visits
Conference

III. Medical Confirmation

Medical Records Complete
No Problems

IV. Educational Assessment

Denver--Developmental Screening Test
LAP-D--Criteria-referenced developmental evaluation

V. Other

Teacher Observations

Recommended for Special Program ☑ — Not Recommended for Special Program ☐

Language Therapy in the Julian Center

Comment:

Exhibit 8-19 continued

Individual Educational Plan

Julian Preschool

Student's Name Alberto Arjona Program Julian Preschool

Birthdate June 18, 1977 Teacher(s) Ms. Gibson

Present Date Oct. 28, 1980

Primary Assignment	Date Started	Expected Duration	Special Media/Materials
Julian Preschool	Nov. 1, 1980	On Going	None

Extent to which the student will participate in Regular Preschool:
Alberto is involved in a regular preschool with itinerant special education services.

Services:

language therapist	Nov. 1., 1980	On going	None

IEP Planning Participants: *Mrs. Arjona - Parent*
Ms. Gibson - teacher
Mr. Zook - language therapist
Mrs. Escovar - teacher (bilingual)
Dr. McGlynn, Psychologist LEA Rep.

Dates for review and/or revision of the IEP Plan: ______

Person responsible for the maintenance and implementation of the IEP Plan: *Ms. Gibson, Preschool teacher*

Exhibit 8-19 continued

Individual Educational Plan

Julian Preschool

Student's Name Alberto Arjona

Instructional Area(s) Problem Solving

Annual Goal(s) To increase on-task behavior

OBJECTIVES	INSTRUCTIONAL METHODS	EVALUATION PLAN and CRITERIA
Alberto will . . .		
a. engage in play/games for increasing lengths of time (or # of tasks) prior to reinforcement.	SHAPING	CHART DURATION OF A BEHAVIOR
b. attend during group "lessons" or activities for 5-10 minutes with some adult prompting.	SHAPING, PROMPTING ATTENTION, VERBAL PROMPTING, VISUAL PROMPTING	CHECKLIST with BEHAVIORAL RATING SCALE-- CHART DURATION OF A BEHAVIOR
c. persist at most age appropriate tasks (e.g., puzzles, art activity) until completion and with minimal prompts from adults	SHAPING	CHART DURATION OF A BEHAVIOR
d. attend for group activities of 10-15 minutes with little prompting from adults (e.g., story times, games circles)	SHAPING	CHART DURATION OF A BEHAVIOR

Exhibit 8-19 continued

Individual Educational Plan

Julian Preschool

Student's Name Alberto Arjona

Instructional Area(s) Own Care

Annual Goal(s) dress/undress without assistance when using the toilet

OBJECTIVES	INSTRUCTIONAL METHODS	EVALUATION PLAN and CRITERIA
Alberto will . . . a. unzip and zip a zipper on pants. b. unbutton and button a button on c. unbuckle and buckle a buckle on belt. d. unsnap and snap a snap on pants. e. put on and remove elasticized pants. f. put on and take off pants with snaps (or buttons) and zipper.	SHAPING MODELING VERBAL, MANUAL AND VISUAL PROMPTING	USE OF A BEHAVIOR RATING CHECKLIST Criteria cannot do it = 0 begins to try = 1 does it with help = 2 does much alone = 3 does it alone = 4 Sample unzips 01234 zips 01234 unbuttons01234

Exhibit 8-19 continued

Individual Educational Plan

Julian Preschool

Student's Name Alberto Arjona

Instructional Area(s) Language Development

Annual Goal(s) To increase verbal experssion skills between peers and teachers.

OBJECTIVE	STRATEGY	EVALUATION
a. uses speech to attract attention of peer or caregiver	shaping	frequency of behavior
b. names several objects	shaping, modeling	frequency of behavior
c. makes one word requests	shaping, modeling	frequency of behavior
d. expresses gratitude verbally	shaping, modeling	critical incidence method
e. describes or designates an object	anecdotal record, modeling	frequency of behavior
f. names, directs, or describes an action	modeling	frequency of behavior
g. uses real two-word combinations	chaining behavior, modeling	frequency of behavior
h. uses varied forms of word combinations (location, possession, nonexistence, negation, questions, action-recipient)	chaining behavior, modeling	frequency of behavior
i. uses 50 words	modeling	frequency of behavior
j. combines several parts of speech	chaining behavior, verbal prompting	frequency of behavior
k. uses compound sentences	chaining behavior, verbal prompting	frequency of behavior
l. ask 3-4 word questions	modeling, verbal prompting	frequency of behavior
m. uses sentences of 4-8 words in length	chaining behavior, modeling	frequency of behavior
n. shares (during conversation or show and tell), information about activities/events experienced	verbal prompting	simple yes-no statement

Exhibit 8-19 continued

	OBJECTIVE	STRATEGY	EVALUATION
o.	retells stories of actual events or from books	verbal prompting	simple yes-no statement
p.	requests favorite activities or objects by asking complete questions or making statements of preference	verbal prompting	frequency of behavior simple yes-no statements
q.	uses staetements of over seven words in length	chaining behavior, modeling	frequency of behavior
r.	converses with other adults and children	chaining behavior, modeling	anecdotal record

Appendix A

Selected Preschool Developmental Scales Useful in Constructing Prescriptive Linkages

Compiled by Marie Bianchianello,
University of Maryland

Test name: Assessment of Children's Language Comprehension (ACLC)

Authors: R. Foster, J. Giddan, and J. Stark

Publisher: Consulting Psychologists Press, Inc.

Date: 1973

Age range: 3-6 years

Purpose of the test—The ACLC was designed to measure the achievement of receptive language skills at a basic level. The authors recommend that it be used as an aid in assessing limitations in language. It taps short-term auditory memory and the processing of syntactic sequences. The ACLC has four parts, A through D. It begins by assessing core vocabulary development (A) and goes on to assess the comprehension of items with an increasing number of critical elements (B through D). The manual offers training suggestions based on the results of the tests.

Standardization/norms—The ACLC was standardized on 311 nursery and elementary school children from Tallahassee, Florida, and rural Vermont Headstart programs. The authors report that the educational and socioeconomic backgrounds of the parents were mixed and that 38 percent of the children were black. Mean scores are presented according to age. The authors agree that normative data are limited and are in the process of collecting new and more complex norms.

Reliability—Internal consistency was measured by generating odd-even reliability coefficients for vocabulary alone and tests B, C, and D combined. Coefficients proved to be .86 and .80 respectively.

Validity—No data on validity are given in the manual.

Administration/scoring—Administration and scoring of the ACLC requires no special training on the part of the examiners, although the authors suggest that they read and become familiar with the manual. On the average, the test can be completed and scored in 15 minutes. The child is required to point to the picture that corresponds with the examiner's word or phrase. If part A is passed, the child is given all of parts B, C, and D. The score is the sum of the correct responses.

Comment—The ACLC requires no verbal response from the child and lends itself easily to use with speech- and language-impaired children. A Spanish translation is provided; and, although norms for the translation are not given, it may be helpful in determining whether a language difference is a critical factor in the child's inability to do well on the English version. Suggestions for training given in the manual are helpful as an aid to program planning.

Test name: Assessment-Programming Guide for Infants and Preschoolers

Author: W. Umansky

Publisher: Developmental Services, Inc.

Date: 1974

Age range: 0-72 months

Purpose of the test—The Assessment-Programming Guide is intended for use (a) as an aid in determining the needs of a child through systematic observation and (b) to provide guidelines and direction in planning a program geared to the child's specific needs.

Standardization/norms—The skills in each developmental area have been grouped according to the ages at which the majority of children can perform them. These determinations are reportedly based on cross-comparisons with data available in the literature and informal observations. References are made available in the manual.

Reliability—No data are given in manual.

Validity—No data are given in manual.

Administration/scoring—The guide is designed to assess the child's level of development in six areas: motor, perceptual motor, language, self-help, personal-social, and academic. Some items may be listed under more than one area. Testing time depends upon the individual situation, since the items are planned for spontaneous exhibition rather than structured administration. Complete evaluation may take several weeks. Basal and ceiling ages are determined, and a functioning age for each developmental area is established.

Comment—The Assessment-Programming Guide is very useful for its intended purpose. It is important to note, however, that the functioning ages are purely estimates and not precise measures of intellectual functioning. An IQ score cannot and should not be calculated from the functioning age. The author strongly suggests that the examiner become familiar with the developmental scales and evaluation procedures before using the guide.

Test name: Battelle Developmental Inventory (BDI)

Authors: John Guidubaldi, Jean Newborg, J.R. Stock, Linda B. Wnek

Publisher: Walker & Company
720 Fifth Avenue
New York, N.Y. 10019

Age range: 0-8 years

Purpose and behavioral content of the test—The BDI was designed to assess the progress of children ages 0-8 years in the broad domains including: cognition, psychomotor performance, communication, personal-social performance, and self-help skills. In total, the test incorporates 563 items.

Three major purposes are served by the instrument:

1. Assessment of the handicapped child.
2. Evaluation of groups of handicapped children in early educational programs.
3. Assessment of normal children.

To best fulfill these purposes, the BDI was developed on a milestone approach, a child's development can be characterized by an attainment of critical skills or behaviors in a particular sequence.

Standardization/norms—Over 4,000 items from published and unpublished tests were analyzed in constructing the milestones utilized by the BDI, then scrutinized by experts before a draft version of the test was run on 152 children in a pilot study. A stratified random sampling procedure, modeled after the norming of the WISC-R, was used to balance age, sex, racial composition, geographic location, and occupational classification. The total sample included 524 children from a variety of types and sizes of schools as well as geographic location.

Reliability–Chronbach's Alph (internal consistency) range from .90-.96 for total scores (across ages), and .81-.90 for individual domain scores.

Concurrent Validity:

BDI—Stanford Binet (MA)	.82
BDI—Stanford Binet (IQ)	.58

BDI—McCarthy Scales	.79
BDI (total)—Minnesota Child Development Inventory	.85
BDI (total)—Bayley (Mental)	.923
BDI (total)—Bayley (Motor Scale)	.925

Predictive validity—In total, five predictive validity studies are reported in the manual comparing the BDI with several widely used instruments. One unique study utilized a team approach in the assessment of kindergarten children, another involved the assessment of 30 infants between the ages of 1 month and 2½ years.

Administration/scoring—Raw scores for the individual domains are converted to scaled scores Y = 10, S.D. = 3. A total score is determined by adding the five domain scores, X = 100, S.D. = 15. Developmental Quotients (DQ) and percentile ranks and a profile analysis can be determined from the manual.

Each of the five domains has a separate administration manual, including standard administration procedures for normal children and those exhibiting the five handicapping conditions: severe motor impairment of the lower body and general musculature, severe impairment of the arms and hands, severe visual impairment, severe hearing impairment, and severe speech impairment.

Critique—The Battelle Developmental Inventory appears to be an instrument which should receive wide use. Figures from the standardization of the scale prove the test to be of sufficient reliability for the developmental assessment of individual children. Validity studies are comprehensive and well illustrate the instrument's usefulness.

Major strengths of the BDI are:

1. It is an appropriate instrument for both handicapped and non-handicapped children.
2. The manual (I reviewed the norming edition) appears straightforward and complete. Scoring instructions are easy to follow. The technical information provided is extensive and hopefully will be precedent-setting for developmental inventories of its kind.
3. Each of the five domains has a separate color-coded administration manual. Every item within a domain is listed on a separate page, along with all the necessary information for its administration. Instructions for handicapped children are provided on the same page, when appropriate. The manuals are well organized and accurately written, making the BDI a relatively easy instrument to administer.
4. The BDI was designed for administration in either a school or clinic setting, with the results to be used in the planning and evaluation of an instructional program.

Test name: Bayley Scales of Infant Development (BSID)

Author: N. Bayley

Publisher: Psychological Corporation

Date: 1969

Age range: 2-30 months

Purpose and behavioral content of the test—The BSID are designed to give a three-part assessment of a child's range of developmental skills within the first 2½ years of life. The three major scales and comparative indices are (a) the Mental Scale-Mental Development Index (MDI), 163 items; (b) the Motor Scale-Psychomotor Development Index (PDI), 81 items; and (c) the Infant Behavior Record—an interview-observer rating scale. The three complementary parts of the BSID provide the clinician with a comprehensive estimate of an infant's development and a means of comparing the infant with age peers.

The following range of functional capabilities is assessed by the BSID: sensory-perceptual activities; discriminations, object-constancy, memory and problem solving; receptive/expressive language; classification, body control; fine/gross muscle control; finger-hand dexterity; eye-hand coordination; and balance and coordination skills.

Standardization/norms—The tasks used in the BSID were selected and adapted from existing infant scales but draw heavily from three California infant and preschool scales. Incorporation of such items and construction of new item-tasks resulted in the 1960 version and 1969 revision of the BSID. The 1960 BSID were normed on 1,400 children between the ages of 1 and 15 months. Revised and expanded, the 1969 version was normed on 1,262 normal children between 2 and 30 months of age and was based on the 1960 census.

Reliability and validity—Test-retest reliability = .75. Split-half reliability coefficient ranges: MDI = .81 to .93; PDI = .68 to .92. Concurrent validity with Stanford-Binet on 350 children from 18 to 30 months of age = .57.

Administration/scoring—The average administration time for the mental and motor scales of the BSID is approximately 45 minutes when given by a trained clinician with extensive experience in testing infants across all age levels. The tasks are adapted to the responsiveness of the child but given in a standard manner according to activities and objects called "situation codes." The scoring of the BSID is done in a pass (P) and fail (F) format, and the PDI and MDI quotients are computed from a norm table utilizing total number of items passed. A deviation developmental quotient (DQ) based upon a mean of 100 underlies the PDI and MDI indices. Age equivalents for individual performances can be computed from the norm tables. The BSID manual represents a model for the construction and organization of other developmental scales.

Comment—The BSID represent the best organized and developed and the most technically adequate of all the comprehensive developmental measures now in existence. Their standardization, content, and conceptual format make them a model for similar scales. The BSID not only provide a method of pinpointing specific developmental deficits but also can be adapted as an aid to individual educational goal-planning. Increasing the age range of the BSID to 5 years would make it indispensable for preschool assessment and evaluation.

A second source can be obtained for handicapped infants (2 to 30 months) through use of the BSID: *Modifications for Youngsters with Handicapped Conditions* (Hoffman, 1974). Standard testing procedures are modified by positioning the child differently, having other persons participate and/or using equipment that allows the child to demonstrate understanding of the required task. Administration of the modification takes from 10 to 90 minutes.

Test name: Callier-Azusa Scales: Assessment of Deaf-Blind Children

Author: R. Stillman, editor

Publisher: Callier Center for Communications Disorders, University of Texas at Dallas, and the Council for Exceptional Children, Reston, Va.

Date: 1975

Age range: 0-9 years

Purpose of the test—The Callier-Azusa Scale was designed (a) to assess the developmental level of children for whom other methods of assessment are inadequate due to language requirements or intact sensory modalities, (b) to measure progress over time for program evaluation, and (c) to provide guidance for program planning. It is composed of five areas: motor development, perceptual development, daily living skills, language development, and socialization. The subscales of each scale are made up of sequential developmental milestones.

Standardization/norms—The scale was compiled by staff members at the Callier Center. The included items described normal developmental milestones observable among deaf-blind children. Each subscale was then classroom tested and revised accordingly. The Callier-Azusa Scale was field tested in the area surrounding Callier, Texas. The 70 teachers who were surveyed indicated that the scale was most effective when used with lower-functioning, deaf-blind and multihandicapped children.

Reliability—No data are given in manual.

Validity—No data are given in manual.

Administration/scoring—Administration and scoring are based on relatively informal observations of classroom behavior. Examiners need not be formally trained, but the authors suggest that they be thoroughly familiar with the child. Completion of the scale should require at least two weeks of observation. Several individuals who have contact with the child in school may take part in the child's evaluation. Five criteria have been set up to determine whether or not the child has attained a specific step on a subscale, and examples are given in the manual.

Comment—The Callier-Azusa Scale has been found to be an effective measure of development in low-functioning, deaf-blind or multihandicapped children. Children functioning above the 6- or 7-year level should be assessed by more appropriate measures. The author warns that the scale should be used not as a program planning device but as a guide for the teacher in planning a child's individual program.

Test name: Carolina Developmental Profile (CDP)

Author: D.L. Lillie

Publisher: Kaplan School Supply

Date: 1976

Age range: 2-5 years

Purpose of the test—The CDP is designed to assist the teacher in establishing long-range objectives to increase developmental abilities in six areas: fine motor, gross motor, visual perception, reasoning, receptive language, and expressive language.

Standardization/norms—The author states that the items on the checklist were developed through "extensive testing of young children and careful review of the literature." Age ranges are given, but these have not been developed through formal standardization measures and should not be applied definitively.

Reliability and validity—The CDP manual states that issues of reliability and validity are not relevant to the use of the CDP since its purpose is not to compare or assess the child in terms of age normative data.

Administration/scoring—The author recommends that the CDP be administered during several sessions. A basal age and developmental age ceiling (DAC) are determined for each skill area. The criterion for establishing the DAC varies from one skill area to another. Presentation of an item may be altered if the examiner feels the child could then accomplish a previously failed task.

Comment—Care should be taken to ensure that the CDP is used solely for what it was intended: facilitating the establishment of objectives to increase developmental abilities. It is not intended as a means of comparing children and should not be used as such. Use of the age levels as diagnostic levels can be misleading and should be avoided.

Test name: Cognitive Skills Assessment Battery (CSAB)

Authors: A. Boehm and B. Slater

Publisher: Teachers College, Columbia University

Date: 1977

Age range: Preschool-Primary Grades

Purpose of the test—The CSAB is a criterion-referenced instrument designed to delineate a profile of skill competencies as an aid in curriculum planning for kindergarten and prekindergarten classes. It provides a profile of skills for the individual child and for the class as a whole. It can also be used to make a year-end evaluation of pupil progress. Five competency areas are covered: (a) orientation toward environment, (b) coordination, (c) discrimination, (d) memory, and (e) concept formation and comprehension.

Standardization/norms—The CSAB was administered to 1,497 kindergarten and prekindergarten children from lower and middle socioeconomic levels in urban, suburban, and rural communities across the country. Norms are in the form of percentages of children who passed and failed each item at the low and middle socioeconomic levels. The data were collected in the fall (N = 898) and spring (N = 599) of the school year.

Reliability—According to the authors, the computation of currently accepted reliability coefficients is inappropriate since total scores and area scores are not obtained and since the content of the battery is such that there is little variability on the items.

Validity—Content validity is established to the extent that the areas included in the battery are among the teacher's curricular goals.

Administration/scoring—The CSAB is designed to be individually administered by a teacher or teacher's aide in approximately 20-25 minutes. Familiarity with the instrument is required. Some areas are scored by a (+) or (−) according to whether or not the child can perform the task. Other areas are scored according to the level of the child's performance. A description of the competency required at each level is provided in the manual. The responses are recorded on both a pupil-response sheet and a class-record sheet.

Comment—The CSAB is a well-designed and helpful criterion-referenced instrument for program planning. It also provides for the evaluation of program design based on the assessment. The user should be aware, however, that the battery has content validity only when the competency areas are included as a regular part of the curriculum.

Test name: Denver Developmental Screening Test (DDST)

Authors: W.K. Frankenburg and J.B. Dodds

Publisher: Ladoca Project and Publishing Foundation, Inc.

Date: 1970

Age range: 2 weeks to 6 years

Purpose and behavioral content of the test—The rationale of the DDST is to screen and identify those children with significant developmental delays in the acquisition of ''landmark'' developmental skills across motor, language, problem-solving, and self-help areas. The screening process serves only to locate gross developmental problems in infants and children that are to be confirmed by more comprehensive testing.

The following major functional areas are assessed by the DDST: gross motor, fine-motor adaptive, expressive/receptive language, and personal-social skills (105 tasks).

Standardization/norms—Potential items were selected after surveying existing infant and preschool tests. The criteria of ease of scoring, quick administration, and no elaborate equipment to perform the item were used to reduce the original 240 items to 105. The items were standardized on 1,036 (543 male, 493 female) normal Denver children between 2 weeks and 6 years of age. Children who were adopted, premature, twins, or who had serious sensory problems were deleted. The standardization group represented racial-ethnic groups in the Denver population according to the 1960 census. Tables present data on the ages at which 25 percent, 50 percent, 75 percent and 90 percent of the total sample performed the task.

Reliability and validity—Test-retest over one week showed that the same items were passed or failed by the same child from 90 to 100 percent of the time yielding total agreement of 98.8 percent. Reliability among examiners ranged between 80 and 95 percent of agreement on previously scored items.

Performance on the DDST tasks was differentiated as abnormal, questionable, or normal. These labels corresponded highly to scores of the same children on the

Standard Binet and the Bayley scales, with 7.2 percent over referrals and 2.95 percent underreferrals.

Administration/scoring—The DDST can be administered quickly, inexpensively and with relatively little training by the examiner. The manual is clear and precise, and scoring guides are explicit. The four sections are analyzed together and any delay in two or more items places the child in the abnormal sector. Performances are scored normal, abnormal, questionable and untestable.

Comment—Although the DDST has met with wide acceptance, one must keep in mind that it is not as reliable, valid, or sensitive as it might be. Use with children under 30 months of age is questionable. At 4½ years of age, the test is quite satisfactory. It is doubtful that an untrained examiner can adequately administer it.

Test name: Developmental Activities Screening Inventory (DASI)

Authors: R. DuBose and M. Langley

Publisher: Teaching Resources Corporation

Date: 1977

Age range: 6-60 months

Purpose of the test—The DASI is a nonverbal instrument designed as a screening measure for children functioning between the ages of 6 and 60 months. The 55 test items in the DASI tap skills in the areas of fine-motor coordination, cause-effect and means-end relationships, association number concepts, size discrimination, and seriation. The manual includes suggestions for teaching the concepts assessed in the DASI in order to provide an interim preintervention program.

Standardization/norms—No standardization data are provided in the manual.

Reliability—No data are reported in manual.

Validity—Concurrent validity: (a) 45 children with multiple disabilities were given the DASI and either the Cattel or Merrill-Palmer Scales. A correlation of .91 was obtained. (b) A study in which 42 delayed and nondelayed children between 7 and 14 months of age were given the DASI, PAR, and DDST generated coefficients of .97 with the PAR and .95 with the DDST. (c) 14 day-care children between 15 and 54 months of age were administered the DASI, PAR, and DDST. Coefficients of .92 with the PAR and .87 with the DDST were obtained. In order to confirm the fact that the DASI did not penalize language-impaired children, the DASI and REEL were administered to 45 children with known language delays. A correlation of .91 was obtained.

Administration/scoring—The DASI was designed for administration by classroom teachers with a basic knowledge of child development. The testing can be completed in 20 to 25 minutes. Basal level is the level at which the child passes all items, and ceiling is the level at which the child fails all items. A response form is provided for recording the child's performance on each task. Plus (+) or minus (−) scores are given according to whether or not the child passes the item.

Comment—The DASI is a useful screening measure for identifying developmental delays in children 6 months to 5 years of age. The instructional suggestions included in the manual for teaching the concepts being assessed are especially helpful for planning and temporary programs prior to formal diagnostic assessment.

Test name: Developmental Profile (DP)

Authors: G. Alpern and T. Boll

Publisher: Psychological Development Publications

Date: 1972

Age range: 6 months to 12 years

Purpose of the test—The DP was designed to assess the development of the child between the ages of 6 months and 12 years. The inventory profiles a child's developmental age-level functioning in each of the following five areas: physical, self-help, social, academic, and communication. There are 217 items arranged by age levels.

Standardization/norms—The DP was standardized on 3,008 subjects in Indiana and Washington. The sample was comprised mainly of black children and white children from urban areas whose mothers had volunteered for the program. The subjects were mostly middle class and were fairly well distributed in terms of age and sex.

Reliability—A study was conducted in which 36 Head Start teachers listened to a parent interview and independently scored the mother's responses. Of these teachers, 71 percent had identical correct scores, 89 percent were within one point of the score, and all of the teachers came within two points of the correct score. A second study was conducted to obtain scorer reliability, reporter reliability, and test-retest reliability. No significant difference was found between the two scores obtained by two interviewers 2 or 3 days apart.

Validity—Studies have indicated that the validity of the mother's reports with the child's actual ability ranged from 81 percent to 87 percent accurate. In another study, 18 retarded children were administered the DP and the Stanford Binet. Correlations found were .55 between the Binet mental age and average functioning age of the DP, .80 between the Binet mental age and the average score from the DP academic and communication age profiles, and .84 between the Binet mental age and the DP's academic age. A third study was done with 70 preadolescent children with an IQ range of 20 to 48. A correlation of .91 was found between the DP's academic scale and the individually administered IQ tests.

Administration/scoring—Administration consists of determining whether the child has mastered the item in question and circling a pass or fail digit on the scoring form. The basal level is the highest age section in which the child passes all items. The sum of all digits circled in the pass column beyond the basal is then added to the basal age to produce a developmental age.

No special training is required to administer the items. If necessary, the administration can be done entirely through an interview with someone who knows the child well.

Comment—The DP is a carefully standardized measure that is easy to administer and score. The authors warn that caution should be exercised in administering the profile to other than white or black children from urban areas.

Test name: Developmental Programming: Infants and Children—vols. 1, 2, and 3

Authors: D. Schafer and M. Moersch, editors

Publisher: University of Michigan Press

Date: 1977

Age range: Birth to 36 months

Purpose of the test—The Developmental Programming instrument was designed to aid in describing the child's comprehensive functioning and identifying the child's strengths and weaknesses. It was also intended to provide information for planning comprehensive developmental programs for children functioning below the 36-month age level. The instrument consists of three parts: (a) assessment and application, (b) an early intervention developmental profile, and (c) stimulation activities. Six different skill areas are examined: perceptual/fine-motor, cognition, language, social/emotional, self-care, and gross-motor development.

Standardization/norms—According to the Developmental Programming manual, the instrument has not been formally standardized. Assignment of the items to specific ages was determined through research on other instruments. Items not taken from standardized tests were assigned the age norms designated by their original source.

Reliability—Interrater reliability: Test-observer paradigm was used in the scoring of 100 profile items. Results ranged from a low of 80 percent agreement to a high of 97 percent agreement between tester and observer with a mean of 89 percent agreement overall.

Test-Retest reliability: (N = 15) (a) three months retest coefficients were .98 with social-emotional, self-care, and perceptual/fine-motor scales; .97 with the gross-motor and cognition scales; and .93 with the language scale. (b) Six-months retest coefficients were .97 with the perceptual/fine-motor and social/emotional scales, .96 with the gross-motor scale, .95 with the self-care scale, .93 with the language scale, and .90 with the cognition scale.

Validity—Concurrent validity studies have generated the following results:

- Bayley (N = 13): Coefficients ranged from a high of .96 with social-emotional and cognition scales to a low of .80 with the self-care scale.
- Bayley (N = 7): Coefficients ranged from a high of .95 with the gross-motor scale to a low of .66 with the self-care scale.
- Vineland Social Maturity Scale (N = 11): Coefficients ranged from a high of .93 with the perceptual/fine-motor scale to a low of .77 with the self-care scale.
- REEL (N = 11):Coefficients ranged from a high of .75 with the language scale to a low of .33 with the gross-motor scale.
- Clinical Motor Evaluation (N = 14): Coefficients ranged from a high of .84 with the gross-motor scale to a low of .36 with the language scale.
- Internal Validity (N = 14): Coefficients ranged from a low of .59 among the language, self-care, and gross-motor scales to a high of .95 between the cognition and social/emotional scales.

Tables are provided in the manual for a more detailed analysis of the validity studies.

Administration/scoring—The Developmental Programming profile was designed to be administered by a multidisciplinary team. Administration time is said to be about 1 hour depending on familiarity with the scale. Administration is done through general observations and structured situations. Basal and ceiling ages are determined (basal = six consecutive passes, ceiling = six consecutive failures). Four scoring levels are provided: pass (P), fail (F), pass-fail (PF), and omitted (O). Complete scoring directions are given for each scale. The profile graph in volume 2 is then charted according to one of the two methods presented in the manual. Stimulation activities for IEPs and general remediation are suggested in volume 3.

Comment—The materials in this instrument are well organized and extremely useful in screening and program planning. The authors have warned that the profile should not be used as a predictive measure or for the diagnosis of handicapping conditions. The instrument was intended to supplement, not replace, data obtained from standardized evaluative measures.

Test name: Gesell Developmental Schedules (GDS)

Authors: A. Gesell et al.

Publisher: Psychological Corporation

Date: 1940

Age range: 4 weeks to 6 years

Purpose and behavioral content of the test—The GDS are designed to provide a functional, clinical assessment of the infant and preschool child's range of developmental skills across major behavioral areas. The scales in their entirety assess the neurological status of the developing infant and also sample more complex developmental progressions. In this respect, the scales are not an intellectual measure but a vivid sampling of interrelated behaviors across maturity-age levels and developmental areas. Separate developmental ranges, instead of a global index, are obtained for each of five developmental domains: gross motor, fine motor, language, adaptive, and personal-social (approximately 350-400 behaviors). Essentially, the child's performance and status are assessed in terms of task skills expected at certain age levels. The scales are particularly useful for identifying and predicting neurological difficulties and retardation.

Standardization and norms—Gesell originally sought to chart longitudinally the development progress of children rather than to create a technically adequate test. The original sample consisted of 107-150 infants and preschoolers between the ages of 4 weeks and 6 years, with approximately 26 to 35 children at each "key" age. The norms were clearly limited in that they focused only on normal individuals from middle-class parents of northern European ancestry in the New England area. The GDS badly need to be restandardized, stressing current norm groups and a review of item placement.

Reliability and validity—Conflicting technical data exist on the GDS; however, the scales are generally viewed as adequately reliable measures of developmental status. More research studies are needed.

Tester-Observer reliability: 44 infants, 40 weeks of age, $r = .90$. Concurrent validity: GDS and Binet, 195 3-year olds, $r = .87$. Predictive validity: GDS (40 weeks) versus Binet (3 years), 195 children, $r = .48$.

Administration/scoring—The GDS require rigorous training and review of several manuals in order to be correctly administered. The administration of the GDS takes about 45 to 60 minutes. In the structure of the examination, standard developmental tasks are adapted to the responsiveness of the child within the framework of "examination sequences."

The scoring of the scales lacks objectivity, yet provides a descriptive, clinical picture of a child's range of developmental skills. Separate developmental ranges are derived for each of five developmental areas based upon the distribution of +, −, and ± scores. A developmental quotient (DQ = DA/CA × 100) can be computed but is not meant to be comparable to the IQ.

Comment—The GDS is the "grandfather" of developmental measures from which all other scales have been directly adapted and organized. The GDS provide an excellent clinical analysis of the neurological, physical, and psychomotor status of developing children. However, the scales need extensive restandardization to be considered a technically adequate diagnostic tool.

Test name: Haeussermann Educational Evaluation—Inventory of Developmental Levels

Author: E. Haeussermann

Publisher: Grune and Stratton

Date: 1958 and 1972

Age range: 2 years to 6-6+ years

Purpose and behavioral content of the test—The Educational Evaluation of Haeussermann offers a structured and pragmatic approach to the educational and developmental appraisal of children between 2 and 6 years of age, or functioning on that level, who exhibit handicaps in sensorimotor and expressive capabilities. The method is the result of experimental exploration rather than statistical computation and compilation. It details a structured interview of performance with suggestions for methodical modification of items depending on the child's functional deficits.

The systematic evaluation determines whether or not a given child can function in all areas related to learning and development and which level he has reached in each functional area. The essential tasks in the evaluation have been devised so as to require neither manipulation nor speech of the child. Such modifications permit a gradual reduction in demand and difficulty so that there can be a gradual retreat to lower levels of functioning.

As Haeussermann (1958) asserts, the approach offers a

> systematic sampling strategy across the child's functional skills and deficit areas with the primary objective of determining the kinds of training and experience that will best promote his own adaptive functional abilities . . . and . . . the special circumstances which are needed to create conditions for learning in the handicapped preschool child (p. ix).

The evaluation provides a basis for planning individualized instructional plans and strategies by comprehensively assessing such skills as comprehension and use of language, recognition of pictorial symbols, ability to discriminate between colors, concept amounts, ability to perceive, differentiate and recall from memory basic symbols, visual-spatial orientation, etc.

Normative and technical data—No normative or technical data are presented in the manual; however, the evaluation is a very pragmatic, clinical method designed to appraise the status of the individual child rather than make comparisons with the normally developing child. Twenty-five years of clinical experience in medical and special educational settings provide the groundwork for the soundness of this approach for children with multiple handicaps.

Administration, scoring, and interpretation—The invaluable Haeussermann Educational Evaluation manual details a structured format for presenting items to the handicapped preschooler. Individual item/task modifications are explained that alter the behavioral/response demand of the items as well as the use of differential materials (objects vs. pictures, edible vs. nonedible items). The intent of the assessment is to define those levels of functioning that represent the child's current levels of performance and those strategies that enable him to respond and learn effectively. Performance is scored pass-fail, but modifications enable one to sample lower demand levels so that one always reaches a representative functional level for each child. The structured appraisal of intact sensory, motor, and language skills enables one to arrive at a plan for intervention; and inventories of developmental levels enable one to derive age levels for generalized functioning.

Test name: Hiskey-Nebraska Test of Learning Aptitude

Author: M.S. Hiskey

Publisher: The Author: 5640 Baldwin, Lincoln, Nebraska 68508

Date: 1966

Age range: 3-16 years

Purpose of the test—The Hiskey-Nebraska Test of Learning Aptitude is designed for use with both hearing and deaf children. The behavior samplings in the areas of memory, picture identification, and picture association for use with the deaf have demonstrated relevance to the school-learning potential of deaf children.

Standardization/norms—In the standardization samples, there were more deaf than hearing children at each age level. Parental occupational levels for the hearing population correspond closely to the U.S. census data. There are no comparable data for the deaf population. However, since the test uses deaf students in the sample, it is superior to many nonverbal tests that are standardized in hearing children but used with the deaf.

Reliability—Split-half reliability for the deaf is reported to be .95, and for the hearing .93, in groups having an age range of 3 to 10 years; and .92 and .90 respectively for the age range of 11 to 17 years. There is no other information reported for these groups.

Validity—Subtest intercorrelations for the deaf range from .33 to .74 for the age range of 3 to 10 years and .31 to .43 for the age range of 11 to 17 years. For the hearing, the intercorrelations range from .32 to .78 for the 3- to 10-year age group and .25 to .46 for the 11- to 17-year age group. A correlation of .86 is reported for IQ comparisons with the S-B, .82 with the WISC.

Administration/scoring—The administrator must be skilled when presenting the Hiskey-Nebraska test to a deaf student. There are instructions for pantomime administration. Experienced psychometricians should give the test. Each of the subtests yields a separate score that converts to a learning age and a learning quotient for deaf students; for hearing children, grade equivalents are given.

Test name: Marshalltown Behavioral Development (MBD) Profile

Authors: M. Donahue, J. Montgomery, et al.

Publisher: AEA #6 Preschool Division

Date: 1975

Age range: 0-6 years

Purpose of the test—The MBD Profile was designed as an aid to individualized prescriptive teaching within the home environment. It was developed for use with handicapped and culturally deprived preschool children (0 to 6 years). Three skill areas are tapped: communication, motor and social. Incorporated into these categories are such skills as receptive and expressive language, cognitive, fine- and gross-motor, personal-social, self-help, and emotional skills.

Standardization/norms—The MBD manual states that the instrument was researched in the summer of 1972 but does not report the results of the research. The arrangement of items is based on the sequence of "normal" child development.

Reliability—The manual does not report reliability data.

Validity—The manual does not report validity data.

Administration/scoring—The MBD Profile is scored on the basis of existing skills, emergent skills, and skills not yet mastered. Those skills clustered between the basal and ceiling items are the ones considered for remediation. Each item on the profile has corresponding behavioral objectives and strategies for implementation.

Comment—The MBD Profile seems to be particularly useful for those involved in program planning or prescriptive teaching for very young children. The behavioral objectives and strategies are especially helpful. The profile should be used only for its intended purpose and not as a test or a comparison among children.

Test name: Maxfield-Buchholz Scale of Social Maturity for Preschool Blind Children

Authors: K. Maxfield and S. Buchholz

Publisher: The American Foundation for the Blind

Date: 1957

Age range: Birth to 6 years

Purpose of the test—The M-B was designed to measure the personal and social development of blind children from birth to 6 years. The scale consists of 95 items divided into seven categories: self-help, general (G); self-help, dressing (D); self-help, eating (E); communication (C); socialization (S); locomotion (L); and occupation (O). The M-B scale generates a social age (SA) and social quotient (SQ).

Standardization/norms—The standardization sample was based on 605 ratings on 398 children who were considered "legally blind" from birth. The manual reports that statistical data on the parents, aside from age, were not available. The children tested were from New York City, New Jersey, Boston, Connecticut, Chicago, and Minneapolis.

Reliability and validity—The M-B manual reports difficulty in reliability and validity testing due to the small size of the population, the diversity in the types of blindness, and the difficulty of diagnosis with very young children. The authors feel that some degree of validity was established by the procedures employed in setting up the scale, such as the percent-passing technique and the refinements that served to distribute the items by category.

Administration/scoring—Good rapport with both the child and the informer is considered essential to proper administration. Experience with the testing and interviewing of children and parents and familiarity with the scale and the specific items are suggested. Five scoring levels are presented: (+) if the child clearly demonstrates the skill; (+F) if the child has formerly demonstrated the skill but did not do so during the session; (+No) if there has been no opportunity for the child to learn the skill due to the restraints of blindness but which could be easily learned if the child were not blind; (±) if the skill is in an emergent state; and (−) if the skill is clearly not evident. Full credit is given to +, +F, and +No scores; half-credit to ±; and no credit for − scores. The number of correct items is added to SA, and SQ scores are determined.

Comment—The M-B scale seems to be well designed and set up. Clearly, there is a need for such a scale for use with blind children. However, the need for further study of its validity and reliability is indicated.

Test name: McCarthy Scales of Children's Abilities (MSCA)

Author: D. McCarthy

Publisher: The Psychological Corporation

Date: 1972

Age range: 2.5 to 8.5 years

Purpose of the test—The MSCA were designed to evaluate the general intellectual level of young children and to indicate both their strengths and weaknesses. There are 18 subtests in the six scale areas. The scale areas are: verbal, perceptual-performance, quantitative, general cognitive, memory, and motor.

Standardization/norms—The standardization sample consisted of 100 normal children at each of 10 age levels. The sample was stratified according to age, sex, color, geographic region, and father's occupation. The group was divided equally among males and females; and the data, in general, closely approximated the latest census estimates (1969-70).

Reliability—Test-retest after a one-month interval generated reliability coefficients ranging from a low of .69 on the motor scale to a high of .91 on the general cognitive scale. Split-half reliability tests generated the following coefficients: verbal scale: .84 to .92; perceptual performance scale: .75 to .90; general-cognitive scale: .90 to .96; memory scale: .72 to .80; and motor scale: .60 to .84.

Validity—General cognitive scale: .63 with the WPPSI-verbal, .62 with the WPPSI-performance, .71 with the SPPSI-PS, and .81 with the Stanford-Binet. Verbal scale: Coefficients ranged from .43 to .66 with the WPPSI-V, P and FS and the S-B. Perceptual-performance scale: .27 with the WPPSI-P, and .41 with the WPPSI-V and the S-B. Memory scale: Coefficients ranged from a low of .39 with WPPSI-P to a high of .67 with the S-B. Motor scale: Coefficients were below .10 with the WPPSI-V and the S-B.

Administration/scoring—The MSCA test is individually administered and usually takes from 45 to 75 minutes depending on the age of the child. Instructions for administration are detailed and clear; however, the manual does not indicate any specific examiner qualifications. Tables are provided for the conversion of raw scores into scale indexes.

Comment—The MSCA are well-standardized and reliable measures for use with nonhandicapped children. There are no norms and no scale equivalents of raw scores earned by exceptional children. One study has indicated that children diagnosed as learning-disabled obtained GCIs in the mentally retarded range where there was no other indication of mental retardation. Until further research is done, caution should be exercised in interpreting the scores of exceptional children.

Test name: Memphis Comprehensive Developmental Scale (MCDS)

Authors: A. Quick et al.

Publisher: Fearon Publishers/Lear Siegler, Inc.

Date: 1974

Age range: 3 months to 5 years

Purpose and behavioral content of the test—The MCDS is the initial step in a system of assessing and programming for the exceptional preschool child. The MCDS, as a teacher-administered, criterion-referenced measure, is designed to determine a child's current level of developmental functioning (present and absent skills) in the following behavioral areas: personal-social, gross motor, fine motor, language, and perceptuo-cognitive. The primary purpose of the assessment is the identification of deficient skill "targets" to form the basis of individualized instructional goal-planning.

Standardization/norms—No normative data are reported in the Project Memphis manual. However, the MCDS and its related programming components are intended primarily as criterion-referenced measures and are not meant to replace traditional comprehensive developmental tests. The item placements and tasks are adapted from these traditional scales.

Reliability—No technical data are reported in the manual.

Validity—No technical data are reported in the manual.

Administration/scoring—The MCDS is administered essentially much like other scales using tasks of increasing difficulty and complexity across different areas. Scoring is accomplished by a simple pass/fail index. A raw score for each developmental area is found by adding the number of tasks passed; developmental ages for each are derived by noting the age level at which the total raw score falls on the scale. ''Information gained from administration of the scale should be used for educational program planning and *not* psychological or developmental diagnosis'' (Quick et al., 1974a, 1974b).

Comment—The MCDS is an excellent teacher-administered developmental measure to guide program planning for the exceptional preschooler. Standardization of the scale would increase its usefulness as both a norm- and criterion-referenced measure. Caution in the use of the MCDS is indicated as a result of the age placement of various items and the questionable precision of the age levels (i.e., 3.25), which would affect reliable developmental assessment.

Test name: Preschool Attainment Record (PAR)

Author: E.A. Doll

Publisher: American Guidance Service, Inc.

Date: 1966-67

Age range: Birth to 7 years

Purpose and behavioral content of the test—The PAR is designed to screen and identify children who possess marked physical, social, communication and intellectual handicaps. It does not allow for strict normative comparison but does permit comparisons of a child with himself or herself on various successive measures. It combines an assessment of physical, social, and intellectual functions in a global appraisal of young children. The PAR is applied by means of both interview and observation that do not require immediate ''testing'' nor the actual presence of the child under consideration. Eight categories of functional skills are assessed by the PAR: ambulation, manipulation, rapport, communication, responsibility, information, ideation and creativity.

Standardization/norms—There has been no standardization of the PAR. Placement of items resulted from information existing in the literature on child development. The PAR extends the method of the Vineland Social Maturity Scale to focus specifically on preschool capabilities.

Reliability and validity—None are reported in the manual. Information on validity comes from a review of the literature on child development plus expert opinion as to the placement and applicability of the items that are similar to those included within traditional developmental scales.

Administration/scoring—The PAR procedure is similar to that of the Vineland Social Maturity Scale. Primarily, a person who is familiar with the child is interviewed. The items on the scale are evaluated by the examiner as to whether the child passes or not. Observation of the child is necessary if information is otherwise unavailable or if double checking seems indicated. Scores include a + if the item passes successfully, ± for intermittent behavior, and − if the child is unable to do the item. The child receives an attainment age divided by life age multiplied by 100.

Comment—The purpose of the PAR is not really to test a child but to obtain descriptions of the child's ordinary or "habitual" behavior. There seem, however, to be some serious difficulties associated with the test. The PAR manual does not explain the relevance or use of the attainment age or quotient. Further, the categories of items often overlap, which may allow for subjectivity of evaluation. The specific item definitions at the end of the manual do give the reader a general knowledge of the time when certain behaviors appear. Much work needs to be done on this test. It can be used with children with handicapping conditions and if used cautiously can be of benefit in formulating programs for handicapped children.

Test name: Preschool Language Scale (PLS)

Authors: I.L. Zimmerman, U.G. Steiner, and R.L. Fvatt

Publisher: Charles E. Merrill Publishing Company

Date: 1969

Age range: 1-8 years

Purpose of the test—The PLS was designed to appraise systematically the early stages of language development. The scale evaluates maturational lags, strengths, and deficiencies as they pertain to developmental progress. The test consists of auditory-comprehension, verbal-ability, and articulation scales. The results are used in the planning of programs for remediation. A Spanish (Mexican-American) version of the scale is also available.

Standardization/norms—The PLS manual indicates developmental age placements of the items representing normative findings from research studies in language development and from experience administering the PLS. No normative data are given. The authors encourage the development of local norms and request that any attempts be shared with them.

Reliability—Split-half reliability was measured using children enrolled in two consecutive year-long Head Start programs. Reliability coefficients ranged from a low of .75 to a high of .92 with a median of .88.

Validity—Predictive validity: PLS with Lee Clark Reading Readiness Test, 79 percent correct prediction; PLS with Burt Reading Test, $r = .24$. Content validity: The PLS manual states that content validity is provided for through the detailed description and rationale given for each of the test items. Concurrent validity: Several studies of concurrent validity were done and a detailed analysis is provided in the manual, a summary of which follows:

- PLS with PPVT: Coefficients ranged from a low of .26 to a high of .66; the lowest coefficients were achieved with middle-class nursery school children and the highest with children in Head Start programs.
- PLS LQ with S-B IQ: 60 Head Start children, $r = .66$; 8 TMR children, $r = .70$.
- PLS LQ with CMMS IQ: $r = .68$.
- PLS LQ with Utah Test of Language Development LQ: $r = .70$.
- PLSACQ with WPPSI PIQ: $r = .33$.
- PLS LQ with ITPA LQ: $r = .97$.

Administration/scoring—The requirements for administration are (a) an examiner who is familiar with the instrument and sensitive to the needs of children, (b) strict adherence to procedure, and (c) correct recording and scoring. Administration and scoring should be completed in about 20 minutes. The point scores obtained can be converted into an auditory comprehension quotient (ACQ), a verbal ability quotient (VAQ), and a language quotient (LQ). The scores can also be plotted as a profile for a quick indication of language-skill strengths and weaknesses.

Comment—The PLS appears to be a well-researched assessment of early language development. Normative data are not available in the manual, and care should be exercised in using the norms provided. The PLS is a useful measure in the recognition of serious language problems and can be helpful as an aid to program planning.

Test name: Preschool Profile

Authors: L. Lynch and M. O'Connor

Date: 1977

Age range: Birth to 6 years

Purpose of the test—The Preschool Profile was designed as a procedure for (a) initial and ongoing assessment, (b) programming, (c) reporting, and (d) curriculum planning. The result of the profile is a chart that can be utilized as an individual record of the child's performance in the following areas: Gross-motor skills; fine-motor skills; preacademic skills; self-help skills; music, art and story skills; social and play skills; receptive language skills; and expressive language skills. It is intended for use with children who have language problems or delays in other areas of development.

Standardization/norms—The language items in the Preschool Profile were taken from the *Sequenced Inventory of Communication Development* (Hendrick, Prather, & Tobin, 1975). The items in the other areas were taken from the *Developmental Age Study* (Baker & Dudrey, 1968) and the *Learning Accomplishment Profile* (Sanford, 1978). No data are reported on the standardization of the Preschool Profile.

Reliability and validity—No data are reported.

Administration/scoring—In each designated area, the items are arranged in blocks that cover a 12-month developmental period. The profile can be administered by anyone who has contact with children and is familiar with normal child development. The profile is administered through observation and individual testing, and the skills are recorded as always performed, sometimes performed, and never performed. Once this is accomplished, a program is designed around the child's strengths and weaknesses.

Comment—The authors state that the Preschool Profile is a working model only and should be added to when appropriate. This is important to keep in mind when using the profile, since it is intended to measure eight skill areas within a 12-month block of time. Twelve months is too long a period in which to assess adequately developmental progress, especially with younger children. Also, these "blocks" contain an average of eight items per block (about one item per skill), which is not enough information to determine accurately strengths and weaknesses.

Test name: Scales of Early Communication Skills for Hearing-Impaired Children

Authors: J.S. Moog and A.V. Geers

Publisher: Central Institute for the Deaf

Date: 1975

Age range: 2-8 years

Purpose of the test—The Scales of Early Communication Skills for Hearing Impaired Children were designed to assess the speech and language development of hearing-impaired children between the ages of 2 and 8 years. The instrument measures skills in four language areas: receptive language, expressive language, nonverbal receptive, and nonverbal expressive.

Standardization/norms—The instrument was standardized on 372 children with no other handicaps aside from their hearing impairment. The children were from 14 oral programs for the hearing-impaired. The sex, race, and geographic locations of these children are not specified in the manual.

Reliability—Interrater reliability was determined through a study done with 31 deaf pupils between the age of 4 to 8. Two teachers who were acquainted with the children's abilities rated each of the children. Reliability coefficients ranged from .76 with receptive language to .91 with expressive language. The nonverbal receptive and expressive skill areas generated coefficients of .81 and .86, respectively.

Validity—No validity data are given in the manual.

Administration/scoring—The Scales of Early Communication Skills for Hearing-Impaired Children were designed for teacher administration as part of an ongoing acquaintance with and observation of the child. Ratings of +, ± or − are given depending on whether the child clearly demonstrates the skill, occasionally demonstrates the skill, or clearly does not have the skill.

Comment—The Scales of Early Communication Skills for Hearing-Impaired Children appear to be a useful instrument for assessing the receptive and expressive skills in both the verbal and nonverbal areas of hearing-impaired children. Caution should be exercised with its use, however, since background information in the form of sex, race, location, and socioeconomic status has not been specified for the standardization sample.

Appendix B

Selected Preschool Curricula Useful in Constructing Prescriptive Linkages

Compiled by Frances Moosbrugger Hunt and Andrea Berger
The Pennsylvania State University

Curriculum: The Cognitively Oriented Curriculum
Author: D.P. Weekart, High Scope Education Research Federation
Publisher: ERIC/NAEYC
Date: 1971

Target population—Culturally disadvantaged and educably mentally retarded children, 3 and 4 years of age.
Theoretical orientation—Piagetian.
Focus of intervention—The development of four different behaviors:

1. the ability to construct and make use of relationships among objects and events in the environment;
2. the ability to construct meaningful representations of self and the environment and to deal with these representations in more and more complex and abstract ways;
3. an increased attention span and concentration, helping to bring the child's behavior under conscious control; and
4. language skills.

Format—This curriculum has four content areas: classification, variation, temporal relations, and spacial relations. Activities are presented for each content area. The curriculum includes an introduction and instructions for use. An activity guide gives examples of activities appropriate to particular conceptual focuses at different levels of symbolization, into which the levels of operations are integrated.

Piaget's outline of the normal, invariant, developmental progression has been used as a framework for structuring the curriculum in two ways:

1. Levels of symbolization: (a) concrete "object level," (b) parts indicating the whole "index level," (c) representational "symbol level," and (d) representation through words "sign level."
2. Levels of operation: (a) directly physical "motoric level," and (b) "verbal level."

Curriculum: COMP Curriculum and Activity Manual
Authors: S. Willoughby-Herb, J.T. Neisworth, K.W. Laub, F. Hunt, and E. Llewellyn
Publisher: The Pennsylvania State University
Date: 1980

Target population—Handicapped and nonhandicapped, birth to 5 years of age.

Theoretical orientation—Behavioral, based on sequences of normal child development.

Focus of intervention—A total of 21 subskill areas organized within four general areas of development: communication, own care, motor, and problem solving.

Format—This spiral-bound curriculum is arranged by subskill areas, with over 800 objectives arranged by normal developmental sequence. The opened curriculum displays objectives, and for each objective there are precision teaching strategies, evaluation methods, and columns for recording child progress. Suggested activities for objective clusters are included. An accompanying manual, the *COMP Curriculum Guide,* contains instructions for implementing the curriculum, including precision teaching strategies, evaluation techniques, behavior management techniques, sample lesson-plan formats and activities, and procedures for placing the child in the curriculum.

The COMP Curriculum serves as an ongoing record of child progress. Evaluation and monitoring of child progress is facilitated by the easy-to-use record-keeping system.

Curriculum: Compet II: Commonwealth Plan to Educate and Train Mentally Retarded Students
Author: S.E. Gerwick, editor
Publisher: Pennsylvania Department of Education and Public Welfare, Harrisburg, Pa.
Date: 1978

Target population—Mentally retarded children from birth to 21 years of age.

Theoretical orientation—Behavioral.

Focus of intervention—Compet II is designed to provide a clear, detailed curriculum plan (individualized educational plan) for mentally retarded school-aged students and to provide the user with an opportunity to develop, expand, and refine the instructional skills needed to implement the plan effectively.

Format—This is a comprehensive curriculum that facilitates a diagnostic-prescriptive teaching approach. Included in the curriculum are the following materials: *Initial Compet* (a handbook) and seven other books, in each of which one of the following units can be found: basic living skills, motor development, perceptual and cognitive development, social living skills, career training, academic skills, motor development, and an inservice manual for teachers. Each unit consists of module objectives under which major objectives, enabling objectives, and activities are categorized. These modules are not in a specific teaching order; therefore, students must be tested in order to find their present instructional levels.

This curriculum was developed to complement and to aid in the development of an individualized educational plan.

Curriculum:	Curricular Programming for Young Handicapped Children—Project First Chance
Author:	C. Bos
Publisher:	University of Arizona
Date:	1980

Target population—Handicapped children of developmental ages from 2½- to 6½-year range who do not have severe visual or hearing impairments.

Theoretical orientation—Cognitive-behavioral.

Focus of intervention—This curriculum covers five skill areas: body management, self-care, communication, preacademics, and socialization.

Format—The color-coded, looseleaf-bound curriculum contains activities for both individual and group instruction; 47 tasks are outlined for individual instruction and 59 programs for group instruction.

Each program sheet specifies the behavior objective, prerequisite skills, and purpose of the program and outlines specific steps, materials procedures—including fading procedures—and recording procedures.

Additional manuals include *Systematic Data Monitoring,* which describes methods for data collection, evaluation, and behavior management, and *Assessment for Instructional Purposes,* which includes a criterion-referenced test that is easily linked to the curriculum.

Curriculum: Distar Language I: An Instructional System
Authors: S. Engelmann and J. Osborn
Publisher: SRA, Chicago, Ill.
Date: 1976

Target population—Data support the use of this program with (a) 4- to 6-year-old children with deficient language skills, (b) children with whom English is a second language, (c) children of primary age who are experiencing difficulty with their school work, (d) children who are involved in speech and language correction groups, and (e) children, 7 to 9 years old, who are labeled EMR.

Theoretical orientation—Behavioral.

Focus of intervention—Language instruction.

Format—The Distar program includes 160, 30-minute daily lessons. Specific teacher directions are included. The program is divided into 30 tracks, each teaching a set of related skills. The tracks are often divided into six groups: description of objects, actions, instructional words, classification, information, and applications.

Materials provided include five teacher-presentation books, which consist of the teacher's script and instruction as well as visual stimuli for the students; a teacher's guide; a storybook of stories to reinforce target skills; and three take-home books of worksheets.

The program is designed for small group instruction. It is based upon concept teaching and a dynamic, forceful, direct instructional style. Throughout the program, there are small sequential steps between tasks and there is continuous review of concepts previously taught.

Comment—Head Start and other evaluation data have consistently demonstrated that the Engelmann-Becker model (from which Distar was developed) was one of the most effective in producing significant gains in academic achievement tests taken by economically disadvantaged children.

Curriculum: The EMI Curriculum Pool Materials
Authors: W.B. Elder, and J.N. Swift
Publisher: University of Virginia Medical Center
Date: 1977

Target population—Multihandicapped infants, from birth to 24 months developmentally.
Theoretical orientation—Diagnostic-prescriptive.
Focus of intervention—Five general areas of development are covered: gross motor, fine motor, social, cognitive, and language.
Format—Infant learning activities are keyed to items from the EMI Assessment Scale. A total of 350 behavioral objectives—with an expanded definition, a rationale, a criterion for mastery, and sample instructional activities for each—are printed in a loose-leaf format with one objective and corresponding information per page.
Comment—The information provided for each objective constitutes a very helpful introduction for the individual who does not have formal training in infant stimulation techniques. However, the manual does not describe backup procedures or techniques that can be used if the child does not respond to the planned activities. A record-keeping system to monitor child progress is not provided.

Curriculum: An Experimental Curriculum for Young Mentally Retarded Children
Author: F.P. Connor and M.E. Talbot
Publisher: Teachers College Press
Date: 1970

Target population—Preschool, educable, mentally retarded children.
Theoretical orientation—Children will improve their ability to modify behaviors and increase coping skills when given increased opportunities across a variety of situations.
Focus of intervention—Seven general areas of development are covered: self-help, social, intellectual, manipulative, imaginative creative expression, and motor.
Format—The curriculum guide includes sections on programming objectives, settings, implementation, and evaluations. Each page of the programming section is divided into two subsections: (a) rating, which describes five levels of curriculum items with a definition and specification for each; and (b) programming, which describes

component prerequisite skills for each level of the curriculum item and provides specific teaching procedures and activity ideas for each level (teachers can delineate gradations in behavior within each level).

Comment—The authors note that significant increments in Stanford Binet scores of children attending an experimental preschool suggest a relationship between use of the curriculum and development in the seven general areas of development (Connor & Talbot, 1970).

Curriculum: Learning Abilities: Diagnostic and Instructional Procedures for Specific Learning Disabilities
Authors: A.H. Adams et al.
Publisher: MacMillan Company
Date: 1972

Target population—Mainstreamed preschool and kindergarten children with any of the following disabilities: learning disabilities, emotional disturbance, mental retardation, physical handicaps, hearing impairment, or language delay.

Theoretical orientation—Experience content approach.

Focus of intervention—This curriculum is designed to aid classroom teachers in identifying the strengths of each child so that they can plan instructional procedures that will be most productive in terms of the child's total growth and development.

Format—The curriculum is in a looseleaf format. Each chapter, prepared by a specialist, focuses on one of the above disabilities. The symptoms of each disability are described so that they may be used in classroom observation. Classroom materials are used in step-by-step procedures to make informal assessments. Progress-record sheets are included to aid in data collection. Instructional extensions of the assessment activities are included in each chapter. Each extension contains a specific objective that is taught through four activities. Evaluation suggestions follow each activity.

Curriculum: Learning Accomplishment Profile (LAP)
Author: A.R. Sanford
Publisher: Kaplan Press
Date: 1974

Target population—Handicapped children of developmental ages from birth to 6 years.
Theoretical orientation—Behavioral.
Focus of intervention—The LAP is designed to help the teacher of young handicapped children to identify developmentally appropriate learning objectives for each child in six areas of development: gross motor, fine motor, social, self-help, cognitive, and language.
Format—The LAP consists of three sections:

- Section I consists of a chart of developmentally sequenced behaviors based on recent normative data, with approximate developmental ages for each and columns for recording dates of assessment, achievements, and teacher comments.
- Section II consists of objectives, each of which is task analyzed into a hierarchy of responses for sequential learning.
- Section III contains 45 weeks of curriculum units with concepts presented hierarchically; the teacher can record specific behaviors demonstrated by each child within the learning units.

Instructions for use of the LAP and other supplementary materials—such as activity books and Early LAP, designed for children younger than 3 years— are also available.

Curriculum: Learning Language at Home
Author: M.B. Karnes
Publisher: Council for Exceptional Children
Date: 1977

Target population—Normal children from 3 to 5 years of age and handicapped children who are at this developmental level.
Theoretical orientation—Behavioral.
Focus of intervention—This curriculum was designed to be used by parents to ensure the continued development of their language-delayed youngster and to teach the parents how to interact with their child so that they are most likely to maximize the child's development.

Format—The program consists of 50 lessons in each of the following four areas: learning to do—motor skills, learning to look—visual, learning to listen—auditory, and learning to tell—speech. These lessons are sequenced in order of difficulty. The activities in the lessons are based on the Illinois Test of Psycholinguistic Abilities Communication Model. A master sequence (1-200) cuts across the four skill areas and lists activities in order of increasing difficulty. Each activity core consists of the objective, materials needed, a step-by-step procedure, and additional related reinforcing activities.

A curriculum manual, available to parents, contains suggestions for a successful lesson, specific suggestions for stimulating language development, techniques for maintaining behavior, and a progress record with directions for its use.

Curriculum: Portage Guide to Early Education
Authors: S.M. Bluma, M.S. Shearer, A.H. Frohman, and J.M. Hilliard
Publisher: The Portage Project
Date: 1976

Target population—Multiply handicapped children of developmental ages from birth to 6 years.

Theoretical orientation—Behavioral/diagnostic prescriptive.

Focus of intervention—The Portage materials are designed for use by parents of handicapped children and by home-based teachers. Activities are categorized as infant stimulation, cognitive, language, self-help, motor, and socialization.

Format—The Portage Guide consists of three components: a checklist of behaviors, a set of color-coded file cards of objectives and activities, and a manual of directions for using the checklist and card file.

- The checklist sequentially orders the objectives and can be used to record and monitor child progress; it can also be used as a criterion-referenced evaluation tool.
- The card file lists the skill title, an approximate developmental level, and several teaching activities.
- The manual outlines procedures for using the Portage materials, describes the preparation of behavior objectives and task analysis, and includes an introduction to correction and reinforcement techniques.

Curriculum: A Prescriptive Behavioral Checklist for the Severely and Profoundly Retarded
Author: D. Popovich
Publisher: University Park Press
Date: 1977

Target population—Moderately and severely retarded individuals with developmental ages from 0 to 3 years of age.

Theoretical orientation—Behavioral.

Focus of intervention—The development of motor skills, eye-hand coordination skills, language skills, and self-feeding skills.

Format—This program consists of a series of checklists that are used as assessment tools to prescribe remedial objectives. Each objective is finely task analyzed, with one objective per page. On the opposite page, materials, prerequisite skills, and procedures for implementation are described. Also included in the book are chapters on the use of the program, data collection, training aids, and parents.

Comment—Graphs are presented, indicating the progress made by the first seven severely retarded students to receive instruction in this program (Popovich, 1977).

Curriculum: Programmed Environments Curriculum
Authors: J.W. Tawney, D.S. Knapp, C.D. O'Reilly, and S.S. Pratt
Publisher: Charles Merrill Publishing Company
Date: 1979

Target population—Moderately, severely, and profoundly handicapped persons.

Theoretical orientation—Behavioral.

Focus of intervention—This curriculum is designed as a teacher's handbook for teaching basic skills to moderately, severely, and profoundly developmentally retarded persons. These skills are organized into eight domains: receptive language, expressive language, cognitive, fine motor, gross motor, eating, dressing, and grooming. The skills are based on normal developmental sequences spanning the period from birth to 3 years of age.

Format—The curriculum is an integrated learning system that includes 79 finely task-analyzed instructional programs in the above domains. Accompanying materials—such as data sheets, class observation forms, and instructions for using and modifying the curriculum—are also included. This system provides a structure for assessment, instruction, documentation of progress, and instructional modification. The components of the curriculum may be used to generate new instructional sequences, and an internal decision-making system provides guidance for program revision. The curriculum contains instructional modules, a video training tape (publishing date—July, 1980), and module posttests that may be used for inservice training.

Curriculum: Project Memphis
Authors: A.D. Quick and A.A. Campbell
Publishers: Kandall/Hunt Publishing Company
Date: 1976

Target population—Developmental ages birth to five years, handicapped children.

Theoretical orientation—Diagnostic-prescriptive. Intervention is based on the identification of deficits, and subsequent developmental programming is based on skill deficits.

Focus of intervention—This curriculum covers five general areas of development: personal-social, gross motor, fine motor, language, and perceptuo-cognitive.

Format—The curriculum's looseleaf format contains a total of 300 objectives and corresponding suggestions for facilitating acquisition of each. Intervention is based on the three-step system of (a) developmental evaluation (using the Memphis Comprehensive Developmental Scale), (b) Individual Educational Program planning using the Developmental Skill Assignment Record, and (c) educational evaluation using the Continuous Record for Educational-Developmental Gain.

Curriculum: Project PAR Sequential Curriculum for Early Learning
Authors: K.J. Cole and A.H. Stevenson
Publisher: Shaginaw County Child Development Centers, Inc.
Date: 1976

Target population—Children from 4 to 6 years of age with minimal learning difficulties.

Theoretical orientation—Developmental.

Focus of intervention—To prevent academic failure and prepare the slow learner for successful placement in a regular mainstreamed classroom when the child is likely to fall behind peers because of learning problems or is less developed in the areas of motor skills, perceptual skills, language, memory, or reasoning.

Format—The Project PAR package includes

- a series of manuals for replicating the Project PAR model,
- a sequenced curriculum for early learning,
- a comprehensive planning guide, and
- a card file of over 500 classroom activities for development of the specific objectives.

The PAR Sequential Curriculum for Early Learning consists of 222 color-coded pages of activities for promoting a series of developmental skills in the 2- through 6-year age range in cognitive, physical, social, and emotional areas. Each page of the curriculum includes a general skill and task, a specific behavior objective, materials, activity, and an evaluation method. Sample evaluation forms facilitate record-keeping.

Classroom Activities for use with Young Children–Strategies for the Development of Specific Teaching Objectives (Alford & Bassett) is a kit of 500 five-by-eight, color-coded cards of classroom activities corresponding to objectives in the curriculum.

Curriculum: The RADEA Program
Author: Dallas County Mental Health/Mental Retardation Center
Publisher: Melton Book Company
Date: 1976

Target population—Children who are functioning between the developmental ages of 0 to 7 years.

Theoretical orientation—Developmental/behavioral.

Focus of intervention—The primary goal of this program is to increase the adaptive behaviors of the child by structuring the rate and direction of behavior change. The intent of the program is to provide structured opportunities for the child to progress normally through the development stages of childhood. The RADEA Program concentrates on the attainment of specific functional processing skills. Areas included are visual perception, auditory perception, perceptual motor, oral language, and functional living.

Format—Each of the five areas of instruction has been analyzed and structured into component tasks representing the steps involved in mastery of that particular function. Materials include

- teacher's manual instructions for using the program
- task cards—each of the 564 cards contains a task objective, sequential teaching steps, materials, mastery criteria, and grouping instructions
- forms for data collection—daily progress charts, an individual progress profile, task trial sheets, and testing and remediation scoring sheets
- sounds and picture cards—3 recorded cassettes and 29 picture cards to use in auditory training
- Radeagraphics—exercise sheets
- Manuscript pages—practice pages that aid in printing the alphabet.

Curriculum: School Before Six: A Diagnostic Approach
Authors: L. Hodgen, J. Koetter, B. Laforie, S. McCord, and D. Schramm
Publisher: Cemrel, Inc., St. Louis, Mo.
Date: 1974

Target population—Children in nursery school to kindergarten from 3 to 5 years of age.

Theoretical orientation—Diagnostic-prescriptive.

Focus of intervention—To diagnose children's needs and strengths in the following areas: language; socioemotional development; and gross, fine, and perceptual motor.

Format—This curriculum is compiled in two volumes. Each chapter starts with a discussion of problems related to the area and then discusses the normal developmental sequence of children in that area. Each content area contains diagnostic procedures, directions for the tasks, simple forms for recording, suggestions for teaching, and specific preschool activities. At the end of each content area relevant research is discussed.

Curriculum: A Step-by-Step Learning Guide for Retarded Infants and Children
Authors: V.M. Johnson and R.A. Werner
Publisher: Syracuse University Press
Date: 1975

Target population—Moderately and severely handicapped children, from 2 to 12 years of age, who are functioning at a level under 4 years of age.

Theoretical orientation—Behavioral.

Focus of intervention—This curriculum is designed to facilitate instruction of handicapped children in the following areas: social, imitation, gross motor, self-care, language, fine motor, and perception.

Format—The curriculum contains 240 developmentally sequenced objectives and includes activity suggestions for developing these objectives. An explanation of the implementation of behavioral techniques is included.

Curriculum: The Teaching Research Curriculum for Moderately and Severely Handicapped
Authors: H.D. Fredericks, C. Riggs, T. Furey, D. Grove, W. Moore, J. McDonnell, E. Jordon, W. Hanson, V. Baldwin, and M. Wadlow
Publisher: Charles C Thomas
Date: 1976

Target population—The moderately and severely handicapped.

Theoretical orientation—Behavioral.

Focus of intervention—To provide individualized programs in the areas of language, self-help, motor, writing, and cognitive skill development.

Format—This spiral-bound curriculum consists of domains divided into major areas of development. An accompanying manual, *A Data Based Classroom for the Moderately and Severely Handicapped,* consists of a placement test and guidelines for the use of the curriculum. The manual explains in detail how to use behavior-modification and classroom-management techniques, how to structure the classroom, and how to implement small-group activities. It also includes methods for data collection and suggestions for the training of parents and volunteers.

Curriculum: Teaching Your Down's Syndrome Infant: A Guide for Parents
Author: M. Hanson
Publisher: University of Oregon
Date: 1978

Target population—Down's syndrome children from birth to 2 years of age.

Theoretical orientation—Behavioral.

Focus of intervention—To teach parents of Down's Syndrome infants to teach their children in four major areas of development: gross motor, fine motor, communication, and social self-help.

Format—This teaching manual contains instructions for implementing the curriculum. It includes teaching strategies, instructions for task analysis, and ongoing evaluation methods. Developmental milestones are outlined in charts, included in the guide, and specific activities are provided for each. Each activity or program includes a teaching objective, materials, and procedures. The specific teaching steps, recommended contingency techniques, and data collection activities are detailed in the procedures section. The manual also includes case studies of actual programs for two children and a chapter with encouraging feedback from parents who participated in the program.

Curriculum: Wabash Guide to Early Developmental Training
Authors: J.T. Tilton, L.M. Liske, and S.R. Bousland
Publisher: Allyn & Bacon
Date: 1977

Target population—Infants to school-age children.

Theoretical orientation—Diagnostic/prescriptive.

Focus of intervention—The Wabash Guide covers five general areas of development: motor, cognitive, language development, self-care, and number concepts and skills.

Format—Approximately 500 loose-leaf pages, bound in a heavy three-ring binder, contain objectives (theme oriented within general areas of development), an extensive bibliography glossary, record forms, equipment lists, and an index. Teaching strategies and activities are described in detail and are cross-referenced to other activities within the manual.

Appendix C

The Perceptions of Developmental Skills Profile (PODS): A Multisource Rating Profile of Functional Capabilities for the Preschool Child

Developed by Stephen Bagnato, D.Ed., Ronald Eaves, Ph.D., and John Neisworth, Ph.D.

A PROFILE OF PERCEIVED CAPABILITIES FOR THE PRESCHOOL CHILD

Few efforts have focused on evaluating adult perceptions of child capabilities. The emerging expectancy literature stresses the real effects that subjective impressions can have on child progress. Such variables are physical attractiveness (Adams & LaVoie, 1974; Clifford & Walster, 1973; LaVoie & Adams, 1974), race (Eaves, 1975; Rubovits & Maehr, 1970), socioeconomic status (Miller, McLaughlin, Haddon, & Chansky, 1968; Neer, Foster, Jones, & Reynolds, 1973), and sex (Jackson & Lahaderne, 1967; Meyer & Thompson, 1956) have been shown to influence teachers' impressions of student performance capabilities. These impressions may lead to significant differences in how teachers and aides work with children.

The work of Iscoe and Payne (1972) is exemplary in providing a method of identifying and recording value judgments about children. "Without doubt, much value judgment is involved in classifying exceptional children, and actually there seems no way to avoid such judgments. In fact, it may very well be that value judgments are an extremely important aspect of dealing with exceptional children" (p. 10). However, because of its focus, the Iscoe and Payne system is not readily applicable to preschool populations. The growing interdisciplinary involvement of school psychologists and educators with preschool populations demands the availability of an instrument designed to detect and summarize the subjective impact made on adults by children.

The Perceptions of Developmental Skills Profile: Goals and Descriptions

The *Perceptions of Developmental Skills Profile* (PODS) (Bagnato, Neisworth, & Eaves, 1977) is a screening instrument for standardizing and profiling the diverse perceptions of significant adults who interact with the handicapped preschooler. It was constructed for use in HICOMP, a comprehensive outreach model program for handicapped preschoolers. The PODS was designed to fulfill five major functions:

1. to screen and assess globally the handicapped preschooler's range of functional capabilities upon entry into a program;
2. to estimate roughly the curriculum entry points for each child;
3. to serve as a general monitor of a child's *perceived* progress through an established curriculum by focusing on the acquisition of functional skills;
4. to facilitate communication between teachers, parents, doctors, school psychologists, and others and to standardize diverse perceptions about the child; and
5. to provide an estimate of the realism with which an individual rater judges a child's status by comparing subjective measures on the PODS with performance estimates obtained elsewhere, so that discrepancies can be reconciled through parent counseling, teaching, agency training, and consultation.

The format for the PODS is a rating scale of functional skills within four major developmental areas: communication, social/emotional adjustment, physical, and cognitive development. Each developmental area is analyzed in terms of the subordinate functions listed in Exhibit C-1.

Each teacher or aide profiles his or her perceptions of the child's level of functional skills on a scale of 1 to 7. A rating of 1 denotes the absence of any perceived deficit in a functional skill, while a rating of 7 indicates the awareness by the adult of a profound problem (see Exhibit C-2). The raters judge the child in terms of their knowledge of normal child development, whatever it may be.

Unique to this scale are operational definitions of the child developmental dimensions that are rated. Because of these operational definitions, gross differences in ratings can be attributed to real differences in judgments rather than to the definitional ambiguity of the characteristics under assessment.

The PODS is not meant to replace performance measures of developmental status but rather to serve as a supplement to them. It provides a measure of the subjective reactions to a child's capabilities that may or may not correspond to more objective measures. The evidence presented in Exhibit C-3 suggests that the rater's judgments are often in close agreement with the results of standardized developmental evaluations. Thus, differences in correspondence between subjective and objective performance estimates can be detected with this approach.

Exhibit C-1 An Example of the PODS Profile

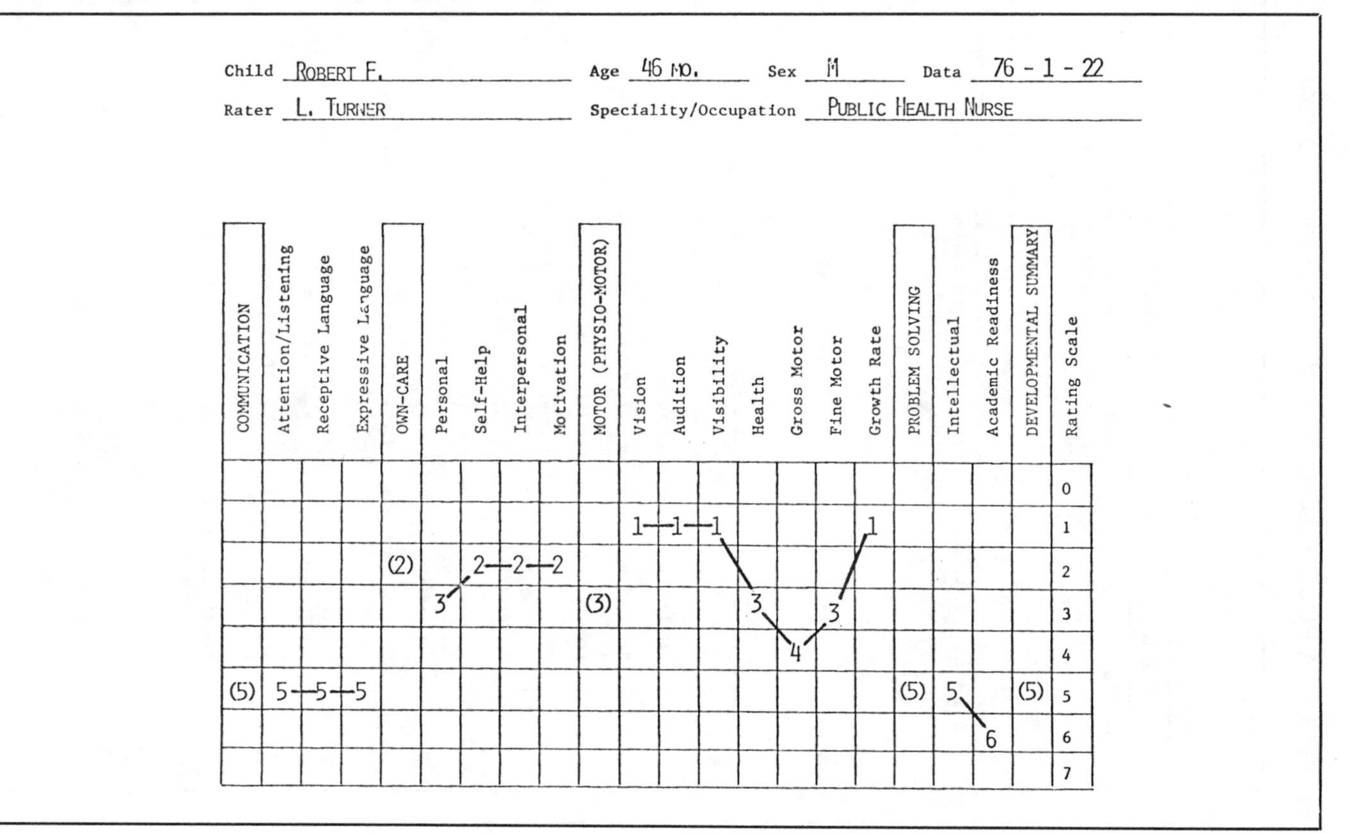

Child ROBERT F. Age 46 MO. Sex M Data 76 - 1 - 22

Rater L. TURNER Speciality/Occupation PUBLIC HEALTH NURSE

Category	0	1	2	3	4	5	6	7
COMMUNICATION						(5)		
Attention/Listening						5		
Receptive Language						5		
Expressive Language						5		
OWN-CARE			(2)					
Personal				3				
Self-Help			2					
Interpersonal			2					
Motivation			2					
MOTOR (PHYSIO-MOTOR)				(3)				
Vision		1						
Audition		1						
Visibility		1						
Health				3				
Gross Motor					4			
Fine Motor				3				
Growth Rate		1						
PROBLEM SOLVING						(5)		
Intellectual						5		
Academic Readiness							6	
DEVELOPMENTAL SUMMARY						(5)		

Exhibit C-2 A PODS Subdomain Scale and Behavior Targets

AREA	CAPABILITY TARGETS
OWN-CARE	personal and interpersonal capabilities with reference to such aspects of behavior as self-statements, appropriateness of behavior, self-help skills, social skills, motivation, and goal-setting.
Self-help Skills Subdomain............	age-appropriate self-help skills in such areas as feeding, drinking, toileting, dressing, washing, etc.

RATING	DEGREE OF CAPABILITY OBSERVED
0	Little or no opportunity to observe.
1	No problem in this area. Independent, self-directed and age-appropriate activity is exhibited in all self-help areas: feeding, toileting, grooming, etc.
2	Slight problem in this area, with generally appropriate self-help skills but some extra supervision and guidance are necessary.
3	Occasional difficulties, with some independent self-help skills, but supervision and guidance are often required beyond expectations for age.
4	Signs of considerable difficulty in demonstrating independent skills relative to age peers.
5	Moderate but clear problem in which demonstration of age-appropriate independent skills is rare.
6	The lack of age-appropriate self-help skills is severe and constantly in evidence.
7	Practically no age-appropriate self-help skills have been acquired.

Exhibit C-3 Congruence between Gesell Developmental Schedules and PODS Results (Child Performance vs. Adult Perceptions)

AN ASSESSMENT/CURRICULUM LINKAGE FOR PRESCHOOL CHILDREN

NAME	Robert F.	DOT	76-02-11
ASSESSMENT PURPOSE	Developmental	DOB	72-04-01
Progress Evaluation		CA	3-10-10 (46 mo.)

COMPREHENSIVE DEVELOPMENTAL ASSESSMENT PROFILE

I. QUANTITATIVE FUNCTIONAL ANALYSIS

The following measures were employed to determine Robert's *current functional levels in major developmental areas and to identify targets to guide individualized instructional goal-planning. The profile below provides a comprehensive estimate of* Robert's *pattern of skill development compared to that expected for his/her chronological age.*

TEST	CURRENT AGE FUNCTION
Gesell Developmental Schedules (GDS)	Motor = 36-42 mo.
	Adaptive = 30-36 mo.
	Language = 24-30 mo.
	Pers-Soc. = 42 mo.
Perceptions of Developmental	Communication = 5; Own-care = 2
Skills Profile (PODS)	Motor = 3; Probl-Solv. = 5

The PODS within the Screening, Assessment, Programming Sequence

The devising of procedures that are capable of providing a comprehensive, functional assessment of the capabilities of handicapped preschool children requires a more pragmatic, clinical perspective on diagnosis than is commonly proposed. The screening, identification, assessment, and programming for handicapped preschoolers is a complex process that necessarily involves the compilation of diagnostic information from diverse sources and the synthesis of such data into a format that facilitates individual instructional programming. To assess functional skills comprehensively, it is necessary to analyze and integrate *subjective, observational* and *performance* estimates of developmental capabilities. Also, to be effective and purposeful, the diagnostic process must be viewed as consisting of "interlinking" phases, each with distinct purposes, but each merging with the purposes of the next (screening → identification → comprehensive assessment → individual programming). The PODS is intended to aid in integrating this diagnostic sequence. It is primarily a screening device for organizing the judgments and subjective impressions of significant adults about a child's range of functional skills. With the multihandicapped preschooler, such perceptions, if well-defined, can be invaluable as guides to more comprehensive assessment and instructional programming.

An Illustration

The initial intake screening on a handicapped preschooler often includes a developmental history derived from the mother, medical reports of significant problems, and a global estimate of skill acquisition based upon performances on "landmark" developmental tasks. The PODS is viewed as serving a vital purpose in this screening process. First, the subjective estimates of the doctor, mother, home health nurse, and the diagnostic specialist can be compared in order to detect the degree of agreement concerning the child's level of disability in major functional areas. If gross judgmental differences exist, conferences could be initiated to determine whether such discrepancies represent situational-behavioral differences, unrealistic perceptions, or merely lack of knowledge of the child and normal developmental patterns in children. Then, if unrealistic judgments and lack of knowledge appear to complicate the view of the child's progress and skill acquisition, ongoing psychoeducational counseling can be initiated for the parent.

The PODS is also viewed as providing a method for guiding and supplementing developmental performance assessments. For example, in the Exhibit C-1 profile, the child was judged by a home health nurse to have significant, major functional deficits in all primary language areas, in cognitive and preacademic areas, and in gross motor capabilities. On the basis of this screening through behavioral ratings, standardized developmental assessment can be guided to focus upon specific skill areas that are perceived as problems, as shown in Exhibit C-3. The PODS is intended to draw attention to deficit areas and to focus upon whether performance measures of developmental status represent the typical in-situ behavior of the handicapped preschooler.

Preliminary Research on the PODS

Recent research (Bagnato et al., 1978) evaluated both the utility of the PODS as a global monitor of perceived child progress and the reliability of the rating scale within a preschool program.

Table C-1 portrays pre-post, gain-score rating results for 10 handicapped preschoolers over a 6-month time period. On the average, teachers and educational support personnel perceived the children as gaining 1.13 units on the profile. The average overall pretest rating for all children was 3.61 within a range of 6.30 to 1.80. The average overall posttest rating was 2.70 within a range of 5.90 to 1.20. On a scale of 1.00 to 7.00, a rating of 3.50 to 4.00 indicates impairment or functional skill deficits of a distinct, moderate nature.

The progress trends support the use of the PODS as a method of utilizing standardized, subjective judgments to monitor child progress. However, such information must be used as *support* data in a wide-range assessment format consisting of subjective, observational, and performance evidence of child progress.

In addition, interrater reliability data on the PODS were collected using the comparative, subjective ratings of eight preschool teachers and three psychologists. Independent, comparative ratings were made on 13 handicapped preschoolers over a 2-week time span within the preschool setting. Table C-2 presents results demonstrating that for the 13 children the average overall rating for teachers was 3.98, while that for psychologists was 3.42. Comparative ratings were also analyzed for each of five major developmental areas (see Table C-3). The average teacher rating was 3.21, while that of the psychologists was 3.05. In general, the teacher-psychologist ratings are described by a correlation of $r = .963$. On the basis of these preliminary results, the PODS holds promise as a reliable method of standardizing and profiling the diverse subjective impressions of significant adults interacting with the handicapped preschool child.

INSTRUCTIONS FOR USING THE SCALE AND PROFILE

Ratings on the PODS may be made by anyone who has had close contact with the child and has observed the child's performance in various situations. Ideally, several ratings should be made by parents, teachers, school psychologists, physicians, and other clinicians so that comparisons between judgments can be observed and differences in perceptions delineated.

Table C-1 PODS Functional Skill Progress Trends

Child	Communication		Own-care		Motor		Problem-Solving		General Development		Grand Gain
	Pre	Post	Pre	Post	Pre	Post	Pre	Post	Pre	Post	
A	4	3.3	3.3	2	3.5	2	5	3.5	5	4	1.2
B	2	1.3	2.3	1.3	3.4	3	2.5	1.5	4	2	1.0
C	5	4	4.5	3	4.5	3.5	6.5	6	6	5	1.0
D	5	4	2.5	1.5	1.5	1.5	5.5	4.5	4	3	1.5
E	2	2	1.5	1	1.5	1.5	2	2	2	2	.5
F	7	6	7	7	4	4	6.5	6.5	7	6	.4
G	3	1	3.5	1.5	3	2	3	1	3	2	1.8
H	4	2	3	1.5	4	1	3.5	2	4	2	2
I	3	1.5	2.5	1	1.5	1.5	3	1	3	1	1.4
J	3	3	3.5	3	2	2	3	3	3	3	.5
	Language 1.0 Units		Self-help 1.1 Units		Motor .7 Units		Cognitive 1.0 Units		Development 1.1 Units		Overall 1.13 Units

Note: Decreasing numbers indicate "perceived" skill acquisition.

Table C-2 PODS Mean Teacher-Psychologist Ratings per Child

	A	B	C	D	E	F	G	H	I	J	K	L	M	Mean Overall
T	4.6	5.2	6.7	1.1	3.7	5.6	2.3	1.5	1.3	1.5	2.4	2.3	3.6	3.98
P	4.3	5.1	6.1	1.7	3.4	5.8	1.9	1.9	1.2	1.7	1.9	2.1	2.6	3.42

Table C-3 PODS Mean Teacher-Psychologist Ratings per Developmental Area

	Communication	Own-Care	Motor	Problem-Solving	General Development	Overall
T	2.77	3.27	3.00	3.08	3.92	3.21
P	2.88	3.12	2.69	3.19	3.38	3.05

Exhibit C-1 presents an example of a finished profile on a particular child. Note the major behavioral areas under consideration: communication, own-care, motor, and problem-solving. Each of these areas is subdivided into more specific functions. These specific functions and their respective behavioral definitions (targets) provide a basis for each person's ratings.

Exhibit C-4 is a sample page from the scale. In order to make your ratings of a particular child's range of functional skills, follow these five steps and refer to the numbered illustrations in Exhibit C-2.

1. Carefully read the area under focus and especially the definition and "capability target-behaviors" that constitute the subdomain.
2. Recall the "capability targets" in the definition. Look to the section "Degree of Capability Observed" and the rating (0-7). Read each level of the scale carefully.
3. Select and circle the number corresponding to that level on the scale that best describes your perception of the child's capability in this area. A rating of 1 indicates normal capabilities or the absence of any impairment or deficiency. A rating of 7 represents extreme or profound impairment or skill deficit. Your rating should take into consideration the child's skills in comparison with those of the normal child of the same age.
4. Place the number corresponding to the capability level you select within the circle to the left of each page. Record any additional comments in the bottom section of each page.

Exhibit C-4 PODS Sample Subdomain Scale

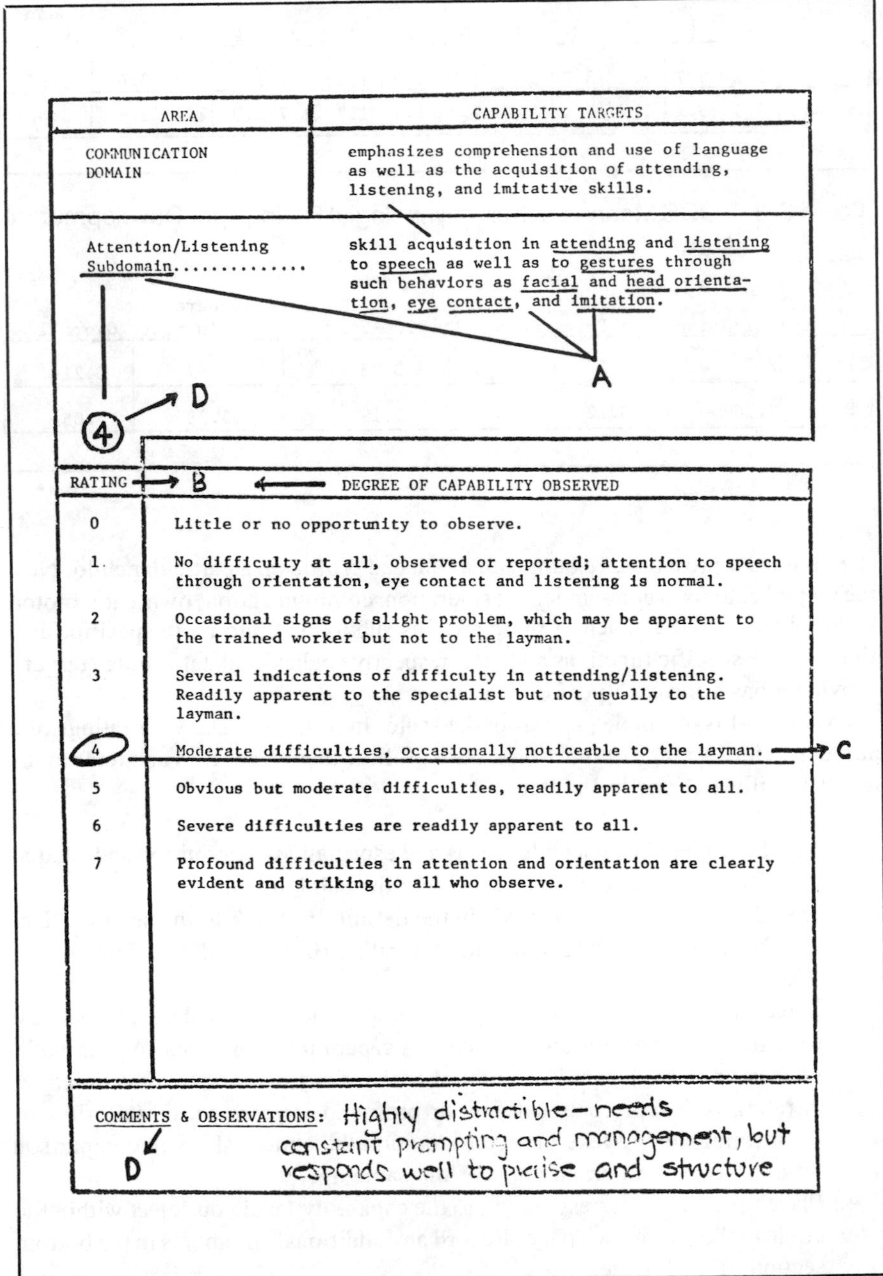

AREA	CAPABILITY TARGETS
COMMUNICATION DOMAIN	emphasizes comprehension and use of language as well as the acquisition of attending, listening, and imitative skills.
Attention/Listening Subdomain.............	skill acquisition in attending and listening to speech as well as to gestures through such behaviors as facial and head orientation, eye contact, and imitation.

RATING	DEGREE OF CAPABILITY OBSERVED
0	Little or no opportunity to observe.
1.	No difficulty at all, observed or reported; attention to speech through orientation, eye contact and listening is normal.
2	Occasional signs of slight problem, which may be apparent to the trained worker but not to the layman.
3	Several indications of difficulty in attending/listening. Readily apparent to the specialist but not usually to the layman.
4	Moderate difficulties, occasionally noticeable to the layman.
5	Obvious but moderate difficulties, readily apparent to all.
6	Severe difficulties are readily apparent to all.
7	Profound difficulties in attention and orientation are clearly evident and striking to all who observe.

COMMENTS & OBSERVATIONS: Highly distractible—needs constant prompting and management, but responds well to praise and structure

5. After completing the entire scale, record your ratings on the profile sheet provided, and connect the numbers by lines to form a profile or graph of the child's overall range of functional capabilities as shown in Exhibit C-1.

As Exhibit C-1 shows, in addition to individual ratings for the subdomains, average group ratings can be calculated for each of the major behavioral areas, for example, for communication (5). However, such averages should be used cautiously since they tend to obscure deficiencies that are evident within specific subdomains.

The full package of PODS subdomain scales, behavior targets, and profile sheet is provided in Exhibits C-5 through C-22. The PODS is not meant to replace performance measures of developmental status but rather serve as a supplement to them. The evidence presented in Exhibit C-3 suggests that the rater's judgments often are in close agreement with the results of standardized developmental assessments.

Exhibit C-5 The PODS Profile Form

PERCEPTIONS OF DEVELOPMENTAL SKILLS (PODS PROFILE)

Child ____________ Age ______ Sex ______ Date ______

Rater ____________ Specialty/Occupation ____________

COMMUNICATION	Attention/Listening	Receptive Language	Expressive Language	OWN-CARE	Personal	Self-Help	Interpersonal	Motivation	MOTOR (PHYSIO-MOTOR)	Vision	Audition	Visibility	Health	Gross Motor	Fine Motor	Growth Rate	PROBLEM-SOLVING	Intellectual	Academic Readiness	DEVELOPMENTAL SUMMARY	Rating Scale
																					0
																					1
																					2
																					3
																					4
																					5
																					6
																					7

Source: Bagnato, S.J. Neisworth, J.T., & Eaves, R.E. *The perceptions of developmental skills (PODS) profile.* University Park, Pa.: The Pennsylvania State University, HICOMP project, 1977. Reprinted with permission. (Exhibits C-5 through C-22)

Exhibit C-6 PODS Format—Communication Domain, Attention/Listening Subdomain

AREA	CAPABILITY TARGETS
COMMUNICATION DOMAIN	emphasizes comprehension and use of language as well as the acquisition of attending, listening, and imitative skills.
Attention/Listening Subdomain.............	skill acquisition in attending and listening to speech as well as to gestures through such behaviors as facial and head orientation, eye contact, and imitation.

RATING	DEGREE OF CAPABILITY OBSERVED
0	Little or no opportunity to observe.
1	No difficulty at all, observed or reported; attention to speech through orientation, eye contact and listening is normal.
2	Occasional signs of slight problem, which may be apparent to the trained worker but not to the layman.
3	Several indications of difficulty in attending/listening. Readily apparent to the specialist but not usually to the layman.
4	Moderate difficulties, occasionally noticeable to the layman.
5	Obvious but moderate difficulties, readily apparent to all.
6	Severe difficulties are readily apparent to all.
7	Profound difficulties in attention and orientation are clearly evident and striking to all who observe.

COMMENTS & OBSERVATIONS:

Exhibit C-7 PODS Format—Communication Domain, Receptive Language Subdomain

AREA	CAPABILITY TARGETS
COMMUNICATION DOMAIN	emphasizes comprehension and use of languag[e] as well as the acquisition of attending, listening, and imitative skills.
Receptive Language Subdomain.............	skill to receive and identify information as in tasks requiring pointing to specific pictures or objects or carry out directions.

RATING	DEGREE OF CAPABILITY OBSERVED
0	Little or no opportunity to observe.
1	No difficulty at all, observed or reported, in the normal reception of information and identification.
2	Occasional signs of a slight receptive language problem which may be apparent to the traines worker but not to the layman.
3	Several indications of difficulties in receptive language capabilities, readily apparent to the trained worker but not usually to the layman.
4	Moderate difficulty, occasionally noticeable to the layman.
5	Moderate but clear difficulty, readily apparent to all.
6	Severe receptive disability is evident.
7	Profound disability is evident in receptive language skills, and obvious to all who observe.

COMMENTS & OBSERVATIONS:

Exhibit C-8 PODS Format—Communication Domain, Expressive Language Subdomain

AREA	CAPABILITY TARGETS
COMMUNICATION DOMAIN	emphasizes comprehension and use of language as well as the acquisition of attending, listening, and imitative skills.
Expressive Language Subdomain.............	use of spontaneous speech and language in producing words and sentences to communicate feelings, wants, and thoughts.

RATING	DEGREE OF CAPABILITY OBSERVED
0	Little or no opportunity to observe.
1	No difficulty at all, observed or reported. Normal capability to communicate feelings wants, and thoughts verbally, through increasingly complex sentence forms.
2	Occasional signs of a slight expressive language problem which may be apparent to the trained worker but not to the layman.
3	Several indications of difficulty in verbal expression, readily apparent to the trained worker but not usually to the layman.
4	Moderate difficulty, occasionally noticeable to the layman.
5	Moderate but clear difficulty, readily apparent to all.
6	Severe disability is evident.
7	Profound disability in verbal expression is apparent and obvious to all who observe.

COMMENTS & OBSERVATIONS:

Exhibit C-9 PODS Format—Own-Care Domain, Personal Adjustment Subdomain

AREA	CAPABILITY TARGETS
OWN-CARE DOMAIN	personal and interpersonal capabilities with reference to such aspects of behavior as self-statements, appropriateness of behavior, self-help skills, social skills, motivation, and goal-setting.
Personal Adjustment Subdomain..............	developing sense of "self" with particular reference to whether overt behavior appears to be in accord with inferred abilities and to whether responses are appropriate to the situation.

RATING	DEGREE OF CAPABILITY OBSERVED
0	Little or no opportunity to observe.
1	No problem observed in this area. The child's self-concept appears consistently high but realistic.
2	Indication of a slight adjustment problem, which is transient and situation-specific and which is evident to a specialist only after observation.
3	Indication of some difficulties less transient but not necessarily of long duration.
4	Considerable difficulties are evident in time, yet not immediately evident to the nonspecialist.
5	Somewhat severe difficulty, immediately apparent to all and less likely to be transient. Several areas exist in which the self-concept is high or realistic but adjustment to situations is poor and in which reactions and responses are inappropriate.
6	Clearly severe problem, in which the child's self-concept is poor and unrealistic, and behavior inappropriate to the situation.
7	The problem is extreme and chronic. Behavior is very inappropriate to the situation and often bizarre, making personal adjustment severely impaired.

COMMENTS & OBSERVATIONS:

Exhibit C-10 PODS Format—Own-Care Domain, Self-Help Skills Subdomain

AREA	CAPABILITY TARGETS
OWN-CARE DOMAIN	personal and interpersonal capabilities with reference to such aspects of behavior as self-statements, appropriateness of behavior, self-help skills, social skills, motivation, and goal-setting.
Self-help Skills Subdomain.............	age-appropriate self-help skills in such areas as feeding, drinking, toileting, dressing, washing, etc.

RATING	DEGREE OF CAPABILITY OBSERVED
0	Little or no opportunity to observe.
1	No problem in this area. Independent, self-directed and age-appropriate activity is exhibited in all self-help areas: feeding, toileting, grooming, etc.
2	Slight problem in this area, with generally appropriate self-help skills but some extra supervision and guidance are necessary.
3	Occasional difficulties, with some independent self-help skills, but supervision and guidance are often required beyond expectations for age.
4	Signs of considerable difficulty in demonstrating independent skills relative to age peers.
5	Moderate but clear problem in which demonstration of age-appropriate independent skills is rare.
6	The lack of age-appropriate self-help skills is severe and constantly in evidence.
7	Practically no age-appropriate self-help skills have been acquired.

COMMENTS & OBSERVATIONS:

Exhibit C-11 PODS Format—Own-Care Domain, Interpersonal Subdomain

AREA	CAPABILITY TARGETS
OWN-CARE DOMAIN	personal and interpersonal capabilities with reference to such aspects of behavior as self-statements, appropriateness of behavior, self-help skills, social skills, motivation, and goal-setting.
Interpersonal Subdomain.............	interaction with adults and children in various contexts emphasizing peer acceptance, cooperative skills and adjustment to new and strange situations.

RATING	DEGREE OF CAPABILITY OBSERVED
0	Little or no opportunity to observe.
1	No problem exists in this area. The child interacts cooperatively with others and adjusts well to new interpersonal situations without evidence of fear or aggression.
2	A slight problem, transient in nature, causing only minor interpersonal difficulties.
3	Occasional yet slight difficulties in adjusting to group situations and usually apparent only to specialists. The child is accepted by the majority of his peers.
4	Evidence of greater interpersonal adjustment difficulties may be noticeable to the layman after observation. The problem is still transient, although general interpersonal adjustment is strained.
5	Evidence of moderate difficulty in interacting cooperatively with others and adjusting to such situations. Peer acceptance is poor.
6	The difficulties are clearly severe, with poorly developed social skills and great difficulties in adjusting to unfamiliar people and situations.
7	Profound problems are apparent, with maladaptive and inappropriate social behavior exhibited which apparently respects a long-standing problem.

COMMENTS & OBSERVATIONS:

Exhibit C-12 PODS Format—Own-Care Domain, Motivation Subdomain

AREA	CAPABILITY TARGETS
OWN-CARE DOMAIN	personal and interpersonal capabilities with reference to such aspects of behavior as self-statements, appropriateness of behavior, self-help skills, social skills, motivation, and goal-setting.
Motivation Subdomain.............	self-direction in various activities and tasks which require concentration, attention, persistence and goal-setting.

RATING	DEGREE OF CAPABILITY OBSERVED
0	Little or no opportunity to observe.
1	No problem in this area. Readily engages in various activities and tasks with a minimum of encouragement by others. Interest level appears to be self-directed and maintained.
2	Slight problem in this area. General motivation is good, but some transient episodes of frustration and boredom are evident.
3	Occasional difficulties, wherein assistance and encouragement are often required.
4	Indications of considerable difficulty in motivation. Encouragement is frequently required to maintain activity level. Frustration, boredom, and distractibility are frequently evident.
5	Moderately severe problem. Use of reinforcement management procedures are continually required to maintain activity level. Little self-direction and goal-setting are apparent.
6	Motivation is severely restricted with constant assistance and external direction required.
7	Motivation is not evident. Frustration, boredom and distractibility evident despite the use of motivational management procedures.

COMMENTS & OBSERVATIONS:

Exhibit C-13 PODS Format—Motor (Physio-Motor) Domain, Vision Subdomain

AREA	CAPABILITY TARGETS
MOTOR (PHYSIO-MOTOR) DOMAIN	range of functional capabilities and physiological status in the areas of: gross-fine motor skills, general health, growth and maturation, and visual and auditory capabilities.
Vision Subdomain.............	visual skills with particular reference to any problems which may hinder performance on tasks requiring visual tracking, orientation, and eye-hand coordination skills.

RATING	DEGREE OF CAPABILITY OBSERVED
0	Little or no opportunity to observe.
1	No apparent or reported disability in this area.
2	Slight difficulty seems evident with no real effect on performance.
3	Some noticeable defect in vision, sufficient to hinder smooth performance in some visual-motor tasks.
4	Moderate visual difficulties, limiting performance in a number of tasks.
5	Moderately severe visual problems which significantly affect performance in many activities and necessitate frequent help and supervision.
6	Severe visual problems with functioning in all areas observably affected; help and supervision needed most of the time.
7	Extremely severe visual problems with functioning in all areas significantly affected and constant help and supervision required.

COMMENTS & OBSERVATIONS:

Exhibit C-14 PODS Format—Motor (Physio-Motor) Domain, Audition Subdomain

AREA	CAPABILITY TARGETS
MOTOR (PHYSIO-MOTOR) DOMAIN	range of functional capabilities and physiological status in the areas of: gross-fine motor skills, general health, growth and maturation, and visual and auditory capabilities.
Audition Subdomain..............	auditory capabilities with particular reference to any problems which may impair the ability to hear (receive) and act on verbally-presented information.

RATING	DEGREE OF CAPABILITY OBSERVED
0	Little or no opportunity to observe.
1	No apparent or reported disability.
2	Slight auditory difficulty seems evident, with no real effect on performance.
3	Some noticeable defect in hearing, sufficient to hinder smooth performance and communication in some situations.
4	Moderate auditory difficulties, limiting performance in a number of tasks.
5	Moderately severe auditory problems which significantly affect performance and communication in many activities and necessitate frequent help and supervision.
6	Severe visual problems with functioning and communication in all areas observably affected; help and supervision needed most of the time.
7	Extremely severe auditory problems, with functioning and communication in all areas significantly affected and constant help and supervision required.

COMMENTS & OBSERVATIONS:

Exhibit C-15 PODS Format—Motor (Physio-Motor) Domain, Visibility Subdomain

AREA	CAPABILITY TARGETS
MOTOR (PHYSIO-MOTOR) DOMAIN	range of functional capabilities and physiological status in the areas of: gross-fine motor skills, general health, growth and maturation, and visual and auditory capabilities.
Visibility Subdomain.............	degree to which physical appearance significantly deviates from that of the physically normal child, and influences interactions with others.

RATING	DEGREE OF CAPABILITY OBSERVED
0	Little or no opportunity to observe.
1	No indication whatsoever of any deviance in physical appearance.
2	Slight indication of some minor deviance which is noticeable after observation to the trained specialist.
3	Several indications of some minor deviance which is immediately apparent to a trained specialist, but not to the layman.
4	Clear signs of relatively minor physical deviance usually apparent to the layman.
5	Clear indications of moderate deviance are readily apparent to the layman at all times.
6	Obvious and significant abnormality in physical appearance.
7	Striking and profound abnormalities in physical appearance.

COMMENTS & OBSERVATIONS:

Exhibit C-16 PODS Format—Motor (Physio-Motor) Domain, Health Subdomain

AREA	CAPABILITY TARGETS
MOTOR (PHYSIO-MOTOR) DOMAIN	range of functional capabilities and physiological status in the areas of: gross-fine motor skills, general health, growth and maturation, and visual and auditory capabilities.
Health Subdomain.............	degree to which health problems are chronic enough to impair performance, to hinder attendance, and to require medical attention.

RATING	DEGREE OF CAPABILITY OBSERVED
0	Little or no opportunity to observe.
1	No significant health problems observed or reported.
2	Recurrent minor health problems are evident or reported but routine responsibilities are not affected.
3	Chronic health problems are evident which occasionally hinder performance.
4	Evidence of chronic, extended health problems which inhibit routine responsibilities and require constant medical attention.
5	Evidence of chronic health problems of major proportions which hinder routine responsibilities are require constant medical attention.
6	Health problems are of major proportion requiring home, out-patient medical care.
7	Health problems are of major proportion requiring frequent hospitalization and continual medical care.

COMMENTS & OBSERVATIONS:

Exhibit C-17 PODS Format—Motor (Physio-Motor) Domain, Gross Motor Subdomain

AREA	CAPABILITY TARGETS
MOTOR (PHYSIO-MOTOR) DOMAIN	range of functional capabilities and physiological status in the areas of: gross-fine motor skills, general health, growth and maturation, and visual and auditory capabilities.
Gross Motor Subdomain.............	level of gross-motor skill development apparent in such activities as climbing stairs, running, jumping, balancing on one foot, and throwing and kicking balls.

RATING	DEGREE OF CAPABILITY OBSERVED
0	Little or no opportunity to observe.
1	No apparent or reported difficulty.
2	Some gross motor difficulties are evident but insufficient to warrant special help.
3	Some gross motor difficulties are evident in moving about but with help seldom needed.
4	Some gross motor difficulties are evident requiring occasional help in some activities and no real help in others.
5	Moderately severe gross motor restrictions necessitating help or direction more than half of the time.
6	Severe gross motor restriction necessitating help and direction most of the time, with only a few activities in which assistance is not required.
7	Extremely severe gross motor restrictions in locomotion, necessitating continual help and direction.

COMMENTS & OBSERVATIONS:

Exhibit C-18 PODS Format—Motor (Physio-Motor) Domain, Fine Motor Subdomain

AREA	CAPABILITY TARGETS
MOTOR (PHYSIO-MOTOR) DOMAIN	range of functional capabilities and physiological status in the areas of: gross-fine motor skills, general health, growth and maturation, and visual and auditory capabilities.
Fine Motor Subdomain.............	level of fine motor skill development apparent in such activities as block stacking, peg-placement, formboard, performance, drawing, and pellet-grasping tasks which require skills in eye-hand coordination and finger dexterity.

RATING	DEGREE OF CAPABILITY OBSERVED
0	Little or no opportunity to observe.
1	No apparent or reported difficulty.
2	Slight difficulty in coordination of fine motor skills but insufficient to warrant special attention.
3	Some coordination difficulties in fine motor skills with help seldom required.
4	Moderate coordination difficulties sufficient to require help in many activities.
5	Severe coordination problems, requiring help more than half the time while failing to complete most fine motor adaptive tasks.
6	Severe coordination problems that require help most of the time.
7	Extremely severe difficulties associated with nearly total lack of coordination in fine motor skills, necessitating constant help and supervision.

COMMENTS & OBSERVATIONS:

Exhibit C-19 PODS Format—Motor (Physio-Motor) Domain, Growth Subdomain

AREA	CAPABILITY TARGETS
MOTOR (PHYSIO-MOTOR) DOMAIN	range of functional capabilities and physiological status in the areas of: gross-fine motor skills, general health, growth and maturation, and visual and auditory capabilities.
Growth Subdomain.............	proportional body-growth rate in reference to that of the physically normal child.

RATING	DEGREE OF CAPABILITY OBSERVED
0	Little or no opportunity to observe.
1	No significant growth problems observed or reported.
2	Minor growth problems apparent to the trained worker but not to the layman.
3	Several indications of variations in proportional growth problems are readily apparent to the trained worker but not usually to the layman.
4	Clear but moderate growth problems, usually noticeable to the layman.
5	Obvious but moderate growth difficulties, readily apparent to all.
6	Severe growth difficulties, readily apparent to all.
7	Profound growth difficulties, obvious and of central concern.

COMMENTS & OBSERVATIONS:

Exhibit C-20 PODS Format—Problem-Solving Domain, Intellectual Subdomain

AREA	CAPABILITY TARGETS
PROBLEM-SOLVING DOMAIN	range and level of cognitive skills and general academic readiness.
Intellectual Subdomain..............	cognitive skill acquisition involving discrimination, classification, sorting, matching samples, stating abstract rules, and reproducing sequences.

RATING	DEGREE OF CAPABILITY OBSERVED
0	Little or no opportunity to observe.
1	No problem in this area. Demonstrates completely appropriate behavior in such activities as classification, sorting, matching samples, reproducing sequences, understanding concepts and stating rules.
2	Generally appropriate in this area but fluctuations appearing in some skill areas.
3	Several areas of difficulty with specific age-appropriate intellectual skills. General skills are still more or less average.
4	Many areas of fluctuation in which intellectual skills are below age expectations, but most general intellectual skills are still probably average.
5	Below average, general intellectual functioning with wide variations in areas of competence.
6	Limited skills, considerably below age peers in all major areas of competence.
7	Profoundly deficient intellectual skills in all areas of competence.

COMMENTS & OBSERVATIONS:

Exhibit C-21 PODS Format—Problem-Solving Domain, Academic Readiness Subdomain

AREA	CAPABILITY TARGETS
PROBLEM-SOLVING DOMAIN	range and level of cognitive skills and general academic readiness.
Academic Readiness Subdomain..............	acquisition of basic skills required in classroom learning situations with special reference to attention, listening, verbal communication, counting, object-labelling, drawing, and direction-following.

RATING	DEGREE OF CAPABILITY OBSERVED
0	Little or no opportunity to observe.
1	No problem in this area. Developing skills in using language, in counting, in solving problems, etc., give clear evidence of readiness for an academic environment.
2	Slight variations in preacademic skills, but general level of readiness is up to or beyond age-appropriate levels.
3	Several areas of difficulty are evident in which readiness is below age-expectations.
4	Many areas of difficulty. General readiness level is slightly depressed with wide fluctuations in specific skill areas.
5	Considerable lack of readiness is evident.
6	Severe lack of readiness is evident across all academic areas.
7	Profoundly deficient range of preacademic readiness skills.

COMMENTS & OBSERVATIONS:

Exhibit C-22 PODS Format—Developmental Summary Domain

AREA	CAPABILITY TARGETS
DEVELOPMENTAL SUMMARY DOMAIN	composite judgment of the developing child's range of functional capabilities in the areas of communication, motor, own-care, and problem-solving with reference to the normal child of the same age

RATING	DEGREE OF CAPABILITY OBSERVED
0	Little or no opportunity to observe.
1	No problem is apparent. Level of skill development in each domain is at or above age level.
2	Slight fluctuation in developmental skills. General level is still age-normal or above.
3	Several variations in developmental areas with slight delays in skill acquisition.
4	Wide fluctuations in development. Considerable delay is evident in one domain area.
5	Developmental delays are evident in at least two domain areas.
6	Severe delays are evident in development. General level is considerably delayed in most areas.
7	Extreme delays in development are apparent requiring extensive training and remediation. General development level is severely impaired.

COMMENTS & OBSERVATIONS:

CONCLUSION

In light of the direct effects that perceptions and biases have on interactions with children, it is vital that we devise methods of analyzing and reporting subjective impressions of child status. The PODS can aid in this effort by standardizing and profiling the diverse perceptions of significant people who interact with the multihandicapped preschooler. Further, the PODS can serve as a valuable supportive adjunct to standardized, developmental assessment.

"Systems of classification do not solve problems. On the other hand, a classification system frequently makes a problem clearer so that one can see the essential elements of a complicated situation and thus take steps towards its partial or complete solution" (Cruickshank, 1969, p. 211).

Glossary

Ability Training: Interventions designed to alleviate ability deficiencies (perceptual, psychomotor, cognitive) which presumably cause academic difficulties.

Adaptive Functioning: "The effectiveness or degree with which the individual meets the standards of personal independence and social responsibility expected of his age and culture group" (AAMD Manual).

Adaptive-Process Scale: Assessment instrument containing special tasks and procedures to partially circumvent the impairments of certain handicaps.

Aptitude Treatment Interaction (ATI): An evaluative and research method which seeks to identify relationships between a person's range of individual differences and the most effective method of instruction for his needs.

Assessment: A multi-facet process which considers performance in a variety of tasks over a variety of settings in all developmental areas in order to give a comprehensive profile of functional development.

Auditory: Of or relating to the sense of hearing or the organs of hearing.

B = P × E Model: Behavior (B) is the result of the Person (P) interacting with the Environment (E).

Baseline: The strength or level (rate, duration, latency) of behavior before an intervention program is introduced.

Basic Skills Approach: A curricular approach emphasizing teaching key or fundamental skills and knowledge.

Cephalocaudal: Development proceeding from head to foot.

Cognition: The process of knowing, perceiving, or recognizing; "thinking."

Cognitive Development: The process of gaining skills related to knowing, perceiving, and recognizing.

Cognitive Style: An individual's personal technique of approaching problems involving cognition.

Criterion: Standard of performance used to indicate when a goal has been achieved.

Criterion-Referenced Test: Instrument designed to identify the presence or absence of specific skills in terms of absolute levels of mastery.

Cross-Over Organization: A curriculum which emphasizes the interrelatedness of developmental objectives which promotes the concurrent progress within and across several developmental areas.

Curriculum: A set of educational objectives (often teaching strategies, materials, and evaluative measures).

Development: The process of change over time in characteristics (biological and behavioral) of the child.

Developmental Age: The current functional level of a child as compared to other children of the same age.

Developmental Ceiling: The specific upper limit of the child's developmental functioning.

Developmental Diagnosis: (1) Process of detailing and analyzing a child's capabilities and deficits as they affect functioning across many interrelated areas of behavior. (2) Comprehensive, specific assessment of young children's range of developmental skills across multiple behavioral areas.

Developmentally Disabled: A disability attributable to mental retardation, cerebral palsy, epilepsy, autism originating before the age of 18 (P.L. 94-103).

Developmental Prescriptive Model: Programs which combine a comprehensive skill analysis with a normal developmental approach.

Developmental Quotient (DQ): Standard score expressing the child's development determined by dividing mental age by chronological age and multiplying by 100.

Developmental Scales: A normal sequence of developmental tasks, skills, and behaviors.

Developmental Task Analysis: The process of identifying and analyzing children's ranges of acquired (+), absent (−), and emerging (±) developmental skills within functional areas for the purpose of selecting tasks and objectives.

Developmental Task Approach: The "whole child" approach; a highly structured, sequenced program fostering progress within and across all areas of development. The use of developmental landmarks or major skills as objectives for instruction.

Diagnostic-Prescriptive Approach: A teaching strategy which consists of analyzing capabilities, determining behavioral objectives, prescribing educational activities, and evaluating progress.

Efficiency Index: A method of expressing a program's instructional impact by dividing a child's developmental progress (in months) by time in the program.

Expressive: Of or relating to speech or language.

Federal P.L. 94-142: Law passed in 1975 that entitles all school age handicapped children to a free appropriate public education in the least restrictive environment.

Functional Assessment: Analysis of a student's strengths and weaknesses in terms of observable behavior, rather than traits or "underlying conditions."

Functional Developmental Domains: Categories of a curriculum or test, e.g., language, motor, social cognitive, etc.

Generalization: The performance of the same behavior across different settings, people, or circumstances.

Genotypic Assessment: Identification of a general underlying problem or condition of an individual, as opposed to phenotypic assessment.

Hierarchy: A sequential list of objectives which roughly corresponds to the sequences of skills displayed by normal children.

Individualized Educational Program (IEP): A program written for a specific child detailing the present level of educational functioning, annual goals, services to be provided, specific evaluation procedures, and objective criteria.

Infant Preschool Assessment: A continuous, general to specific process of defining functional capabilities and establishing treatment goals.

Informal Tests: Nonstandardized tests designed and used by professionals and nonprofessionals.

Instructional Objective: A precise specification of a goal which defines the behavior to be changed, the conditions under which it is to occur, and the criteria for mastery.

Intervention: Modifying services, programs, and strategies to maximize the child's progress.

Intraindividual Differences: The relative differences of a child's performance across several areas.

Linkage: Matching assessment findings to curricular objectives.

Mainstreaming: Integrating handicapped individuals into the regular social, recreational, and educational activities of the community.

Multidomain: Wide range coverage of functional skills across several behavioral areas, e.g., language, motor, cognitive, and perceptual skills.

Multihandicapped: An individual who exhibits two or more handicapping conditions.

Multimeasure: The employment of diverse types of scales and approaches to analyze child functioning.

Multisource: Combining information about child functioning from a variety of perspectives; e.g., parent-teacher ratings, interviews, curriculum-based records, etc.

Nonverbal Test: Test that does not require the use of words in the item or the response to it.

Normalization: Process to help children become more "normal" and adequate in their functioning and appearance. Process of progressively modifying goals and methods towards those typically employed with nonhandicapped persons.

Norm-Referenced Test: A comparative index which compares a child's performance to the performance of his peers who are most like him along several dimensions.

Parallel Organization: A curriculum organizational method in which each domain contains separate and unrelated hierarchical lists of objectives.

Phenotypic Assessment: Identification of observable characteristics and capabilities an individual does or does not display.

Plasticity: Theory stating that the function of some damaged neural structures can be learned and carried out by other parts of the brain.

Preacademic Approach: Curriculum concerned with getting children ready for the academic content of regular school.

Predictive Validity: Refers to how accurately an individual's current test score can be used to indicate future learning success.

Preventive Assessment: Identifying the problem(s) to formulate and execute treatment plans before a secondary problem emerges.

Process Variables: Those techniques which an individual uses to approach problems (e.g., persistence, attention, organizational approach, need for feedback).

Program: A plan for teaching and evaluating instruction of a skill.

Proximodistal: Growth and development proceeding from the body midline to extremities.

Psychological Constructs Approach: A curriculum emphasizing the development of alleged psychological processes; i.e., motivation, self-concept and need reduction.

Psychosituational Assessment: The use of multiple methods and sources of data collection integrating subjective, observational, interview, and performance data.

Qualitative Data: Refers to the quality of the child's response behaviors and skills used to earn the score.

Quantitative Data: A numerical indication of the average functioning of an individual across multiple skills and domains.

Reliability: The extent to which a measurement device is consistent in measuring what it measures.

Remedial Approach: Curriculum focusing on the child's developmental problems or delays.

Screening: Global process of surveying the individual's behavior to detect the existence of developmental problems.

Sensorimotor: Motor responses to sensory stimuli (visual, auditory, tactile, etc.).

Sensory Impairment: Damage, injury, or incapacity within the sense organs or central nervous system (hearing impaired, visual impairment).

Spiral Organization: A curriculum which consists of sequences of interrelated modules or units across several domains, and where the same skills appear throughout a curriculum in progressive, more complex forms.

Tactile: Of or relating to the sense of touch.

Target Population: Individuals for whom assessment, screening and curricula are intended.

Task Analysis: Breaking down of learning tasks into their component parts so that the skills involved in performing the task can be identified and more readily taught.

Testing: Exposing a person to a particular set of verbal and/or nonverbal items to obtain a score.

Validity: The extent to which a measurement device measures what it claims to measure.

References

Adams, G., & LaVoie, J. The effect of student's sex, conduct, and facial attractiveness on teacher expectancy. *Education,* 1974, *95,* 76-83.

Aliotti, N.C. Covert assessment in psychoeducational testing. *Psychology in the Schools,* October 1977, *14*(3), 438-443.

Alpern, G.D., & Boll, T.J. *The developmental profile.* Aspen, Colo.: Psychological Development Publications, 1972.

Ames, L.B., Gillespie, C., Haines, J., & Ilg, F. *The Gesell Institute's child from one to six: Evaluating the behavior of the preschool child.* New York: Harper & Row Publishers, 1979.

Anastasiow, N.J., & Mansergh, G.P. Teaching skills in early childhood programs. *Exceptional Children,* 1975, *41,* 309-317.

Bagnato, S.J. The efficacy of diagnostic reports as individualized guides to prescriptive goal-planning. *Exceptional Children,* 1980, *46*(4), 554-557.

Bagnato, S.J. Developmental diagnostic reports: Reliable and effective alternatives to guide individualized intervention. *Journal of Special Education,* 1981, *15*(1), 65-76.

Bagnato, S.J. & Llewellyn, E.A. *Assessment/curriculum developmental linkages.* University Park, Pa.: HICOMP Project, The Pennsylvania State University, 1979.

Bagnato, S.J., & Neisworth, J.T. Between assessment and intervention: Forging an assessment/curriculum linkage for the handicapped preschooler. *Child Care Quarterly,* 1979, *8*(3), 179-195.

Bagnato, S.J., & Neisworth, J.T. The intervention efficiency index (IEI): An approach to preschool program accountability. *Exceptional Children,* 1980, *46*(4), 264-269.

Bagnato, S.J., & Neisworth, J.T. Developmental scales and developmental curricula: Forging a linkage for early intervention. *Topics in Early Childhood Special Education,* in press.

Bagnato, S.J., & Neisworth, J.T. Subjective judgment vs. child performance measures: Congruence in developmental diagnosis. *Analysis & Intervention in Developmental Disabilities,* in press.

Bagnato, S.J., Neisworth, J.T., & Eaves, R.E. *The perceptions of developmental skills (PODS) profile*. University Park, Pa.: The Pennsylvania State University, HICOMP Preschool Project, 1977.

Bagnato, S.J., Neisworth, J.T., & Eaves, R.E. A profile of perceived capabilities for the preschool child. *Child Care Quarterly,* Winter 1978, *1*(4), 326-335.

Banus, B.S. *The developmental therapist*. Camden, N.J.: Charles B. Slack, Inc., 1971.

Bayley, N. *Manual for the Bayley scales of infant development*. New York: Psychological Corporation, 1969.

Bell, V.H. An educator's approach tc assessing preschool visually handicapped children. *Education of the Visually Handicapped,* 1975, *25,* 84-89.

Bereiter, C., & Engleman, S. *Teaching the disadvantaged child in the preschool*. Englewood Cliffs, N.J.: Prentice-Hall, 1966.

Bersoff, D.N. *The psychological evaluation of children: A manual of report writing for psychologists who work with children in an educational setting*. Unpublished manuscript, 1973.

Bijou, S.W. Practical implications of an interactional model of child development. *Exceptional Children,* 1977, *44*(1), 6-14.

Bloom, B.S. (Ed.). *Taxonomy of educational objectives: The classification of educational goals*. New York: Longmans, Green, 1956.

Brigance, A.H. *Brigance diagnostic inventory of early development*. Worcester, Mass.: Curriculum Associates, Inc., 1978.

Burgemeister, B.B., Blum, L.H., & Lorge, I. *Columbia mental maturity scale* (3rd ed.). New York: Harcourt Brace Jovanovich, 1972.

Caldwell, B.M., & Drachman, R.H. Comparability of three methods of assessing the developmental level of young infants. *Pediatrics,* 1964, *34,* 51-57.

Capute, A.J., & Biehl, R.F. Functional developmental evaluation: Prerequisite to habilitation. *Pediatric Clinics of North America,* 1973, *20*(1), 3-26.

Cartwright, G.P., Cartwright, C.A., & Ysseldyke, J.E. Two decision models: Identification and diagnostic teaching of handicapped children in the regular classroom. *Psychology in the Schools,* 1973, *10*(1), 4-11.

Cattell, P. *Cattell infant intelligence scale*. New York: The Psychological Corporation, 1969.

Chase, J.B. Developmental assessment of handicapped infants and young children: With special attention to the visually impaired. *The New Outlook for the Blind,* October 1975, pp. 341-348.

Chinn, P.C., Drew, D.J., & Logan, D.R. *Mental retardation: A life cycle approach*. St. Louis: C.V. Mosby Company, 1975.

Clifford, M., & Walster, E. The effect of physical attractiveness on teacher expectations. *Sociology of Education,* 1973, *46,* 248-258.

Cromwell, R., Blashfield, R.K. & Strauss, J.S. Criteria for classification. In N. Hobbs (Ed.), *Issues in the classification of children* (Vol. I). San Francisco: Jossey-Bass, 1975.

Cruickshank, W.M. The multiply handicapped cerebral palsied child. In J.W. Wolf & R.M. Anderson (Eds.), *The multiply handicapped child.* Springfield, Ill.: Charles C Thomas, 1969.

Diebold, M.H., Curtis, W.S., & Dubose, R.F. Developmental scales vs. observational measures for deaf-blind children. *Exceptional Children,* 1978, *44*(4), 275-279.

Doll, E. *Vineland social maturity scale.* Circle Pines, Minn.: American Guidance Service, 1965.

Doll, E.A. *Preschool attainment record.* Circle Pines, Minn.: American Guidance Service, 1966.

Drew, C.J., Freston, C.W., & Logan, D.R. Criteria and reference in evaluation. *Focus on Exceptional Children,* 1972, *4,* 1-10.

Dubose, R.F., & Langley, M.B. *The developmental activities screening inventory.* New York: Teaching Resources, 1977.

Dubose, R.F., Langley, M.B., & Stagg, V. Assessing severely handicapped children. In E.L. Meyen, G.A. Vergason, & R.L. Whelan (Eds.), *Instructional planning for exceptional children.* Denver, Colo.: Love Publishing Co., 1979.

Eaves, R.C. Teacher race, student race, and the behavior problem checklist. *Journal of Abnormal Child Psychology,* 1975, *3,* 1-9.

Erickson, M.L. *Assessment and management of developmental changes in children.* St. Louis: C.V. Mosby Co., 1976.

Forsberg, S.J., Neisworth, J.T., & Laub, K. *COMP curriculum.* University Park, Pa.: HICOMP Preschool Project, The Pennsylvania State University, 1977a.

Forsberg, S.J., Neisworth, J.T., & Laub, K. *COMP-curriculum and manual.* University Park, Pa.: HICOMP Project, The Pennsylvania State University, 1977b.

Fowler, W. A developmental learning approach to infant care in a group setting. *Merrill-Palmer Quarterly,* 1972, *18,* 145-175.

Frankenburg, W., Dodds, J., & Fandal, A. *Denver developmental screening test.* Boulder, Colo.: University of Colorado Medical Center, Ladoca Publishing Co., 1975.

French, J.L. *The pictorial test of intelligence.* Boston: Houghton-Mifflin, 1964.

Garwood, S.G. Special education and child development: A new perspective. In S.G. Garwood (Ed.), *Educating young handicapped children.* Germantown, Md.: Aspen Systems Corporation, 1979.

Gearhart, B.R., & Litton, F.W. *The trainable retarded.* St. Louis: C.V. Mosby Company, 1975.

Gesell, A. *Gesell developmental schedules.* New York: Psychological Corporation, 1949.

Gillespie, P.H., & Sitko, M.C. Training preservice teachers in diagnostic teaching. *Exceptional Children,* 1976, *42,* 401-402.

Gordon, R. *Evaluation of behavioral change: Study of multihandicapped young children.* New York: New York University Medical Center, 1975.

Guidubaldi, J., Newborg, J., Stock, J.R., & Wnek, L.B. *Battelle Developmental Inventory.* New York: Walker & Co., in press, 1981.

Guilford, J.P. *The nature of human intelligence.* New York: McGraw-Hill, 1967.

Haeussermann, E. *Developmental potential of preschool children: An evaluation in intellectual, sensory, and emotional functioning*. New York: Grune & Stratton, Inc., 1958.

Hammill, D.D. Evaluating children for instructional purposes. *Academic Therapy,* 1971, *6,* 341-353.

Hatch, E., Murphy, J., & Bagnato, S.J. Comprehensive evaluation of handicapped children. *Elementary School Guidance and Counseling Journal,* 1979, *13*(3), 170-187.

Havighurst, R.J. Research on the developmental task concept. *School Review,* May 1956, pp. 215-223.

Havighurst, R.J. *Developmental tasks and education* (3rd ed.). New York: David McKay Company, Inc., 1974.

Hewett, F.M., Taylor, F.D., & Artuso, A.A. The Santa Monica project. *Exceptional Children,* 1968, *35,* 523-529.

Hiskey, M. *Hiskey-Nebraska test of learning aptitude*. Lincoln, Nebr.: Union College Press, 1966.

Hoffman, H. *The Bayley scales of infant development: Modifications for youngsters with handicapping conditions*. Commack, N.Y.: Suffolk Rehabilitation Center, 1975.

Horowitz, F.D., & Paden, L.Y. The effectiveness of environmental intervention programs. In B.M. Caldwell & H.N. Riccuiti (Eds.), *Review of child development and social policy*. Chicago, Ill.: University of Chicago Press, 1973.

Hunt, D.E., & Sullivan, E.V. *Between psychology and education*. New York: Dryden Press, 1974.

Hunt-Moosbrugger, F. *HICOMP lesson plan chart*. University Park, Pa.: HICOMP Project, The Pennsylvania State University, 1980.

Hymes, J.L. *Early childhood education: An introduction to the profession*. Washington, D.C.: National Association for Education of Young Children, 1968.

Illingworth, R.D. *The development of the infant and young child: Normal and abnormal*. London: E. & S. Livingstone, 1970.

Iscoe, I., & Payne, S. Development of a revised scale for the functional classification of exceptional children. In E.P. Trapp & P. Himelstein (Eds.), *Readings on exceptional children: Research and theory* (2nd ed.). New York: Appleton-Century-Crofts, 1972.

Jackson, P., & Lahaderne, H. Inequalities of teacher-pupil contacts. *Psychology in the Schools,* 1967, *4,* 204-211.

Jedrysek, E., Klapper, Z., Pope, L., & Wortis, J. *Psychoeducational evaluation of the preschool child.* New York: Grune and Stratton, 1972.

Johnston, R.B., & Magrab, P.R. *Developmental disorders: Assessment, treatment, education*. Baltimore, Md.: University Park Press, 1976.

Jordan, J.B., Hayden, A.H., Karnes, M.B., & Wood, M.M. *Early childhood education for exceptional children*. Reston, Va.: Council for Exceptional Children, 1977.

Kamii, C., & Elliott, D.L. Evaluation of evaluations. *Leadership,* 1971, *28,* 827-831.

Keogh, B. Psychological evaluation of exceptional children: Old hangups and new directions. *Journal of School Psychology,* 1972, *10*(2), 141-145.

Knobloch, H., & Pasamanick, B. The developmental behavioral approach to the neurological examination in infancy. *Child Development,* 1962, *33,* 181-198.

Knobloch, H., & Pasamanick, B. *Developmental diagnosis.* New York: Harper & Row, 1974.

Knobloch, H., Stevens, F., & Malone, A.F. *Manual of developmental diagnosis* (Revised edition). New York: Harper & Row, Publishers, 1980.

Kurtz, P.D., Neisworth, J.T., & Laub, K.W. Issues concerning the early identification of handicapped children. *Journal of School Psychology,* 1977, *15*(2), 136-140.

Lambert, N.M., Wilcox, M.K., & Gleason, W.P. *The educationally retarded child: Comprehensive assessment and planning for slow learners and the educable mentally retarded.* New York: Grune and Stratton, 1974.

LaVoie, J., & Adams, G. Teacher expectancy and its relation to physical and interpersonal characteristics of the child. *Alberta Journal of Educational Research,* 1974, *20,* 122-132.

Leiter, R.G. *General instructions for the Leiter international performance scale.* Chicago, Ill.: Stoelting Company, 1969.

LeMay, D.W., Griffin, P.M., & Sanford, A.R. *LAP's examiner manual.* Winston-Salem, N.C.: Kaplan School Supply, 1977.

LeMay, D.W., Griffin, P.M., & Sanford, A.R. *Learning accomplishment profile: Diagnostic edition* (Rev. ed.). Winston-Salem, N.C.: Kaplan School Supply, 1978.

Lewis, M. Infant intelligence tests: Their use and misuse. *Human Development,* 1973, *16,* 108-118.

Llewellyn, E. *Teacher's sequence record.* Unpublished teacher inservice workshop, The Pennsylvania State University, University Park, Pa.: August 1980.

Louttit, C.M. *Clinical psychology of exceptional children.* New York: Harper & Row, 1957.

MacTurk, R.H., & Neisworth, J.T. Norm- and criterion-based measures with handicapped and nonhandicapped preschoolers. *Exceptional Children,* 1978, *45*(1), 34-39.

Maxfield, K.E., & Buchholz, S. *A social maturity scale for blind preschool children.* New York: American Foundation for the Blind, 1957.

Mayer, R.S. A comparative analysis of preschool curriculum models. In R.H. Anderson & H.G. Shane (Eds.), *As the twig is bent.* Boston: Houghton-Mifflin, 1971.

McCall, R.B., Hogarty, P.S., & Hurlburt, N. Transitions in infant sensorimotor development and the prediction of childhood IQ. *American Psychologist,* 1972, *27,* 728-748.

Meeker, M.N. *The structure of the intellect.* Columbus, Ohio: Charles Merrill Publishing Company, 1969.

Meier, J. *Screening and assessment of young children at developmental risk.* Washington, D.C.: U.S. Government Printing Office, 1973.

Meier, J. Screening, assessment and intervention for young children at developmental risk. In N. Hobbs (Ed.), *Issues in the classification of children* (Vol. 2). New York: Jossey-Bass, 1975.

Meier, J. *Developmental and learning disabilities*. Baltimore, Md.: University Park Press, 1976.

Meier, J.H. Developmental inventory—profile and base for curriculum planning. In J. Meier (Ed.), *Developmental and learning disabilities*. Baltimore, Md.: University Park Press, 1976.

Meyer, W., & Thompson, G. Sex differences in the distribution of teacher approval and disapproval among sixth grade children. *Journal of Educational Psychology,* 1956, *47,* 385-396.

Miller, C., McLaughlin, J., Hadden, J., & Chansky, N. Socioeconomic class and teacher bias. *Psychological Reports,* 1968, *23,* 806.

Morrison, D., & Potheir, P. Two different remedial motor training programs and the development of mentally retarded preschoolers. *American Journal of Mental Deficiency,* 1972, *77*(3), 251-258.

Naer, W., Foster, D., Jones, J., & Reynolds, D. Socioeconomic bias in the diagnosis of mental retardation. *Exceptional Children,* 1973, *40,* 38-39.

Neisworth, J.T., & Madle, R.A. Normalized day care: A philosophy and approach to integrating exceptional and normal children. *Child Care Quarterly,* 1975, *4*(3), 93-104.

Neisworth, J.T., Willoughby-Herb, S.J., Bagnato, S.J., Cartwright, C.A., & Laub, K.W. *Individualized education for preschool exceptional children*. Rockville, Md.: Aspen Systems Corporation, 1980.

Newland, T.E. The psychological assessment of exceptional children and youth. In W.M. Cruickshank (Ed.), *Psychology of exceptional children and youth* (3rd ed.). Englewood Cliffs, N.J.: Prentice-Hall, 1973.

Palmer, J.O. *The psychological assessment of children*. New York: John Wiley & Sons, Inc., 1970.

Peter, L. *Prescriptive teaching*. New York: McGraw-Hill, 1967.

Peter, L. School psychologist as coordinator of prescriptive teaching. In J.F. Magary (Ed.), *School psychological services*. Englewood Cliffs, N.J.: Prentice-Hall, 1967, 693-694.

Quick, A.D., & Campbell, A.A. *Lesson plans for enhancing preschool developmental progress: Project MEMPHIS*. Dubuque, Iowa: Kendall/Hunt Publishing Company, 1976.

Quick, A.D., Little, T.L., & Campbell, A.A. *Memphis comprehensive developmental schedules*. Belmont, Calif.: Fearon Publishers, 1974a.

Quick, A.D., Little, T.L., & Campbell, A.A. *Project MEMPHIS: Enhancing developmental progress in preschool exceptional children*. Belmont, Calif.: Fearon Publishers, 1974b.

Rogers, S.J., D'Eugenio, D.B., Brown, S.L., Donovan, C.M., & Lynch, E.W. *Early intervention developmental profile*. Ann Arbor, Mich.: University of Michigan Press, 1977.

Safford, P.L. *Teaching young children with special needs*. St. Louis: C.V. Mosby Company, 1978.

Salvia, J., & Ysseldyke, J.E. *Assessment in special and remedial education*. Boston: Houghton-Mifflin, 1978.

Sanford, A. *Learning accomplishment profile*. Winston-Salem, N.C.: Kaplan School Supply, 1978.

Sattler, J.M. *Assessment of children's intelligence*. Philadelphia, Pa.: W.B. Saunders Co., 1974.

Sattler, J.M., & Tozier, L.L. A review of intelligence test modifications with cerebral palsied and other handicapped groups. *Journal of Special Education,* 1970, *4,* 391-398.

Schafer, D.S., & Moersch, M.S. *Developmental programming for infants and young children* (Vol. III) Stimulation activities. Ann Arbor, Mich.: University of Michigan Press, 1977.

Scriven, M. The methodology of evaluation. In R.W. Tyler & R.M. Gagne (Eds.), *Perspective of curriculum and evaluation*. Skokie, Ill.: Rand-McNally, 1967.

Shearer, D. *The Portage guide to early education: The Portage project*. Portage, Wis.: Cooperative Educational Service Agency 12.

Shearer, D., Billingsley, J., Frohman, S., Hilliard, J., Johnson, F., & Shearer, M. *Developmental sequential checklist*. Unpublished manuscript, the Portage Preschool Project, Cooperative Educational Service Agency 12, Portage, Wis., 1971.

Shearer, M.S., & Shearer, D.E. The Portage project: A model for early childhood education. *Exceptional Children,* 1972, *39,* 210-217.

Simeonsson, R.J. Infant assessment and developmental handicaps. In B.M. Caldwell & D.J. Stedman (Eds.), *Infant education*. New York: Walker & Company, 1977.

Simeonsson, R.J., & Wiegerink, R. Accountability: A dilemma in infant intervention. *Exceptional Children,* 1975, *41,* 474-481.

Smith, R.M., & Neisworth, J.T. *The exceptional child: A functional approach*. New York: McGraw-Hill Book Company, 1975, 262-269.

Song, A., & Jones, S.E. *Wisconsin behavior rating scale*. Madison, Wis.: Center for Developmentally Disabled, 1980.

Spungin, S.J., & Swallow, R. Psychoeducational assessment: Role of the psychologist to the teacher of the visually handicapped. *Education of the Visually Handicapped,* October 1975, pp. 67-75.

Staats, A.W. *Learning, language, and cognition*. New York: Holt, Rinehart, and Winston, 1968.

Stellern, J., Vasa, S.F., & Little, J. *Introduction to diagnostic-prescriptive teaching and programming*. Parsippany, N.J.: Exceptional Press, 1976.

Stillman, R.D. *The Callier-Azusa scale: Assessment of deaf-blind children*. Reston, Va.: Council for Exceptional Children, 1974.

Tano, T. *Considerations for the formulation of regulations for Public Law 94-142*. Unpublished manuscript, Harrisburg, Pa.: Pennsylvania Department of Education, 1976.

Tawney, J.W., & Deaton, S.L. *Curricula for the severely developmentally retarded: A survey and primer on the curriculum process* (Final report, Vol. 1, Grant numbers OEG-0-72-5361 and OEG-0-75-00669). Washington, D.C.: U.S. Office of Education, 1979.

Thomas, H.T. Psychological assessment instruments for use with human infants. *Merrill-Palmer Quarterly,* 1970, *16*(1), 179-223.

U.S., Congress. Developmental disabilities act (1978 revision), Federal Public Law 91-517. *Congressional Record,* 97th Cong., 1978, *145*(8), 1118-1190.

U.S., Congress. Federal Public Law 94-142. *Congressional Record,* 94th Cong., November 29, 1975, *12,* 773-796.

Valett, R. A developmental task approach to early childhood education. *Journal of School Psychology,* 1967, *5*(2), 136-147.

Valett, R.E. Developmental task analysis and psychoeducational programming. *Journal of School Psychology,* 1972, *10*(2), 127-133.

Valett, R.E. *Developing cognitive abilities.* St. Louis: C.V. Mosby Company, 1978.

Vane, J.R. Problems in and strategies for evaluating preschool programs. *Journal of School Psychology,* 1976, *14*(1), 39-46.

White, B.L., Castle, P., & Held, P. Observations on the development of visually-directed reaching. *Child Development,* 1964, *35,* 349-364.

Wolf, J.M., & Anderson, R.M. *The multiply handicapped child.* Springfield, Ill.: Charles C Thomas, 1969.

Wolfensberger, W. *Normalization: The principle of normalization in human services.* Toronto, Canada: National Institute on Mental Retardation, 1972.

Wood, M.M., & Hurley, O.L. Curriculum and instruction. In J. Hordan, A. Hayden, M. Karnes, & M. Wood (Eds.), *Early childhood education for exceptional children.* Reston, Va.: Council for Exceptional Children, 1977.

Yang, R.K., & Bell, R.Q. Assessment of infants. In P. McReynolds (Ed.), *Advances in psychological assessment* (Vol. 3). San Francisco: Jossey-Bass, 1975.

Ysseldyke, J.E., & Bagnato, S.J. Assessment of exceptional students at the secondary level: A pragmatic perspective. *High School Journal,* 1976, *59*(7), 282-289.

Ysseldyke, J.E., & Salvia, J. Diagnostic-prescriptive teaching: Two models. *Exceptional Children,* 1974, *41*(3), 181-185.

Index

Note: Numbers set in italics indicate tables, figures, or exhibits.

C

D

E

F

G

Q

R

S

T

V

About the Authors

STEPHEN J. BAGNATO, D.ED., is a developmental school psychologist and assistant professor of child psychiatry at the Milton S. Hershey Medical Center, The Pennsylvania State University College of Medicine and the Elizabethtown Hospital for Developmental Disabilities. Dr. Bagnato formerly served as assistant professor of school psychology at both the University of Maryland and the Pennsylvania State University, where he was also instructor in early special education and psychological supervisor in the CEDAR Child Diagnostic Clinic. He has also functioned as a child developmental psychologist and consultant for a neonatal diagnostic program at the John F. Kennedy Institute for Handicapped Children and Johns Hopkins Hospital. He is consulting editor for an early special education journal, *Topics in Early Childhood Special Education,* and a field reviewer for HCEEP (Handicapped Children's Early Education Program).

Dr. Bagnato has published and coauthored several articles, books and applied materials for school psychologists and early special educators concerning the linkage between adaptive developmental assessment and intervention for handicapped infants and preschoolers.

JOHN T. NEISWORTH, PH.D., is Professor of Special Education at the Pennsylvania State University. His research and articles have appeared in numerous journals. He is author or coauthor of six widely used textbooks in special and early education. Dr. Neisworth is codirector of the HICOMP Early Intervention Project, a federally funded demonstration and dissemination project in early education for the handicapped; consulting editor for several journals, as well as coeditor for *Topics in Early Childhood Special Education*; and a vigorous proponent of noncategorical approaches to the treatment of children with educational problems.